D1583025

This
b

3023149

GENETICS, MOLECULAR BIOLOGY and the LAW

John Candlish

UNIVERSITIES AT MEDWAY LIBRARY
344'
041
96
CAN

Wildy, Simmonds & Hill Publishing

Copyright © 2010 Wildy, Simmonds & Hill Publishing

Genetics, Molecular Biology and the Law

ISBN 9780854900404

The right of John Candlish to be identified as the authors of this Work has been asserted by them in accordance with sections 77 and 78 of the Copyright, Designs and Patents Act 1988

First published in Great Britain 2009 by Wildy, Simmonds & Hill Publishing

Website: www.wildy.com

All rights reserved. No part of this publication may be reproduced, stored in a retrieval system, or transmitted, in any form or by any means, electronic, mechanical, photocopying, recording, scanning or otherwise, except under the terms of the Copyright Designs and Patents Act 1988 or under the terms of a licence issued by the Copyright Licensing Agency, 90 Tottenham Court Road, London W1P 9HE, UK, without the permission in writing of the publisher.

British Library Cataloguing-in-Publication Data:

A catalogue record for this book is available from The British Library

First published in 2010 by
Wildy, Simmonds & Hill Publishing
58 Carey Street, London WC2A 2JB
England

Printed and bound in Great Britain by
CPI Antony Rowe, Chippenham, Wiltshire

2 0 MAY 2010

To our younger generation:
Aileen, Gina, Hsuan, Kerensa, Nick, Steve and Zarel

ACKNOWLEDGEMENTS

My sincere thanks to Mr Andrew Riddoch and Dr Brian Hill of Wildy, Simmonds & Hill Publishing for putting the book togther and to the law, science and medical librarians of the National University of Singapore for their generous resources. It is hoped that mistakes are minimal but intimation thereof would be gratefully received at jkcandlish@gmail.com

INTRODUCTION

This volume is intended as a reference source for the novel intrusion of multifarious biological molecules, DNA in particular, into various areas of law. (The urge to entitle it something like 'Molecular Law' was resisted.) It has been a demanding task. ' The greater part of a writer's time is spent on reading, ' said Dr Samuel Johnson, ' a man will turn over half a library, to make one book.' That is putting it mildly, especially in the information-laden twenty first century. The concentration here is on English and US law, particularly with respect to Chapters 2 (Criminal) and 4 (Intellectual Property). Just as US scientists have driven much of the technology, so have the US courts driven much of the interaction of science with that technology, and so their business is full of interest. (There have of course been some notable UK contributions, such as the establishment of the structure of DNA in 1953 in Cambridge and the development of DNA fingerprints some thirty years later in Leicester.) Unless at the highest (Federal Court) level US law can be difficult to penetrate owing to the legislative autonomy of each state, and this is noted at various points. (In that too extensive diversity throughout the US is thought to be undesirable, there is a National Conference of Commissioners on Uniform State Law.[1] It has promulgated, for example, the Uniform Parentage Act of 2002 which has some relevance to Chapter 3 herein.) However it has to be remembered too that there are at least three separate legal systems within the UK; in addition, concentrating on England and the US is not to deny the importance of, say, Canadian, Australian and Continental European (as well as many other) jurisdictions;[2] trying to be any way internationally comprehensive however would take decades for a single author and would predicate a sort of Forth Bridge painting activity in reverting to the first chapter, to bring it up date, as soon as he had finished the final few pages.

Chapter 1 (the molecular biological technicalities) has been pared to the minimum necessary in order to proceed on with the legal issues; it deals mainly with the language of biotechnology, but precise language is the bedrock of all disciplines. Mastering the language presented here takes time, but anybody conversant with both molecular biology and the law has acquired a formidable vocabulary.

---

1   The National Conference website is: <www.nccusl.org>.
2   Consideration of Commonwealth cases is sometimes absolutely essential, for example the Australian *Victoria Racing* (Chapter 2) and the Canadian *Schmeiser* (Chapter 5).

Much cross-referencing has been necessary, since the same topic tends to crop up in variety of contexts. (The nature of DNA in jurisprudence is nothing if not protean.) Tables have been included where they may possibly be useful and the modern tendency of incorporating boxes (sometimes called sidebars) has been tentatively adopted so that they can be referred to as the argument progresses.

The text is considered up to date as at mid-2008.

ABBREVIATIONS

ACSLD	Association of Criminal Science Laboratory Directors
AIA	Advance Informed Agreement
BINAS	Biosafety Information Network and Advisory Service
BWC	Biological Weapons Convention
CAFC	Court of Appeals for the Federal Circuit
CBD	Convention on Biological Diversity
COP	Conference of Parties
CODIS	Combined DNA index system
CWC	Chemical Weapons Convention
DNA	Deoxyribonucleic acid
EIA	Environmental impact assessment
EPA	Environmental Protection Agency (USA)
EPC	European Patent Convention
EPO	European Patent Office
EST	Expressed sequence tag
EU	European Union
ECHR	European Court of Human Rights
FBI	Federal Bureau of Investigation (USA)
FDA	Food and Drug Administration (USA)
FSS	Forensic Science Service (UK)
GMF	Genetically modified food
GMC	Genetically modified crop
GMO	Genetically modified organism
GRAS	Generally Regarded as Safe
HGDP	Human Gene Diversity Programme
HVR	Hypervariable region
HUGO	Human Genome Organsation
ICC	International Criminal Court

IRRO	Information Resource for the Release of Organisms
LH	Likelihood ratio
LCJ	Lord Chief Justice
LCN	Low copy number
LMO	Living modified organism
LR	Likelihood ratio
MVR	Minisatellite variable repeat
mtDNA	Mitochondrial DNA
NRC	National Research Council (US)
NIH	National Institutes of Health (US)
NGO	Non-governmental organisation
OECD	Organisation for Economic Cooperation and Development
PCR	Polymerase chain reaction
rDNA	Recombinant DNA
RFLP	Restriction fragment length polymorpism
RMP	Random match probability
RNA	Random match probability
SGMPlus	Second Generation Multiplex Plus
SLP	Single locus probe
SNP	Single nucleotide polymorphism
STR	Short tandem repeats
TRIPs	Trade Related Intellectual Property
UNEP	United Nations Environmental Programme
UNESCO	United Nations Educational, Social and Cultural Organisation
UNIDO	United Nations Industrial Development Organisation
USDA	United States Department of Agriculture
USPTO	US Patent and Trademark Office
VNTR	Variable number tandem repeats
WIPO	World Intellectual Property Organisation
WTO	World Trade Organisation

A Note on Citations

Combining law and science poses something of a problem in referencing; in an effort like the present one both areas are to be cited, but the conventions in the two disciplines are quite different. Most biomedical journals now tend to the Vancouver system which, for an article, requires the names of the authors, the title of the paper, the year of publication, the volume, and pagination. [1] There are a standard set of conventions for abbreviating the titles of the journals. Herein, however, the full titles have been spelt out, should the abbreviated form be unfamiliar to the reader, and full pagination is avoided in the interests of some economy.

In respect of legal citations, the standard abbreviations are used herein. A comprehensive guide is provided by Blackstone Press. [2] The abbreviations of US case reports can be difficult, sometimes next to incomprehensible to those better acquainted with English /Commonwealth law. In general terms the format is volume number, 'reporter' (that is, source), page number and year. A guide to both Commonwealth and US styles is provided by the very helpful Wikipedia site.[3] There is also an authoritative guide from the Harvard Law Review. [4]

The Internet, like DNA, has changed everything. Indeed it has made life easier in many ways. Once the tedious business of typing out the site address is accomplished, then all the other details are revealed when the page is sourced. There is not much point in noting the date of accession of a site since there is no certainty that it will yield the same information when subsequently visited.

1. For information on the Vancouver system see <http.www.le.ac.uk/li/sources/subject3/boil/ist/Vancouver.html>

2. French D. *How to Cite Legal Authorities*. Blackstone Press Ltd, London, 1996

3. <http://en.wikipaedia.rg/wiki/Court_citation>

4. *The Blue Book: a Uniform System of Citation*, 15th edn. Harvard Law Review, Cambridge (1991)

GENETICS, MOLECULAR BIOLOGY and the LAW

Diagrams

Tables

Boxes

Chapter 1

The Basics of Molecular Biology

1.1 The Absolute Basics

Molecular biology is a branch of science dealing with the properties and manipulation of large biological molecules, principally deoxyribonucleic acid (DNA), ribonucleic acid (RNA) and proteins. Henceforth these abbreviations will be used, as is the custom both in laboratories and in the courts. There is no reason why other biological molecules, even small ones like glucose, should not be considered under the rubric of molecular biology. They can also be important forensically – consider for example hypoglycaemia as an automatism defence - but the definition has settled on the macromolecules only. Ventures like stem cell manipulation and therapeutic cloning, which are becoming important in medical and family law, are usually considered to be part of the discipline of cell biology rather than molecular biology. Dogma was formerly the province of religion, but the late Francis Crick (an atheist by all accounts) in the sixties formulated what he called the central dogma of molecular biology:

DNA makes RNA makes protein.

Like all dogmas, it admits of some minor exceptions, largely irrelevant to the present themes.[1] Coming back to DNA and RNA, together they are called *nucleic acids*. Why 'acids'? We think of acids as chemicals which are markedly corrosive. However in chemistry an acid is simply any molecule which is able to donate a hydrogen ion (otherwise known as a proton), however reluctantly it does so. Both DNA and RNA consist of long strands of repeated units, one part of which is phosphate, and this is weakly acidic, or proton donating. DNA and RNA also contain bases. Many may remember from schooldays that a base is something which reacts with an acid to give a salt. In DNA and RNA the bases are the informational components and they are merely so called because they have attracted hydrogen ions/protons under the particular conditions of the body fluids. The five bases are listed in Fig. 1.1; conveniently, before their biological roles became known, they were all given names with different initial letters, and so A,T,C,G and U unambiguously identify each of them. The bases are arranged in a linear

---

1 The exceptions are the RNA viruses and the prions, infective protein particles which infect the brain cells causing bovine spongiform encephalopathy in ruminants and Jacob-Creutzfeldt disease in humans.

2

Fig 1.1 A guide to the Language of DNA

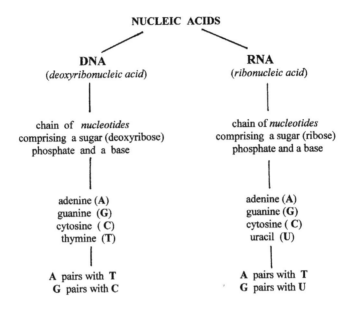

NUCLEIC ACIDS

DNA	RNA
(deoxyribonucleic acid)	*(ribonucleic acid)*
chain of *nucleotides* comprising a sugar (deoxyribose) phosphate and a base	chain of *nucleotides* comprising a sugar (ribose) phosphate and a base
adenine (A) guanine (G) cytosine (C) thymine (T)	adenine (A) guanine (G) cytosine (C) uracil (U)
A pairs with T G pairs with C	A pairs with T G pairs with U

fashion on a phosphate sugar backbone, and since this can be very long, an infinite series of base sequences can be envisaged. Intuitively, the sequences are informational.

Complementariness of bases

The concept that the bases interact in a specific manner with each other, as in Fig. 1.2, is one of the most fundamental concepts to grasp. It allows the famous double helix to form. The interaction is possible by means of the formation of hydrogen bonds; these are weak individually but collectively they hold the two DNA stands together quite cohesively. However they can be disrupted by heat. This disruption is called *denaturation* or melting; importantly it is reversible - on cooling again there is *annealing*, that is the two strands can regain their specific base-to-base bonding. The two strands also part company during replication – each one forms a daughter strand aligned with it and thus two double helices appear in place of the original. Finally, here, we can note that the sequences can be cut at specific points. Enzymes known as *restriction endonucleases* recognise particular base

3

Fig 1.2 DNA Unwinding

A representation of DNA unwinding (melting, denaturing) upwards from the bottom part of the diagram, hydrogen bonds (........) between A and T, as well as G and C, breaking.

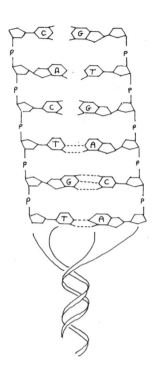

sequences and catalyse scission at those points. (As a catalytic factor, of course, the enzyme is not consumed during its activity and can perform the same task numerous times.) Enzymes are important components within the corpus of DNA technology as a whole. Apart from the cutting enzymes, there are synthesizing enzymes - the DNA polymerases link up nucleotides to form DNA stands. The nucleotides are considered the basic unit of nucleic acid structure. A nucleotide is a base combined with a sugar (ribose or deoxyribose) and phosphate. When lined up, there is a sugar-phosphate-sugar –phosphate etc, etc backbone, with the bases linked to each sugar along its length (Fig 1.2). At this point the following concepts in respect of DNA can be adopted:

- complementariness of bases
- specific (informational) sequences of bases
- melting and annealing properties
- susceptibility to specific scission
- replicability.

Introns and exons

The DNA in living cells contains the information to make enzymes and other proteins. Each three base sequence codes for a single amino acid, so that a linear array of these is set up, and when they are joined together they form a protein. Many of the proteins synthesized in the cell are enzymes, and these in turn catalyse the synthesis of all the other body components like the cell membranes. A sequence of bases which have the information for - code for - a protein is a *gene*. However not all the base sequences in DNA code for proteins. Much of the DNA is of no known function although it has been theorised many times that it is not really 'junk'.[2] Some of the theories as to the nature of these sequences are:

- they are the remains of accumulated viruses

- they represent a pool of bases which may be employed for the construction of new genes, according to evolutionary dictates

- they are spacers, allowing enzymes to be interact with functional elements

- they may indeed have function, wholly or partly, but such has remained undetectable to date

- they tend to mop up, as it were, undesirable mutations during replication, sparing the functional sequences to some extent.

Be that as it may, much of this non-coding DNA (as it is presently regarded) contains sequences of bases that repeat themselves from a few to many thousand times and these are known as *introns*. (the coding sequences are known as *exons*, - they are *ex*pressed.) Some introns turned out to be so-called *short tandem repeats* (STRs), now the choice for forensic and paternity investigation. ("Tandem" because they sit one behind the other.) They consist of repeat units of two to seven bases, and are usually highly polymorphic, ('hypervariable') that is they vary markedly from individual to individual. (They are sometimes also called *microsatellites*. They are distinguished from *minisatellites*, or variable number tandem repeats (VNTRs) which are repeat units of several hundred base pairs - these were used forensically until a few years ago but gradually were replaced by the microsatellites.) The principles of the investigation of individual differences in STRs are surprisingly simple as long as a few essential points are borne in mind. First of all, we all have two chromosomes of each type, one with base sequences inherited from the

---

2 Non-coding sequences constitute about 98% of the total DNA in human cells. See <http://en.wikipedia.org/wiki/Junk _DNA>.

Fig 1.3   A Chromosome in Two Individuals – One Homozygous and One Heterozygous for an AT Short Tandem Repeat

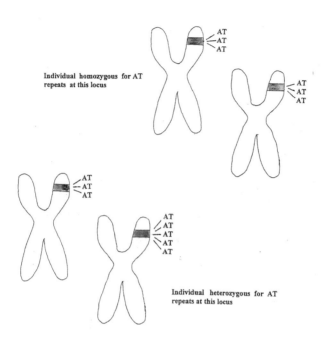

Individual homozygous for AT repeats at this locus

Individual heterozygous for AT repeats at this locus

mother, and the sister chromosome containing the sequences from the father. If an individual inherits the same version of a gene from both father and mother he or she is *homozygous*. If the gene exists on the two chromosomes in different forms, then he or she is *heterozygous*. The different forms of a gene are termed *alleles*, and it is important to grasp the meaning of this word, for it is much used in the discussion of forensic DNA evidence. Thus, for each gene there can exist hundreds of alleles each one slightly different in base sequence from the other. However an individual can only possess two at most, one from each parent – indeed there is only one variant if he or she is homozygous for that gene. The word allele is also applied to variants of non-coding sequences, that is DNA which does not appear to have the information for functional protein molecules, like STRs.

Box 1.1 The Hardy-Weinburg Equilibrium

In the process of matching two DNA samples, the issue is whether the profile of the testee (usually suspect or putative father) is rare enough to exclude that suspect from the population at large with a high probability. But what is to be the population? It is the group to which the suspect belongs, considered at the present time to be coterminous with his ethnicity. But further consideration raises the proposition that the reference population must be genetically stable. If it is drifting in some way, how can the comparison be made? The answer is that stability is tested by the Hardy-Weinberg equation. In a homogenous population, this states that:

$$p^2 + q^2 + 2pq = 1$$

Thus if a gene with two alleles is selected, and if the frequencies of these alleles among the parents are p and q, then the genotype frequencies among the progeny are p^2, $2pq$ and q^2, and they must summate to unity. If there is a palpable rate of mutation or if mating is non-random, then the Hardy-Weinberg relationship will not hold. It is always possible for the defence to bring this up or ask for the proof thereof – although actual instances of such challenges are difficult to find in the cases.

Another , perhaps neglected point is: quantitative calculations inevitably suffer from a degree of error, error in the sense of scatter about or deviation from the true value. The Hardy-Weinburg equation will never yield exactly unity in practice. So how near unity must it be to allow the assumption that it holds. It is open, again, to the defence to ask for the raw data on which the calculation is made and check it.

The derivation of the equation can be found in standard genetic texts, for example Falconer DS. *Introduction to Quantitative Genetics*. (Longman Scientific and Technical, 3rd edn, 1989) at p 7.

Suppose one parent transmits, to a heterozygous offspring, an allele such as:

GC- AT-AT-AT-AT-AT-AT- GC

And the other parent transmits

GC- AT-AT-AT-GC

If we can somehow arrange to cut the DNA between G and C, we will be able to obtain two fragments

C-AT-AT-AT-AT-AT-AT-G and C-AT-AT-AT-G

which can be sorted by size (6 and 3 repeats of AT respectively).[3] Fragments of the same size will be found in related individuals but unrelated individuals can be distinguished as such because they will yield differently sized fragments due to variations (polymorphisms) in the lengths of the repeats. Alternatively, instead of cutting with a restriction endonuclease, if we can somehow make multiple copies of each of these sequences, then on examination each will have a specific size and will be characteristic of the individual. This is done by the polymerase chain reaction (PCR) which is considered further below.

Suppose on the other hand there exist, on a particular chromosome, three base repeats in tandem, say GAG and TAT, and that the repeats are not uniform, as in:

GAG-GAG-GAG-TAT-GAG-GAG-GAG-TAT-GAG

On the corresponding chromosome, from the other parent, we might have

GAG-GAG-GAG-TAT-TAT-GAG-GAG-GAG-GAG

The differences are underlined. Now label GAG and TAT as X and Y respectively. If we have some way of reading the bases linearly along the chromosome we can more conveniently compare the two sequences:

X X X Y X X X Y X

X X X Y Y X X X X

For a given site, there are three possibilities. X is in the same site in both alleles (call that condition 1), Y is on the same site in both alleles, call that situation 2, or both X and Y are at the site, condition 3. So we can further write:

1112331111

which is a ternary code easily handled by a computer programme and is unique for each unrelated individual. This technique types individuals by allelic variability, following sequencing, rather than size as described above and is known as minisatellite variant repeat-polymerase chain reaction mapping (MVR-PCR).[4] It will be appreciated that some of the techniques

---

3   A word on the language used may be apposite here, for misunderstanding it could be fatal to any challenge to expert evidence in court. If an allele has 6 repeats of (say) a three base sequence, it is known as the 6 allele; if 3 repeats, it is the 3 allele - not 'allele (number) 6' or 'allele (number) 3'. At a different locus on the same chromosome there may be another 6 allele, and another 3 allele.
4   Jeffreys, AJ, Royle, NJ et al 'Minisatellite repeat coding as a digital approach to DNA

are based on sorting DNA fragments by size and some are accomplished by determining the sequence of bases along the length of a chosen segment. Size sorting has in general been the choice for forensic applications, MVR-PCR being comparatively laborious and used mainly in connection with the investigation of difficult cases, such as those where identification is required in the absence of a mother, and also in such medical scenarios as bone marrow transplantation, even when donor and recipient are closely related; that is, the technique will enable monitoring of the origin of the white cells at any chosen time. The other application for techniques involving sequencing relate to mitochondrial DNA, as below.

Obviously too, any of the procedures for identifying variations in DNA, either in terms of the sequences of bases in VNTRs/ STRs, or their sizes, when applied to populations *en masse,* reveal the frequency with which these variants occur. The findings are catalogued to construct databases for particular populations and when an unknown sample, of blood say, is used to prepare DNA fragments it can be compared with the reference data. Suppose a certain allele exists in the reference population at a frequency of 5%. If that allele is found in a particular individual there is only a 5 % chance that he is a member, genetically, of that population. Or, we can say, the odds are twenty to one against. Such statements assume that populations are in *Hardy-Weinburg equilibrium* (Box 1.1).

The population frequencies of STR loci are being continuously published to expand the data necessary for the calculation of *random match probabilities* in both criminal and family cases (see Box 1.2). To take a random example, in the March 2005 issue of the *Journal of Forensic Sciences,* data are presented for four different mainland Chinese groups, as well as for Brazilians and Northern Thais. Eventually all possible ethnic groups and subgroups will be surveyed and catalogued although there are signs that some may well object to this, as mentioned in both Chapter 3 and Chapter 4. DNA databases are now being compiled, not only for forensic purposes, but to try to detect patterns of disease and in the Human Genome Diversity Project (Chapter 3). Nonetheless the best-established databases exist for the support of criminal investigation and to some extent immigration. They are maintained in the USA by the FBI (which operates what is known as the Combined DNA Index

---

typing' [1991] Nature vol 354 at p 204. Jeffreys, A J 'Minisatellite repeat mapping by PCR: 1992 William Allan Award Address ' [1993] *American Journal of Human Genetics* vol 53 at p 1. For a glimpse of the pioneering work see Jeffreys, AJ Wilson, V et al 'Individual specific "fingerprints" of human DNA [1985] *Nature* vol 316, at p 76; Farr, CJ and Goodfellow, PN. 'New variations on the theme' [1991] *Nature* vol 354 at p 104.

Box 1.2 Random Match Probabilities

Each individual has two chromosomes of each type, and at a given locus one chromosome has an allele inherited from the father, the other has an allele from the mother. To calculate the random match probability (RMP) a population – properly stated, a population sample – is selected, usually numbering more than 100. In the US there are, at the time of writing, separate databases for Caucasians, African Americans, Hispanics, and American Indians. In UK the ethnic groups sampled are Caucasians, Blacks and Pakistanis. Databases for other ethnic groups and sub-groups appear continuously in the literature.

Suppose an investigator chooses a group of 100 and types a particular locus which has two possible alleles A1 and A2. In the group A1 occurs five times and A2 three times. The frequency of the genotype A1, A2 by the product rule is then:

$$2 \times 0.05 \times 0.03 = 0.003$$

(Why multiply by two? This is because there are two ways in which an individual can receive the genotype. He could receive A1 from either parent and A2 from either parent. So the chances are doubled.) Thus it is assumed that figure 0.003 represents the probability of finding the genotype in the parent population.

Another locus, independent of the first one, is chosen to count its alleles B1 and B2. They occur six times and four times respectively. So the probability of occurrence is:

$$2 \times 0.06 \times 0.04 = 0.0048$$

Again by the multiplication rule, the probability of both these genotypes occurring in a single individual selected at random, the RMP, is:

$$0.003 \times 0.0048 = 0.0000144$$

Mathematicians would prefer to express this as 1.44×10^{-5}. Nonetheless it generates the assumption that 14 persons in every million in this ethnic group will have the A,B genotype - or one in about 70,000. It represents the odds of two unrelated individuals in the same population having the same A, B genotype as being about one in 70,000 against. (Odds = probability / [1 - probability].) However if this exercise had been performed with the caucasian population of UK, for example, one would expect there should be about 800 matching individuals in the country. In a typical criminal case, of course, most of these could be eliminated as suspects because of sex, age, alibi, and so on, making the data from only these two loci extremely probative. It can readily be appreciated that if multiple loci are sampled, the RMP might indicate with extremely high probability that no other person in the whole world could possess the genotype of the suspect.

System, or CODIS),[5] and in UK by the Government's Forensic Science Service (known by them as the National DNA Database).[6] The UK database is said now to contain about three million samples - a formidable number; it seems then that perhaps one in every 25 of the population, man woman or child, is thus fingered today. Evidently, they are not all criminals.

Mitochondrial DNA (mtDNA)

Mitochondria (singular, 'mitochondrion') are often referred to as the powerhouses of the living cell, and enable us to utilise oxygen for the capture of energy. They contain DNA in the form of a circular, double stranded chromosome, like that in bacteria (indeed mitochondria are thought to be the descendants of archaic bacteria). The complete base sequence of human mtDNA was elucidated as long ago as 1981 and any allele detected in an individual can be checked against it. Technically, the information is known as the Cambridge Reference Sequence. Importantly, mtDNA is inherited solely from the mother, the spermatozoon having negligible mitochondria, which in any case generally do not enter the ovum at fertilisation. Thus males are irrelevant to relationship assessment if mtDNA is used for investigation - it traces maternal lineage. Everyone in the maternal line though shares some mtDNA – it is not unique for a few individuals. Its genes exist in high *copy number* (HCN), meaning high concentration. Each nucleus in a cell contains only one two copies of a specific gene or allele. Since there are hundreds or even thousands of mitochondria in a cell, each mitochondrial allele is present as very many copies in a given cell. (The red cells in the blood however are unusual in having no nucleus, and also no mitochondria; when a blood sample is taken for DNA fingerprinting, it is the white cells which yield the information.) MtDNA therefore comes in useful when the nuclear DNA is degraded. It was used, for example, in the identification of the Tsar of Russia's remains.[7]

In the case of mtDNA, generally two hypervariable regions of the chromosome are examined. Segments of these are amplified by PCR and sequenced to reveal variations – these are not minisatellite STRs and do not lend themselves to sorting merely by size. Occasionally during fertilisation the mitochondrion in the neck segment of the spermatozoon penetrates the

---

5   The FBI DNA site is < www.fbi.gov/hq/lab/handbook/examsdna.htm>.
6   The UK Forensic Science Service (FSS) site is <www.forensic.gov.uk>.
7   For more technical information on mtDNA examination, see Steighner, RJ and Holland, M 'Application of sequencing of mitochondrial DNA in forensic casework' [1996] *Methods in Molecular Biology* vol 109, at p 107. For the Romanov family specifically see Koblinsky, L Liotti, TF and Oeser-Sweat, J *DNA: Forensic and Legal Applications* (Wiley Interscience, 2005) p 121.

ovum, so that the child will have two types of mtDNA in his or her cells. This is known as *heteroplasmy* and can make the interpretation of results difficult. It appears to have first been an issue in the *Pappas* case in the US.[8]

In the US there are guidelines for mtDNA profiling published by the Scientific Working Group on DNA Analysis Methods (SWGDAM)[9] and in UK the Forensic Science Service has its own standards.[10]

Summary of 1.1

- Molecular biology entrains a central dogma.

- Information for protein synthesis is provided by sequences of bases in DNA.

- The DNA double helix owes its cohesion to the complementariness of the bases.

- Some stretches of DNA have sequences with no coding function, the introns.

- Some introns can be described as STRs.

- The STR lengths and sequences are characteristics of individuals.

- The STR pattern can be checked against its known frequency in a population to calculate random match probability.

- Most DNA is in the nucleus of the cell, but mtDNA can also be examined.

- mtDNA is of high copy number but heteroplasmy can be a problem.

1.2 Some Genetics

The genome is the total informational DNA in a cell (and therefore in whole organs). Although each cell contains the total genomic information, genes are switched off (repressed) or activated, in the interests of cell specialization.[11]

---

8   Walker, MD 'Mitochondrial DNA evidence in State v Pappas' [2003] *Jurimetrics* vol 43, at p 427.
9   <http://www.fbi.gov/hq/lab/fsc/backissu/april2003/swgdammitodna.htm>.
10   <http://www.forensicsci-goc.uk/forensic_t/inside/news/list_casefiles_pjp?case=2>.
11   There are various interlocking definitions of a gene:

The information is contained in each cell in 46 chromosomes, 23 pairs, but only in females. One variant of the gene (allele) is one chromosome, the other allele on the corresponding chromosome If the allele is the same on each chromosome, the individual is said to be homozygous; if they differ, he or she is heterozygous (Fig 1.4). Males have 22 paired chromosomes plus one X- and one Y- rather than the two Xs in females. Recall that there are two types of cell division – meiosis, in which the chromosome number is halved for the production of reproductive cells (gametes) and mitosis, which involves the replication of each of the 46 chromosomes to produce two new cells from each parent cell.

Haplotypes are groups of genes in the same region of a chromosome which thus tend to be inherited together during meiosis. However members can become separated during the process of recombination. If the observed haplotype frequencies in a population do not agree with their frequencies as predicted by multiplying frequencies of individual alleles (and of course this is usually the case since the alleles are close together on the chromosome and therefore occur together more often than chance would indicate) this is termed *linkage disequilibrium*. Linkage *equilibrium*, the opposite, is when random reassortment of alleles is observed. When DNA is being examined to determine human relatedness, multiple alleles are usually tracked. These should be far apart on the genome, avoiding linkage disequilibrium, for the probabilities of their individual occurrence are multiplied to give final probabilities, and this is only valid (by the multiplication rule) if they are inherited independently (see Chapter 2.4).

Mutations

The word *mutation* has two meanings – either the process by which a change occurs in the base sequence of DNA, or the alternatively the result of that change. Evidently mutations are responsible for evolution, and also disease. They are classifiable into two modes, either spontaneous, or induced (as by radiation and chemicals). Of the former, the one constituting the most immediate forensic interest and application is the substitution of one base/ nucleotide in a sequence by another. These are examples of *point mutations*, now known as *single nucleotide polymorphisms* (SNPs, sometimes

---

A a segment of DNA containing the information for the synthesis of a protein
B a unit of heredity, that is something ensuring inheritance of a trait (after Mendel)
C an entity which can result in disease when mutated
D a template for RNA synthesis
E an entity which uses energy supplied by the body to accomplish its own replication (the 'selfish gene', in other words).

Fig 1.4   A Pedigree Showing the Inheritance of STR Alleles

The father (□) possesses the 6 and 3 alleles on this particular chromosome,
the mother (O) the 4 and 2 alleles. Since the chromosomes randomly segregate
during meiosis the alleles 6,4, 3 and 2 randomly occur in the sons and daughters.
None of the children, of course has a 6,3 or 4,2 combination. The lower part
shows the electrophoretic pattern which might be obtained, corresponding to the
pedigree. Either the 6 or the 3 from the father is found in all the children. In the
case of uncertain parentage, the more alleles from the father detected, the grater the
probability of the relationship.

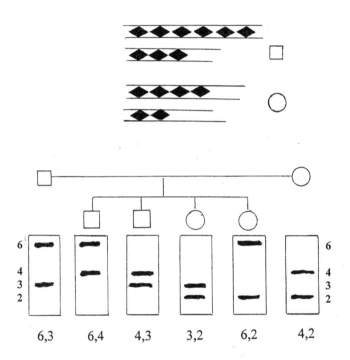

pronounced as 'snips'). They are in fact old mutations scattered throughout
the chromosome in manner unique for each individual, and the distribution is
of course inherited by progeny, from both father and mother. Therefore they
are (potentially) valuable in kinship and exclusion assessment procedures.
Over a million have been identified and are accessible on the Internet. Already
a commercial company can survey 176 SNPs in a DNA sample to assess

whether the donor is a pale skinned Caucasian, dark skinned Caucasian, African/Caribbean, South Asian, North Asian, or Middle-Eastern.[12]

They are not yet extensively used for forensic purposes, although that is said to be on its way, and are perhaps of most interest legally in that attempts have been made to patent them, or rather the knowledge of them (Chapter 4). SNPs generally do not much alter the nature of a protein if they occur on the gene for that protein and many of them are in non-coding sequences.[13] (There are exceptions - sickle cell anaemia is caused by the substitution of a single nucleotide in one of the genes for haemoglobin.) However expressed proteins are altered, or sometimes not expressed at all, as a result of other types of mutations such as large scale *deletions* and *frameshifts*. Deletions of chunks of bases compromise RNA synthesis (*transcription*) and subsequent protein synthesis for the RNA template (*translation*). So do frameshift mutations - these are the result of the additions or deletions of nucleotides and in that they distort the three base sequence coding for the amino acids since they alter the *reading frame*, usually adversely, in other words they cause disease. These mutations are evidently relevant to insurance and medical law.

Spontaneous mutations - that is, not inherited - do occur. Obviously, when relationships are being investigated, scientists try to examine regions of chromosomes where this is least likely to occur.

The Y-chromosome

The Y-chromosome, which has become increasingly important in forensics, has the property of *hemizygosity* (not to be confused with homozygosity, see above), meaning that it presents only one copy of each allele to the cell. The X-chromosome pair in females (and the others, the autosomes) between them of course carry two copies. The Y-chromosome contains few exons but has many non-coding and repetitive sequences which have been used forensically, especially in rape cases, since the Y-alleles, of course, are in no danger of being confused with the DNA from a female victim. Otherwise, if autosomal STRs are examined, a high preponderance of female material can mask any material from the assailant. The mutation rate of Y-STRs is rather

---

12   The SNP Consortium site is < http://snp.cshl.org>. For the technicalities see further Diune, AM Allen, M. 'A DNA microarray system for forensic SNP analysis' [2005] *Forensic Science International* vol 154, at p 111; Sobrino, B Brion, M et al ' SNPs in forensic genetics: a review on SNP typing methodologies [2005] *Forensic Science International* vol 154, at p 181.
13   Sutherland, G R and Richards, R I 'DNA repeats, a treasury of human variation' [1994] *New England Journal of Medicine* vol 331, at p 191.

high, however, which is a potential difficulty, but it can be overcome by examining multiple loci.[14] Mutation rates are taken into account in paternity cases when the father is not available and inferences are made from the analyses of male relatives.

The multiplication method (see Chapter 2-3) cannot be used to calculate probabilities of the occurrence of alleles, since they are not inherited independently, rather linked in a haplotype. The way round this is to calculate the probability of finding the entire haplotype in a random individual within the ethnic group of the suspect. If the biological material and the suspect both yield an unknown haplotype then the frequency of its occurrence is related to the number of individuals in the group database. So, if there are 1000 individuals in the database, the novel haplotype has a frequency of 2 in 1000, or one in 500. If the haplotype is not novel but matches two individuals in the database then the frequency is four in 1000 or one in 250 and so the suspect material might come from one out of any random 250 individuals in the group. So there is only one in 250 chance that the suspect is not the perpetrator. There are obvious problems of trying to explain such niceties to a jury. Evidently too, it is important to construct reliable databases, and this is being accomplished for European ethnic groups at least.[15]

The Y-chromosome is used to track migration and descent patterns[16] and it has in this instance an analogy to family names, usually transmitted, like the Y-chromosome, from father to son. The police are interested in the relationship between the Y-chromosome polymorphisms and name polymorphisms. For example if they know that the Jones family has a certain alleles in the Y-chromosome, and they find a stain with that same pattern, they might start looking for a criminal called Jones. In practice Y-SNPs are even more useful for this type of work, since they are stable from generation

14   Gill P Brenner C et al 'DNA Committee of the International Society for Forensic Genetics: recommendations on forensic analysis using the Y-chromosome [2001] *Forensic Science International* vol 124, at p 5; Kayser, M and Sajantila, A 'Mutation rates of Y-STR loci: implications for paternity testing and forensic analysis' [2001] *Forensic Science International* vol 118, at p 116. The Y- Chromosome Consortium is on <ycc.biosci.arizona. edu>. See also <http://ystr.org> for the European minimal haplotype.

15   See Koblinsky et al note 7, p 158 for a discussion of this difficulty.

16   Shreeve J 'Human journey' [2006] *National Geographic Magazine* vol 209, at p 60. Jefferson's pedigree is discussed at length by Watt, W J *DNA Detectives* (Hale, 2005) p 97. There have even been identification cases which employed the full cannon: Y- and mt-DNA plus the conventional STRs. See Irwin JA, Edson, SM et al 'DNA identification of "Earthquake Mc Govern", 50 years post mortem' [2007] *Journal of Forensic Science* vol 52, at p 115.

to generation after they have been established (originally they themselves were mutations, of course.)[17]

Summary of 1.2

- Each individual is either homozygous or heterozygous for an allele.

- Males however have one X and one Y chromosome; the latter is hemizygous.

- Alleles which are grouped together on a chromosome as haplotypes exhibit linkage disequilibrium, and in combination are avoided for forensic studies.

- Mutations create SNPs, the distribution of which is also individually characteristic.

- The Y-chromosome is useful in detecting specifically male biological material.

1.3 The Genome and its Manipulation

The total genetic information in an organism is called the genome. The human genome project was, and is, an effort to determine the sequence of bases in every chromosome in the human body. Some of the sequences of bases in humans are found throughout all living things (leaving aside such lowly forms as bacteria, moulds and the like). Such sequences from different species are said to have high homology, and to be highly conserved (in the course of evolution). There was some surprise among the general public, apparently, when it was announced that the chimpanzee genome had about 99% homology with that of humans. To a biochemist it was not at all surprising – we have almost all our metabolic pathways in common with the chimps, which means our enzymes and structural proteins must be very similar and so necessarily must be the DNA coding for them. The 1% or so of difference presumably codes for higher cognitive function and certain obvious but fairly superficial somatic differences. Of course this 1% is not neglected by forensic scientists - it is being explored to try to find if it can

---

17   Wetton, J H Tsang, KW et al 'Inferring the population of origin of DNA evidence within the UK by allele-specific hybridization of Y-SNPs' [2005] *Forensic Science International* vol 152, at p 45; Lessig, R, Zoledziewska M F et al 'Y-SNP genotyping – a new approach in forensic analysis' [2005] *Forensic Science International* vol 154, at p 128; Jones, S *Y - the Descent of Men*. (Little Brown, 2002) p 155. This book is goldmine of sociological and scientific lore on the Y-chromosome.

predict subtle human traits, like being ethnically European or having red hair, or even being bald, to give the police a better idea of who they (visually) are looking for. The SNPs, mentioned above, are likely to come into prominence within this context.

Some important techniques

Obtaining DNA fragments by cutting the VNTR regions with enzymes and then sorting them by size was the pioneer technique for identifying individual uniqueness. It was very laborious, involving the extraction and purification of the DNA, the measurement of its quantity, incubation with the restriction endonuclease to cut it, separation of the fragments (called restriction fragment length polymorphisms or RFLPs) by means of migration on an electrically polarized agarose gel, and hybridisation of the RFLPs, after separation. to a radioactive complementary DNA (cDNA) probe (that is, a piece of DNA which allows the A-T and G-C complementary binding). Finally the hybridised fragments were visualized by exposure to an X-ray film. Patterns like those in Fig 1.4 were obtained, depending on whether a single locus is examined, using a single locus probe (SLP) or a number of probes simultaneously, a so-called multiplex method. The end-stage fragments are sorted by size, and this is universally done by electrophoresis. This term is a general one referring to the separation of closely related molecules by the application of a direct current to the in mixture which they reside. In DNA work there are two principal modes, *gel electrophoresis* (the traditional method) and *capillary electrophoresis*. The former yields bands (*biobands*) on the agarose gel after an electrical current has been run though it. The smaller fragments migrate faster in the electrical field than do the bigger ones (Fig 1.4) and the pores in the gel have an added separation effect by seiving. The pattern obtained is sometimes referred to as an *electropherogram.* The bands are not visible to the naked eye, so various methods of staining or otherwise detecting them have been devised.

Comparatively large amounts of DNA are required for the above and there is often not enough DNA in a blood spot or stain to allow it to be conducted successfully. Fortunately even small amounts of DNA in a sample of blood or other body fluid can be multiplied by PCR,[18] the introduction of which was just as revolutionary as the earlier elucidation of individual variance in VNTRs. The endonucleases are not now required for PCR-based

18   All the standard texts go into PCR in some detail, see for example Koblinsky note 7, p 70; Butler, JM. *Forensic DNA Analysis* (Elsevier, 2005) p 63. In addition all texts of biochemistry and molecular biology hold descriptions.

procedures, but the first two steps of the traditional methods, preparation and quantitation of the DNA yield, remain essential. Subsequent to these preliminary steps, the genomic DNA is denatured by heat to yield single strands, and two *primers,* short lengths of DNA complementary to the flanking region of the locus of interest, are introduced. A DNA polymerase, that is an enzyme which links the nucleotide units one to another, is then added, and this accomplishes the synthesis of the sequence at that locus, complementary to each of the two denatured strands (Fig. 1.5). The longer the STR repeat in the part of the genome being examined, the longer will be the amplified fragments produced. Thus the various lengths of DNA are synthesized rather than cut out with enzymes. As a technique it does not in itself seem to have been successfully challenged in court. The essential point is that the amplification is exponential – the first phase of the treatment yields two copies of each primer-directed segment of the sample of double-stranded DNA, the second yields four copies, the third eight and so on to millions. The analogy is with an old urban legend which relates how a recruit to a new job told his boss that he did not want much of a salary, only a penny for the first day at work, two pence on the second, four on the third, *et sequitur,* and did not want to be paid till the end of the year. At that later date the formerly delighted boss found his employee had become a millionaire.

The gel electrophoresis technique is still used to separate the products of PCR but is rapidly being superseded by capillary electrophoresis.[19] This technique involves taking the unsorted DNA fragments and forcing them under pressure though a narrow tube across which there is an electrical potential. The tube contains a polyacrylamide derivative which adds a sieving effect to the separation due to charge differential As the separated fragments reach the end of the tube they are detected by a fluorimeter, a fluorescent marker having been added to them at an earlier stage, and this feeds the information to a computer which yields a retention time (characteristic of the size of the fragment) and a peak height (characteristic of its quantity) (Fig 1.6).

The techniques described above are not quantitative in the normal sense, that is they are not measurements on a continuous scale, which is what science is popularly supposed to produce.[20] The measurement of the

---

19   Capillary electrophoresis is dealt with in some detail by the standard texts. See Koblinski note 7, p 102 Butler note 18, p 318.
20   In ordinary life a number is just a number; however science has to particularise. Cardinals and ordinals are no doubt familiar. But we have to recognise numbers from an interval scale, like temperature, wherein the zero is arbitrary, and numbers on a ratio scale (like the LR). See also note 3 above.

Fig 1.5 The Principle of the Polymerase Chain Reaction

The preliminary step, the unwinding of the double helix of the sample of DNA, is omitted. After this, the two primers (■) allow extension of the selected segment, after which there is further unwinding, further primer-directed replication, and so on exponentially.

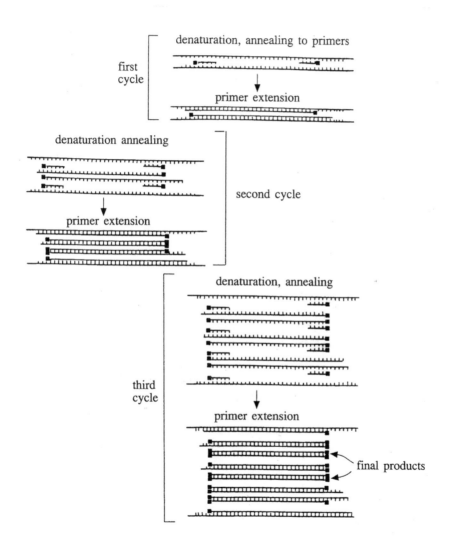

distance a fragment travels on a gel or the speed with which is moves through a capillary is not performed for the sake of recording such measurements in themselves, rather to discover whether another fragment from another bodily sample shows the same mobility. Of course a quantitative element enters at the stage of the statistical evaluation of the results, producing probability estimates, and this is where DNA technology has an advantage over the other prime means of forensic identification, the fingerprint/thumbprint. (The statistics relating to DNA are dealt with in Chapter 2.4 and Chapter 3.3).

Quite recently the technique of low copy number (LCN) DNA profiling has come to the fore. This simply means the ability to examine DNA from very small samples, as little as 100 pg, that is, the DNA in a single cell, a blood sample too small to be detected by the naked eye, or a fingerprint smear. (See Box 2.4) It supports 34 PCR cycles, beyond which there tends to be too much artefactual interference. The technique is enabled by a commercial company, Applied Biosystems, which markets a kit entitled Second Generation Multiplex Plus (SGM Plus).[21]

The ability to profile smaller and smaller samples comes with some disadvantages, however. There is the problem of 'stutter' - this when a small band accompanies the authentic STR band. This is a PCR artifact related to certain sequences. It does not generally interfere with interpretation since the stutter bands are small compared to the authentic ones. If it is large however it might be presumed that the DNA sample being examined represents a mixture from two individuals. Another problem is that of allele dropout. In its simplest manifestation this occurs when the PCR primer fails to bind to its complementary strand on the flanking region after which of course it will not serve to amplify the adjacent allele. It follows that the flanking region should be stable, that is, not subject to mutation. Fortunately however allele dropout appears to be relatively uncommon.

The preceding techniques relate mainly to relationship or identification requirements. The other important branch of biotechnology has a broad scope in agriculture and medical science, in that it involves transferring DNA fragments, or more importantly whole genes, from one chromosomal site to another. In food technology usually the gene is transferred from one species to another, whereas in gene therapy an unmutated human gene is

---

21   Gill, P Whitaker, J et al 'An investigation of the rigor of interpretation rules for STRs derived from less than 100 pg of DNA' [2000] *Forensic Science International* vol 112, at p 17. (A picogram (pg) is 10-12 g or a billionth of a gram. Multiplex techniques have needed about 1 nanogram (ng) or 10-9 g.) A succinct account is given by Goodwin, W Linacre, A et al *An Introduction to Forensic Genetics* (John Wiley, 2007) p 68.

Fig 1.6 Two Modes of Visualising the Assortment of DNA Fragments

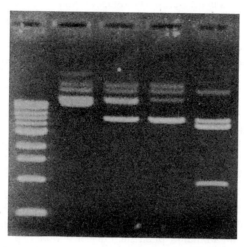

This shows the electrophoresis gel obtained from a blood sample found at a crime scene compared with samples from three suspects. Two alleles were examined in each individual, giving four bands, so each sample exhibited heterozygosity. That is, each person carried two different versions of the same allele. On the left is a 'ladder' consisting of DNA size standards. The probability of 'B' being the culprit can be inferred from the frequency of these alleles in the parent population, as explained n the text.

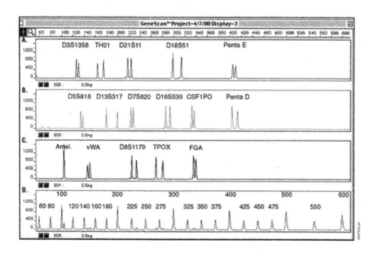

This shows a print-out following capillary electrophoresis of DNA fragments. The alleles, here 16 from a single individual, are also sorted by size, with the concentration of each being indicated by the height of its peak, rather than by the density of its band, as in gel electrophoresis above. All alleles are automatically identified (e.g. Amel for Amelogenin). The names accorded to the alleles in themselves have no significance. The peaks below represent, again, a set of size standards. Obviously the pattern obtained can readily be compared with that from another individual. However multiple samples cannot be accommodated on the same run, as is the case with gel electrophoresis. (Chart by courtesy of Promega Pte Ltd.)

---

identified for splicing, although there is no reason why therapeutic genes could not be obtained from animals. As a whole these procedures are known as *recombinant DNA technology*, of which Fig 1.7 attempts a simplistic representation. Unlike the modern forensic PCR-based techniques, it remains heavily dependent on the restriction endonucleases necessary for excision of the relevant gene before its ligation into its new site. Producing a gene for recombination by excising it with enzymes is one thing, but inserting it into the cells of an animal or plant such that it will be expressed is another. Scientists have had to exercise a great deal of ingenuity in this direction.[22] Techniques for the creation of transgenic animals include:

- Microinjection of DNA into the pronucleus of a fertilised oocyte (zygote)

- Integration of a retroviral vector into an early embryo. (Retro viruses are RNA viruses which will direct translation, that is the formation an amino acid chain from the information in the virus bases sequence.)

- Incorporation of genetically manipulated pluripotent cells. These are cells which have the capacity to differentiate into end-stage cells - stem cells is an alternative term, most often used in the media.

- Transfer of genetically altered nuclei into enucleated oocytes

The use of DNA technology for forensic purposes has evoked little or no public concern, in contrast to its use for food production, which has caused frank outrage (Chapter 5). Gene therapy has remained legally uncontroversial, perhaps because it has not so far been a proven success. If dispute arises it

---

22 Standard texts on the less technical aspects of recombinant DNA technology are: Primrose, SB and Malden, MA *Principles of Gene Manipulation and Genomics* (Blackwell, 2006); Murrel, J C and Roberts, M *Understanding Genetic Engineering* (Ellis Horwood, 1989); also see <http://news.bbc.co.uk/2/hi/health/4902150.stm> for a journalistic viewpoint.

Fig 1.7 The Construction of Recombinant DNA

The process is dependent on two enzymes, first the restriction endonuclease (RE) which cuts both DNAs at a known, specific point, and the ligase, which joins the 'sticky ends' together.

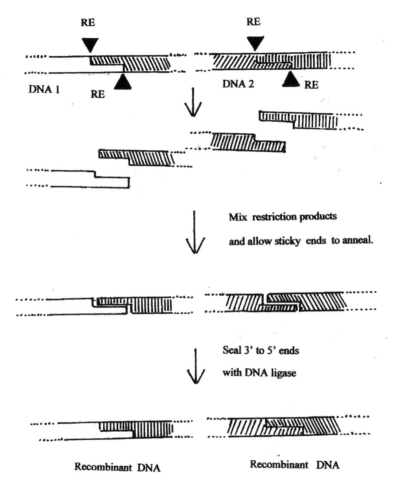

is likely to be in the context of the allocation of scarce resources by health authorities. The herceptin issue will no doubt be quoted as a precedent. Herceptin is a drug useful in the treatment of early breast cancer, but it costs around 20,000 pounds sterling per year per patient. The Swindon health authorities refused to allow it to be prescribed for a Ms Rogers. After the usual progress through the lower courts the Court of Appeal ruled that the policy of the authorities was 'irrational and unlawful', mainly on the grounds that there was no justification in favouring one patient over another as long as the clinical criteria for treatment were met. Any form of gene therapy is likely to be even more expensive, and may attract the same sort of issues.

The future

The future is becoming the present as one writes. Databases are being compiled for insects which are important forensically. Also, there has been one case at least in which a victim was identified via of his DNA as removed from the larvae which had been feeding on his remains. Analysis of the postmortem fragmentation of DNA is being investigated as a means of assessing the time of death.

The process of preparing, measuring, and amplifying the DNA sample then applying it to a gel or column demands skill and experience, and a modern endeavour is to achieve automation sufficient to (largely) eliminate the human element, and if possible make determination of the profile a matter of minutes rather than days or weeks. This is rapidly being perfected, mainly by commercial companies such as Promega and Applied Biosystems. One drawback of contemporary PRC techniques is that the double-stranded DNA in a sample must unwound and then annealed by heating and cooling (in a 'thermal cycler'), but there are now moves to use helicases, enzymes which achieve the unwinding of double stranded DNA in the cold. Detectives are anxious to have access to instruments sufficiently 'deskilled' and speeded up to be used at the crime scene itself. Scientists are said to be lukewarm about this because any results obtained in the field might still have to be validated in the laboratory.

Another innovation is the genomic matching technique, which examines blocks of DNA in the human histocompatibility complex, rather than single alleles. This is said to be promising in that it will be cheaper than existing techniques and allow enhanced throughput.[23] It will soon be possible to detect and analyse foetal DNA in maternal serum - this will have profound effects on paternity testing (Chapter 3).[24] Other techniques are arriving which may be just as revolutionary as the original Jeffreys RFLP breakthrough - for example Matrix Assisted Laser Desorption Ionisation – Time of Flight Mass

---

23   Laird, R., Dawkins, RL et al 'Use of the genomic matching technique (GMT) to complement multiplex STR profiling reduces DNA profiling costs in high volume and intelligence led screens' [2005] *Forensic Science International* vol 151, at p 249.
24   Lo, D Y M. 'Fetal DNA in maternal plasma: biology and diagnostic applications' [2000] *Clinical Chemistry* vol 46 at p 1903

Spectrometry or MALDI-TOFMS. This offers a STR size sorting technique, analogous in a way to the gel methods, but extremely fast. Some scientists are working on size sorting by the detection of unwinding temperature – the more nucleotides in a STR, the higher its melting temperature. STRs are heated after hybridization to a segment of synthetic DNA labeled with fluorescent dyes. The temperature of melting, detected by a colour change, is correlated with the STR size. Many other developments are in the offing.[25]

Summary of 1.3

- PCR is used to amplify segments of DNA in biological samples.

- Different types of electrophoresis allow the amplified segments to be sorted by size.

- The resultant patterns are compared against suspect samples or databases.

- Recombinant DNA technology depends on restriction endonucleases.

- These enzymes cut DNA at specific points in a chromosome so that another segment of DNA (a recombinant gene) can be inserted.

- Recombinant technology is important in production of genetically modified food and (potentially) in human gene therapy.

1.4   Proteomics

Molecular biology is concerned with molecules other than nucleic acids. There is a relatively new area of study termed *proteomics* (sometimes *peptidomics*, a peptide being a smaller version of a protein) which sets out to examine, not the genetic makeup of a cell, but rather it seeks to determine which proteins a cell, or a tissue for that matter, is actively expressing. DNA, as genes, represents only the synthetic potential of the cell, important though that may be. In most tissues, a large proportion of genes are permanently repressed (turned off) anyway. One could say that proteomics asks, simplistically, 'what is the cell doing in the way of protein synthesis?'[26] (The suffix *–omics,* by

25   Mennel, J and Shaw, I 'The future of forensic science Part 1. A UK forensic science and user and provider perspective' [2006] *Forensic Science International* supplements 157S, and S7.

26   Soloviev, S and Finch, P 'Peptidomics, current status' [2005] *Journal of Chromatography* vol B 815, at p 11. See also <http://www.jdi.ucl.ac.uk/cs_networls/cs_

the way, has been hijacked to define a series of new candidate disciplines.[27])
Proteomics has little to do with matching individuals, as is the case for DNA
profiling. However it offers potential for yielding information on state of
health, lifestyle, or behaviour. In other words, proteomics offers another
biomarker in addition to (digit) fingerprints, DNA profiles/fingerprints,
iris configuration, and others. Suppose a piece of tissue is found at a crime
site. Of course first of all it is mined for its DNA, as common sense would
indicate. But what else can it reveal? Suppose the tissue is a piece of bone,
and bone usually contains marrow, which as an alternative description is the
haemopoietic tissue synthesizing haemoglobin. Suppose a proteomic scan
of its proteins reveals sickle cell haemoglobin. This might indicate a search
of hospital records in addition to DNA databases. Admittedly proteomics
patterns are very complex (Fig 1.8) but assessment techniques for them are
being rapidly developed.

If not proteins, then messenger RNA (mRNA) as the intermediary
between the genomic information and the synthesis of proteins outside
the cell nucleus, representing expressed protein, can be the subject of
investigation. Examination of mRNA in a specimen found at the scene of a
crime can reveal the biological nature of the specimen, whether it is saliva,
semen, sputum, gastric fluid, and so on.[28] This has always been forensically
desirable, but previous techniques were immunochemical, that is, to detect
saliva, say, one had to create an antibody specific for a protein in the sputum,
such as histatin 3, and allow it to react with specimen in such a way that this
could be detected, were the specimen to be what was suspected. RNA as a
vehicle for forensic investigation was problematic due to its instability (in
contrast to DNA) but it can now be stored safely at room temperature by a
process which is basically one of dehydration.

Proteins come into prominence in many areas of forensics. The famous
Lindy Chamberlain case in Northern Australia (filmed as *Cry in the Dark*)
substantially hinged on whether haemoglobin found in the car was in fact
foetal haemoglobin, which persists in the blood of young babies. One can
recall the role of ricin, derived from castor beans, in killing Georgi Markov

---

contacts/soloviev.php>.

27   There are other 'omics', e.g. lipidomics, the pattern of expression of lipids by cells.
See <http://omics.org/.org>.

28   Jusola, J and Ballantyne, J. ' Multiplex mRNA profiling for the identification of body
fluids' [2005] *Forensic Science International* vol 152, at p 1: Nussbaumer, C Gharehbagli
–Schnell, E et al ' Messenger RNA profiling: a novel method of body fluid identification
by real time PCR' [2006] *Forensic Science International* vol 157, at p 181.

Fig 1.8 A Typical Proteomics Pattern

The tissue under investigation here produces hundreds of proteins, which indicate its functions and output; in contrast, knowledge of the DNA sequences in the cells of the tissue only indicates its potential for synthesizing proteins. The individual spots can be identified as required. This is a two dimensional process, the current being run through the gel a second time at right angles to the first. It is obvious that much skill is required for interpretation. (Courtesy of Dr Neil Langlois and the editors of *Medicine Science and the Law*.)

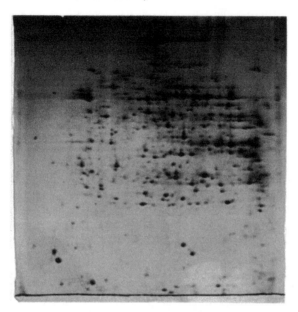

in 1978.[29] The p53 protein monitors a cell's DNA. If damage to the cell is detected, p53 causes the cell to enter a process of DNA repair, and if this fails, it induces apoptosis, that is, programmed cell death. Thus p53 is a response to injury. It has forensic importance, therefore, in that if a deceased person exhibits trauma, the p53 protein will be present in the injury site, only if the injury was caused before death, but it will be absent if the injury was caused after death.[30] This is something any investigating team might well wish to know.

29   Walsh, NP. 'Markov's umbrella assassin revealed' *The Guardian* 6th June, 2005.
30   Tarran, S Dziewulski, P et al 'A study of p53 expression in thermal burns of human skin for the determination of wound age' [2004] *Medicine, Science and the Law* vol 44, at p 222.

Finally, many of the important intellectual property cases (Chapter 4) deal with proteins rather than DNA. Insulin, tissue plasminogen activator, and erythropoietin have all engendered keynote cases in the patents courts. Erythropoietin threw up a challenge to one patent court's grasp of technicalities, in that it had to consider the degree of glycosylation of this protein (*Amgen* v *Transkaryotic Therapies*, Chapter 4, p 193). Many proteins, although basically a set of amino acids in end-to-end linkage, are joined to other molecular species in the process of posttranslational modification (translation it itself being the linkage process for the amino acids). The argument in the case mentioned turned on whether Amgen's erythropoietin, which was more glycosylated (posttranslationally bound to carbohydrate) than the equivalent protein found in human urine, and which was well characterised, was novel or not.

One of the many aims of biotechnology has been to produce therapeutically valuable proteins and prophylactic vaccines in the milk of mammals. As everybody knows, a cow has a tremendous capacity for the synthesis of milk and harvesting relatively massive quantities of protein from it is an attractive prospect. (Of course much skill has to applied to separate out the desired protein and purify it.) Fibrinogen, the protein converted to fibrin in shed blood and therefore promoting clotting, is one example of a desirable product, useful in treating haemophilia and perhaps battleground wounds, for example. In a US patent case *Verlander* v *Garner* (2003)[31] the court had to consider the following claim: 'A non-human mammal carrying in its germline DNA segments encoding Aα, Bβ and γ chains of fibrinogen, wherein female progeny of said animal express DNA segments in a mammary gland to produce biocompetent fibrinogen.' This relatively short sentence conceals much that is important in biotechnology law. First of all, 'non-human' is carefully inserted. In all countries whose legislatures have addressed the matter, tampering with the human germline is illegal. However in the context of the said patent the modification has to be made to the germline since insertion of the gene into a series of animals in every generation would be prohibitively expensive. Then, it is apparent that the protein consists of three separate chains; a separate gene has the information for each chain and these must be made to a associate to yield the integral protein, so that appreciation by the court of the technical difficulties involved in that goes to the concept of inventive step. Finally, the fibrinogen is described as 'biocompetent', that is, it fulfills it function in that it can be split by thrombin to yield fibrin. It

---

31 [2003] CAFC 02-1366, interference no 104,242. This was an interference action, that is a dispute between the filers of a second patent (Garner) and the owners of a preceding patent (Verlander) over the identity or non-identity of claims in the two patent applications.

would be quite possible to produce a three chain protein vaguely describable as fibrinogen but in which the chains are in the wrong alignment or have the wrong conformation. (The case in itself hinged on the obviousness of the techniques.) (See Chapter 4 for more extended discussion of molecular aspects of patenting.)

For completeness, it must be mentioned that a tissue can yield information on the basis of many different types of molecules detected in it. In the case of small molecules such as carbohydrates, the science is termed 'metabolomics.' In summary, protein and metabolic profiles can be representative of the state of health, lifestyle, behavioural patterns, sample origin, severity and type of trauma, as well as time of death.

Summary of 1.4

- An alternative aspect of molecular biology in forensics, called proteomics, relies on examination of proteins in cells and tissues.

- Protein patterns can offer information on health, lifestyle or behaviour.

- Examination of mRNA can also offer information as to the nature of a specimen.

- The technicalities of protein chemistry have been important in the area of intellectual property law.

1.5 Some Overviews

The public acceptance of DNA technology is presumably grounded on the perception that it can be seen to work, and the fact that what is presented in court in most civil and criminal proceedings remains in essence a probability rather than a certainty (Box 1-2) seems no drawback to this acceptance. (Placid acceptance does not of course extend to defence attorneys, as will be mentioned in Chapter 2.) The situation is different for the other arm of DNA technology, the engineering of genetically modified organisms (GMOs), which is actively demonised outside governmental and scientific circles. GMOs will inevitably be blamed by an individual or a group who imagine that significant harm has accrued from them. In the event of suit alleging this, the civil courts will have to construe the scientific evidence using principles which appear to have been already laid down both in England and US. Cases analagous to *Reynard* v *NEC Corporation* (1995) may occur; the plaintiff in this case claimed damages for suffering from a brain tumour claimed to

Table 1.1 Summary of Applications of DNA Technology to Law in General

Application	Area of Law	Page ref
Matching of biological materials; time of death	Criminal	36
Baby switching; human and organ trafficking	Criminal	116
Identity theft	Criminal	44
Paternity /relationship testing	Family; immigration	116
Gene patenting	Intellectual property	165
Identification after mass burials/ disasters	Humanitarian; international	37
Genetically modified organisms and foods	Food; EU; international	203
Personal privacy	Privacy; tort	131
Employment discrimination	Employment	156
Genetic defects and predictive diagnosis	Medical; insurance	154
Identification of smuggled animals	Wildlife (CITES)	243
Biopiracy/biodiversity	International (CBD)	245
Gene doping in sport	Sports	*
Manufacture of new pathogens	International/ humanitarian	258
Tracing materials and products	Forgery; international trade	202

Probably most have ramifications in administrative law and certainly all in the law of evidence.

* This aspect is just becoming apparent. See Custer KF 'From mice to men: genetic doping in sport' *Hastings International and Comparative Law Review* [2007] vol 30, at p 183.

be caused by the use of a cellular telephone.[32] It may not be long before we see claims that genetically modified foods have caused colon cancer, for example.

When this situation arises, useful developments in the law relating the presentation use of scientific evidence (in the US) will apply. In *Daubert* v *Merrel Dow* P*harmaceuticals* (1993) the plaintiffs attempted to prove that birth defects had been caused by a pregnancy sickness therapy. The case went to the Supreme Court on the issue of whether the appropriate legal

32 *Reynard v NEC Corporation* [1995] 887 F. Supp 1500 (M.D. Fla).

standard for the admissibility of scientific evidence was a general acceptance of the evidence by the scientific community at large, or the more liberal one of reliability and relevance.[33] The latter was held to be correct. The points to be tested have been summarized as:

- Whether the underlying theory or technique can be or has been tested for its validity.

- Has the theory or technique been subjected to peer review and publication?

- What is the known or potential rate of error of the technique and do standards for it exist?

- What is the degree of acceptance within the scientific community?

Some states however use Rule of Evidence 702: ' If scientific.... knowledge will assist the trier of facts to understand the evidence or to determine a fact in issue, a witness qualified as an expert by knowledge, skill, experience, training or education may testify thereto in form of an opinion or otherwise.' It was modified in 2000 to add: ' A witness... qualified... may testify if (1) testimony is based on sufficient facts or data (2) the testimony is the product of reliable principles and methods, (3) the witness has applied principles and methods reliably to the case.

In the Commonwealth the rules for expert witnesses and the mechanism of *voir dire* may be adopted. In England the Civil Procedure Rules which came into force on April 4, 2005 apply.[34] (The criminal procedure rules seem still to be pending at the time of writing.) Some of the relevant points are:

- The expert must give details of his qualifications.

---

33   There is a large literature on admissibility standards in the US courts. The Frye hearing is the most venerable - 293F. 1013,D.C. Cir. 1923 - and takes account of the generality of scientific opinion with respect to the underlying principles at issue. In many states it was superceded by the rules formulated in *Daubert v Merrill Dow Pharmaceuticals* [1993] 509 US 579. For an informative discussion see Brixen, CE and Meis, CE 'Codifying the "Daubert Trilogy": the amendment to the Federal Rule of Evidence 702' [2000] *Jurimetrics Journal* vol 40, at p 527. In James, SH and Nordby, T J *Forensic Science* (CRC Press, 2002), there is a list of state admissibility standards, variously Frye, Daubert or Rule of Evidence 702, plus relevant statutes state by state.

34   Rules for expert witnesses in UK, see the website of the Department for Constitutional Affairs, specifically <http://www.dca.gov.uk/civil/procrules_fin/contents/practice_directions/pd_part35.htm>. Also < http://www.ucl.ac.uk/jdi/cs_network/cs_contents/> For a general review see Kershaw, A 'Expert evidence: managing the risks. *New Law Journal* 29 July 2005, p 1166.

- The expert must make clear which of the facts stated are within his own knowledge.

- Where there is a range of opinion the expert must summarise the range of opinion.

- The expert must give reasons for his own opinion.

- The report must contain a statement that the expert understands his duty to the Court.

Obviously these points are concerned not only with scientific testimony as such. The liability of expert witnesses received an extensive airing in the English courts following the Sally Clark case.[35] She had been convicted, at least partially, on the statistical evidence given by the paediatrician Sir Roy Meadows. He calculated the odds against two children in the same family suffering cot deaths as 73 million to one against. At the time of the trial the Royal Statistical Society was concerned enough to issue a statement, pointing out that that Meadows made the assumption that such deaths occurred independently within families, which was invalid. Nonetheless, Sally Clark's first appeal was turned down. Eventually it came back to the Court of Appeal via the reference by the Criminal Case Review Commission and on other evidence (although the statistical evidence was reviewed in depth) the sentence was quashed. Professor Meadows was subsequently struck off the medical register by the General Medical Council on the grounds of serious professional misconduct, and he appealed, in his turn, to the High Court. A single judge heard the case and decided that expert witnesses could be entitled to immunity from disciplinary proceedings (by their professional bodies), largely on the grounds that it could not be right for an expert witness to be faced with the loss of his livelihood subsequent to disciplinary action when an equivalent civil action in professional negligence would result only in a financial penalty by way of damages. Thence on to the Court of Appeal, wherein three judges including the Master of the Rolls decided otherwise - largely on the grounds that the professional disciplinary bodies had an ultimate responsibility to the public in assessing competence to practice. This last finding was not welcome to the Expert Witness Institute[36] which

---

35   *R v Clark* [2003] EWCA Crim 1020. For a transcript of the Court of Appeal judgement, see <http://www.sallyclark.org.uk/Judgment03.html> For the many ramifications of the case see Magner, T 'To err is human....' *New Law Journal* 24th Feb, 2006 p 301; also Montgomery C. 'Forensic science in the trial of Sally Clark' [2004] *Medicine, Science and the Law* vol 44, at p 185.

36   The Expert Witness Institute site is: <www.ewi.org.uk>.

expressed fears about the willingness of its members to come forward in the face of the decision.

Molecular biology as represented by nucleic acids and proteins is relevant to a surprising number of areas of law (Table 1-1) and new comminglings will no doubt come to light in due course. Of course regulation, the province of administrative law, lags behind the science, for the legislators could hardly be expected to envisage the technology before the scientists. Public fears and concerns, plus misconceptions, tend to be reflected first in advisory bodies and commissions of enquiry, recommendations from which can eventually be promoted to domestic legislation (Tables 1.2 and 1.3) and then on to international instruments, which on the whole tend as yet to be merely declaratory. The new areas of administrative law are said to represent a departure from tradition in UK at least where the authorities for long preferred to work within the established organs, the legislature (select committees for example) and the civil service. The US was more attracted to the *ad hoc* agency (the Tennessee Valley Authority for example). UK has gone much the same way, with a plethora of agencies having a variety of advisory and regulatory roles, such as the Human Genetics Commission, the Human Fertilisation and Embryology Authority, and the Food Standards Authority; there is a proposal for a Council for the Registration of Forensic Practitioners, and if gene therapy ever becomes general it may regulated in part by the National Institute for Clinical Excellence. DNA changes everything.

Summary of 1.5

- In general public acceptance of DNA technology extends to the criminal process but not to genetically modified food.

- When the relevance and reliability of DNA technology is disputed the courts have evolved mechanisms to allow or disallow the presentation of evidence.

- In the US the *Daubert* rules and or Rule of Evidence 702 are applied.

- In England and the Commonwealth either a *voir dire* and/or Civil/Criminal Rules of Evidence are apposite.

- The scientist as expert witness is subject to these rules.

- Aspects of DNA are now the direct concern of many statutes and regulatory/licencing bodies.

Table 1-2 Legislation, Regulation and DNA Technology in UK

Statute

Disability Discrimination Act (1995) s 1	Disability defined as actual, not genetic potential incapacity.
Data Protection Act (1998)	Provisions generally considered to apply to DNA databases
Criminal Justice and Police Act (2001) s 80	Samples from arrestees not convicted retainable by police
Criminal Justice Act (2003) ss 76-78	Autrefois acquit abolished
Human Tissue Act (2004) s 45	Theft of DNA introduced

Regulatory/advisory

Human Genetics Commission (1999)	Watching/advisory brief on genetics
Human Fertilisation and Embryology Authority (1991)	Indirect brief on genetics as regulator regulator of ovum/sperm technology
Genetics and Insurance Committee (1999)	Non-statutory advice on insurance issues
Food Standards Agency (2000)	To monitor safety of, and give advice on, novel foods
Medicines and Healthcare Products Regulatory Agency (2003)	Regulation of genetic testing devices
National Institute for Health and Clinical Excellence (2003)	Advice on national policy for, inter alia, gene therapy

Westminster legislation may not necessarily be applicable to Scotland and Northern Ireland, and regulatory/advisory bodies too are sometimes territorial; nor does this claim to be exhaustive.

Table 1-3 Legislation, Regulation and DNA Technology in the US

Federal Statutes

Economic Espionage Act (1996)	Combatting industrial espionage (clearly importing DNA technology)
Health Insurance Portability and Accountability Act (1996)	Restriction on the use of health records (including genetic information)
DNA Identification Act (1994)	To establish national DNA bank by FBI
DNA Database Compilation Act (2003) ('Debbie Smith' Act)	Financing backlog of DNA testing
Justice for All Act (2004)	Funding for postconviction DNA testing
Genetic Discrimination Act (2008)	Insurance/employment protection in the face of genetic information

Regulatory/advisory bodies

Scientific Working Group on DNA Analysis (1999) (FBI)	Technical guidelines for DNA analysis
National Council on the Future of Evidence (defunct)	Advice to Attorney General
DNA Advisory Board (FBI) (1994)	Advice on quality, support of CODIS
Centers for Disease Control (Office of Genomics and Disease Prevention) (1997)	Integration of efforts in human genetics
Advisory Committee on Genetic Testing (National Institutes of Health) (1998)	Policy advice to the Dept of Health and Human Services
Recombinant DNA Advisory Committee (National Institutes of Health (1974)	Oversight of gene therapy research
President's Council for Bioethics (2001)	Independent advice to President

Not necessarily exhaustive

Chapter 2

Criminal Law

2.1 Biology of Molecular Transfer Processes

The Locard principle, that any physical contact between two entities predicates transfer of material, however minute, is of course the basis of molecular forensics. However in the case of transfer of macromolecules there must be, in addition, consideration not just of their transfer but also of their stability. Further, if a molecule with potentially probative value is frankly unstable, the degradation product has to be considered. Obviously, instability is seldom a problem with paint, hairs, fibres, and so on, but it must be considered in the context of biological materials. Stability is relative. Within the range of biological materials, DNA is much more stable than RNA, and more stable than most proteins, which are subject to what is termed denaturation by heat and many chemicals. DNA can also be denatured, in the sense of having its two complementary strands separated, but it retains its information because that exists in a linear array, not in three-dimensional space. Protein molecules however possess most of their functional information in their spatial configurations and charge distributions, and these are disrupted on denaturation. Conventional blood protein typing, that is the examination of polymorphisms in red cell antigens and enzymes, cannot be performed on most ancient remains to detect relationships, especially under humid and hot conditions, due to denaturation. When denatured these proteins lose their reactivity to the antibodies designed to detect them by immunological techniques and that is why DNA has opened up new vistas in this area.

The relative stability of DNA is manifested by the successful profiling of the long dead, such as Joseph Mengele,[1] Egyptian mummies,[2] and Tsar Alexander III and his family. The question of stability arose specifically in respect of this last example. The original examination of the mtDNA from the bones of the Russian imperial family was conducted in 1993, but in 2004 a group of scientists in USA called into question the results, maintaining that DNA of sufficient integrity could not have survived for seventy years in a shallow moist grave.[3] Coming up to date, the deceased from the December

---

1 Jeffreys AJ, Allen MJ et al. Identification of the skeletal remains of Josef Mengele by DNA analysis. [1992] *Forensic Science International* vol 56, at p 65.
2 <www.pbs.org/wnet/pharaohs/secrets3.html> ; also Paabo, S 'Molecular cloning of an ancient Egyptian mummy' [1985] Nature vol 314, at p 644
3 Highfield, R 'Scientists reopen the Romanov enquiry' *Daily Telegraph* 12th July, 2004. There was also an argument about heteroplasmy in the remains - some groups of

26th 2004 tsunami are being identified by their DNA, but again stability will limit the investigations - DNA although a famously robust molecule has its limits in the hot and humid conditions of South East Asia. From the forensic point of view, despite its stability, DNA must be handled carefully, and in trials it is always open to the defence to challenge evidence obtained from improperly or carelessly handled specimens. Defence attorneys have not been slow to proceed down this avenue (see 2.4 below). Degradation was a persistent problem when the pioneering RFLP techniques were used. The more modern STRs technique which examine shorter repetitive segments of DNA rather than VNTRs are an improvement in this direction.[4]

2.2 Possession and Ownership of DNA

Before going on to discuss the theft of DNA, as genetic material, it is necessary to consider what sort of property DNA, or alternatively, its genetic information, might consist of. On the principle that the old cases are the best, discussions of the nature of property often begin with the Australian classic of *Victoria Park Racing and Recreation Grounds* v *Taylor* (1937).[5] The plaintiff race-track owners brought an injunctive action against three parties. One of these had a property overlooking the racecourse, to enable a second to comment on the races and relay the results to a third, a radio broadcasting company. The result was that punters stayed away from racecourse and placed their bets at home. The essence of the plaintiff's claim was in nuisance, which allegedly had deprived it of the enjoyment of, and profit from, its land. Three of the judges of the Supreme Court of New South Wales refused the injunction, two would have allowed it. Between them, they surveyed almost every aspect of property rights. It is agreed on all sides that the judgements in the case reveal that the idea of property is elusive, and further, is dynamic. A novelty in the facts of *Victoria Park Racing* was the use of radio to transmit the results in real time (to use the modern jargon); it

---

scientists detected this, others failed to do so. See also Butler, JM *Forensic DNA Typing* (Elsevier, 2nd edn, 2005) p 252.

4   For an account of the changeover from VNTRs to STRs at the time see Lygo, J 'Sharpening the focus – "shift to mixtures" ' [1991] *New Law Journal* April 5, p 448. Other accounts of STRs are by Butler, note 3, p 373 ; Rudin, K and Inman, R *Forensic DNA Analysis* (CRC Press, 2001) p 150 and by Koblinsky, L, Liotti, TF and Oeser-Sweat, J *DNA: Forensic and Legal Applications* (Wiley-Interscience, 2005) p 107. For an advanced treatment see Gill, P, Curran, J et al 'A graphical simulation of the entire DNA process associated with the analysis of STR loci' [2005] *Nucleic Acid Research* vol 33, at p. 632.

5   [1937] 58 CLR 479 An informative modern exposition of Victoria Racing it is to be found in Mossman, M J and Flanagan, WF. *Property Law: Cases and Commentary.* (Edmond Montgomery Publications Ltd, 1998) p 1.

Box 2-1 Questions Apposite to the Ownership of Genetic Material

(1) Does a person own the physical DNA which is inside his body?

(2) Does a person retain ownership pf the physical DNA isolated from his cells by some other party?

(3) Can a person own knowledge of the base sequence in the DNA of another individual (either the entire genome or in part) without the acquiescence of the donor?

(4) Does a person own, in perpetuity, the base sequence of his own DNA, given that it is unique (even if he has a monozygotic twin, since spontaneous mutations may occur)?

(5) If a person can own the knowledge of partial base sequences from the genome of

  a.   an individual, or

  b.   a group of individuals such as a tribe

     must such sequences code for specific proteins ?

(No doubt the list could be expanded.)

---

was that factor which caused the loss to the plaintiff – delayed publication of the results in newspapers would not have had the same impact. One can reasonably expect that DNA, or at least a knowledge of its sequences, will throw up fresh dynamic aspects of the law of property. Also, in so far as DNA consists of information, one would expect that the timing of the release of the information, as in *Victoria Park*, might be the nub of the matter. The Richard Crossman diaries case hardly needs to be cited - therein the House of Lords decided that information which might be inexpedient as public knowledge at an early stage loses the quality of confidential information over time. Thus the UK Human Tissue Act (below) exempts sequencing the DNA of individuals dead for over a hundred years from any criminal sanction.

Common law is said to be particularly protective of property - 'Property and law were born together,' as Jeremy Bentham wrote. Real as distinct from personal property, tangible and intangible assets, conversion, confidential information as an equitable resource, copyrighting and patenting are only superficially marginal to molecular biology. What has to admitted is that clarity is lacking, and the concepts are intellectually obscure. To try to analyse the dilemmas it is useful initially to pose certain questions, which are entered in Box 2.1 and for convenience they can be referred to in turn. As one proceeds, it must always be borne in mind that all authorities stress that in common law, title is always relative, not absolute – the best claimant, in effect, is the owner.

To go to Question 1, there is much legal literature surrounding the anomaly that in common law the human body cannot constitute property, that it is *nullis in bonis,* to invoke the Latin. The starting point is usually taken as *Williams* v *Williams* (1882).[6] Briefly, commentators hold that while there is no property in a dead body as such, there is a right of possession by the executors for burial or other means of disposal.

Possession, of course, is far from being the same as ownership. The question of property in the *living* human body can be rapidly disposed of – this is prohibited by the anti-slavery provision of both international law and the constitutions of all countries which possess one. In fact, one cannot even sell oneself.

However it seems uncontestable that I possess and own the DNA in my own cells, and I can choose to sell it or discard it (encapsulated as it is in exfoliated epidermis, sputum, urine, faeces, and hair roots, to name some examples of the relevant biological detritus). It would be bizarre to suggest that I could not own and sell my own urine for medical research, or my hair to make wigs. So the question is summarily answered on a purely commonsense basis and there is little or nothing in the literature to contradict this. In the context of organ donation, nobody has ever suggested that I do not own my own kidneys; the legislation (in UK, the Human Tissue Act, 2004, s 32) as well as the moral obloquy, merely forbids selling one of them. The same applies to blood; if I do not own my own blood, who does? I have possession of it, I control it (I can choose to bleed myself or not) and it is a resource which can be utilised for a number of purposes (medically, industrially, or even as a fertiliser). In many countries selling one's blood is quite legal, and therefore in such circumstances there must be ownership

---

6 Williams is cited as [1882] 20 Ch.D. 659. Examples of the large literature on the ownership of the body and its parts are: Dworkin, G. and Kennedy, I 'Human tissue: rights in the body and its parts' [1993] *Medical Law Review* vol 1, at p 291; Kaan, T 'Rights, ethics and commercialisation of the human body' [2000] *Singapore Journal of Legal Studies* Dec 2000 at p 483; Andrews, L. and Nelkin, D ' Whose body is it anyway? Disputes over body tissue in a biotechnology age' [1998] *Lancet* vol 351, at p 53 ; Brahams, D 'Body parts as property' [1998] *Medico-legal Journal* vol 66, at p 45. The matter is of great interest also to those US organisations devoted to cryopreservation, that is freezing of the body in the interests of immortality. See website <ImmInst.org> for an example.

of it and its components. The legislation in more restrictive locales merely pertains to purchase by blood banks and hospitals, not to private contracts. But what is and what is not, a component of the human body? This may be a side issue, but what of my colonic bacteria? Technically, they are not part of my body, merely denizens in a tube open to the environment at both ends. Suppose, of the 400 species which have been identified in the human colon, one of the streptococci among them, in my own gut, turns out to be capable of synthesizing a novel antibiotic. Could I claim a proprietary interest in such a novelty? Suppose I develop a fungus on my skin, do I own that? These may be whimsies, but they are legally untested and when one begins the study of law one becomes aware that there is nothing too bizarre within human affairs not to turn up in court sooner or later.

Question 2, as to whether in all circumstances I own the physical DNA removed from my body, is more difficult. It can reasonably be assumed that if I allow a waiter to remove a napkin from my dinner table then any smear of saliva on it is considered to be abandoned, becoming in effect *res nullius*. That biological material as such can in many circumstances be considered to be abandoned was essentially the decision in the influential and much discussed Californian case of *John Moore* v *The Regents of the University of California*,[7] which involved spleen cells, but these cells had been differentiated into a tumour, and therefore had been made scientifically and commercially valuable by the unique sequences in their DNA. A related case in UK is that of *Dobson v North Tyneside Health Authority*.[8] Here, the patient had died and during autopsy a part of the brain was removed and processed for histology. The sample was disposed of, but in the view of the family of the deceased it was needed for a medical negligence action. The Court of Appeal held that the plaintiffs had no claim in conversion. There had been no property in the dead body per se and processing of the tissue had demanded care and skill which firmly removed any claim they might have had. The sample had been - in effect - legitimately abandoned by the hospital. Thus if my DNA is prepared from a smear of saliva abandoned on my wine glass, somebody would have had to put care and skill into preparing it, and this would certainly remove title from my grasp. One may further cite the case of *R* v *Kelly* (1999),[9] wherein an artist persuaded a technician

---

7   793 P.2d 479 (Cal. Sup. Ct. 1990). The John Moore case is also discussed by Andrews and Neilkin as well as Dworkin and Kennedy (note 6); a contextual review is by Lang, A. 'What is the body? Exploring the law, philosophy and ethics of commerce in human tissue' [1999] *Journal of Law and Medicine* vol 7, at p 53.

8   *Dobson v North Tyneside Health Authority* [1996] 4 All E.R. 474.

9   *R v Kelly* [1999] 3 All ER 741. See now s 32 of the Human Tissue Act (2004) for a statutory confirmation.

at the Royal College of Surgeons to provide him with numerous museum specimens, including arms, legs, heads and feet. It is not clear what he wanted them for, but both participants were convicted of theft, and appealed on the basis that body parts were not entities capable of being stolen. However the Court of Appeal upheld the conviction on the basis of section 1 of the 1968 Theft Act, in that is these parts constituted property because they had been subject to some skill such as dissection or preservation. So an abandoned sample of DNA belonging to nobody could acquire an owner though his skill in its preparation. The analogy is with capturing a wild bird, initially *ferae naturae* and belonging to nobody, and stuffing it. It could then be stolen because it has been rendered property by the skill of the taxidermist. (Further to the circumstance of abandonment, and illustrative of the bizarre outcomes of DNA technology, in August 2006 it was reported in the media that one Ms Marchese picked used condoms from the rubbish bin of psychiatrist, the better to use the garnered DNA to accuse him of rape. Further details are mercifully hidden from us, but she was convicted of harassment, not theft.) It must be concluded then that the answer to Question 2 is 'no' if the DNA is isolated and/or purified by the party acquiring it.

Turning to Question 3 in Box 2.1, suppose, however, that my abandoned, purified DNA to which at that point (as decided above) I have no title, is subject to sequencing by the party with possession of it. If I abandon my DNA in saliva, urine, hair roots, or shed blood, am I at the same time abandoning the knowledge of the base sequences? In England the entire landscape has been altered by the Human Tissue Act (2004) which came into force early in 2005, and of which more below. The holder of the DNA, sequencing it without my permission, could spend three years in jail and/or be fined (s 45). Evidently there is tacit admission that I have some sort of title in my own DNA. But is it exclusive ownership? My total genome is undoubtedly unique to myself, but I might have sequences also unique in their own way, not individually but to a group or tribe. Might the group not have have some claim, as discussed again below? And what of the state's claim? It certainly claims title to the DNA sequences of criminals (and others), maybe to us all.

If the DNA contains a gene which can be adapted to some useful purpose such as making a vaccine or acquiring a patent I may also be held to be aggrieved. I can claim like John Moore that I have an interest in any commercial benefit which may arise from a knowledge of the base sequence. John Moore failed in this, but who knows if other jurisdictions will follow the California Supreme Court in allowing patenting of the DNA of genetic material assumed to be abandoned (for evidently the decision is not binding outside its home state)? This brings us to other aspects of civil law in the absence of a criminal prosecution against secretly sequencing an individual's

DNA (and we will see how many other countries follow UK in respect of the 2004 Act). I am unlikely, as a normal citizen, to have prior knowledge of the sequences prior to the hypothetical abandonment or theft of the DNA. Of course I know that I possess genes for certain proteins, otherwise I would not be here, but I do not know whether I carry mutations in those genes. And in the case of VNTRs and STRs, almost certainly I am uniquely endowed. If somebody takes my DNA and sequences it, either secretly or against my will, what claim do I have on the knowledge of this sequence? It cannot have the quality of confidential information, since I did not have the information in the first place. Invasion of my personal privacy is a possible head of action if the relevant jurisdiction is flexible enough to accommodate this. (The law of privacy is discussed in Chapter 3.3).

In respect of Question 4, if my DNA is sequenced by the holder with my permission, with or without payment or other consideration, presumably simple principles of contract would apply. However if I belong to a group of individuals which have some commercially valuable mutation, and I allow my DNA to be sequenced there is the possibility of a move by the group to conserve it, or possibly exploit it as a collective resource. This aspect could pertain to a family exhibiting a founder effect, which in genetics means a disease or trait running in a family can be traced back to a spontaneous mutation in a single ancestor, or to a tribe like the Penans of Sarawak, who have some unexplained genetic apparatus which makes them resistant to malaria. The genome of the Penans is therefore potentially commercially valuable. The sequences in a single member of the tribe will not be informative, only a mutation or an unknown gene common to the whole group. Class actions become a possibility if the DNA is acquired under less than ethically sound circumstances. A Penan who wanted to sell the genes with this trait to say, a pharmaceutical company is at least prime facie reprehensible because the gene, like the tract of land on which they haunt and grow food surely in some sense belongs to the whole tribe. The concept of relative title has some meaning here, the group versus the individual. The same issue is becoming important in medical law where the genetic information can be regarded either as personal, or familial.[10] Again, this point is reconsidered, in Chapter 3. This aspect goes to the question of whether genetic material is common property and the conviction that it is indeed that underlines the intense opposition to gene patenting (Chapter 4).

10   Parker, M and Lucassen, AM. 'Genetic information: a joint account' [2004] *British Medical Journal* vol 329, at p 165.

There are no easy answers to Questions 3 and 4. If there is any way to boil the issues down, they may very well principally devolve on consent, which in one form or another is the theme of the above. If there is no consent, there can be breaches of criminal law, privacy, confidential information, and equity. Hohfeldian principles may well be of interest, in that property is a relationship between persons in respect of things (including information) and this must inevitably apply to genetic information as elsewhere.[11]

This takes us to Question 5, which propels the enquiry firmly into patent law, (see my Chapter 4 herein). It is inserted for completeness, and relates to the attempted patenting of so-called expressed sequence tags (ESTs). Again this aspect is considered later and the answers to (a) and (b) are almost certainly 'yes' and 'no' respectively.

In respect of owning DNA, there are other interesting analogies in law, unlikely as they are to arise in court, or are they? In the opening paragraph I mentioned real and personal property. Of course it would be ridiculous to maintain that legal aspects of DNA can be solved by the application of the laws of real property, but DNA has in common with land the ability to be passed down from generation to generation and of being indestructible (unless for those who die without issue), unlike personal property which can be disposed of intergenerationally. This rebounds on the remarks above about DNA being considered as a collective resource, as in a family.

One can also consider DNA, especially one's own, as a resource among many. It has been pointed out in that new forms of property keep arising, such as professional licences.[12] Knowledge of one's DNA sequence is presumably merely another form of entitlement. Other forms of property evolve, then cease to be so, such as slaves and married woman. The situation is dynamic. The modern citizen has claims to a number of resources, and that success (however defined) lies in maximizing these claims. Thus in addition to a salary and a severance payment if terminated, there are numerous entitlements like legal aid, subsided night classes, a public library card, certain medical services, free bus rides in old age, perhaps a pension. Most of these may be considered intangible property, or choses in action, in that they have no

---

11   Hohfeld's analysis is in all the textbooks of jurisprudence. For a modern view see Lazarev, N 'Hohfeld's analysis of rights: an essential approach to a conceptual and practical understanding of the nature of rights' *Murdoch University Electronic Journal of Law* 12, nos 1 and 2 on website <file:///A:E%20Law.htm>.

12   Beloff, Lord. 'Property and the pursuit of hapiness' In Kolbert, C (ed) *The Idea of Property* (The MacAlpine Trust, 1997) p 1. An earlier form of the same idea was proposed by Gray, KJ and Symes, PD *Real Property and Real People* (Butterworths, 1981) p 11.

value as the enabling pieces of paper, rather as promises or contracts which must be fulfilled on demand. Free bus rides are of no value to me now, in my forties, I have to redeem the promise by living long enough. Can we put DNA into the same category? It is a physical entity, true, but its value is only realisable when sequencing has taken place. It is a resource waiting to be tapped, and it is my resource, for it is unique to myself. And if I have some salient characteristic, like height, intelligence, beauty, stamina, or resistance to disease, so much more is it valuable.

Thus, property in DNA is not a simple thing. To quote one practitioner: 'Bemused English lawyers do not know whether to treat DNA as tangible property or intellectual property or human tissue of information. It is rather worrying that an area of law so important should be so chaotic.'[13] One can only agree.

DNA Banks and Databases

The first DNA bank was a criminal one set up in 1995 by the Home Office (that is, the government department responsible for the police) in London. The co-discoverer of the structure of DNA, Dr J D Watson, advocates DNA profiling of everyone at birth and is quoted as saying that the sacrifice of this particular form of anonymity does not seem an unreasonable price to pay provided that the laws see to a strict and judicious control over access to public data. He might well be accused of displaying the characteristic naiveté of the scientist, for those with power, in this case the controllers of the genetic information, are seldom reluctant to use it. The controllers would seem to be on his side, however - DNA databases are proliferating everywhere. Sir Alec Jeffreys has gone on record as agreeing that everybody in the country should be represented on a DNA database, not for investigative purposes, for it should not be held by the police, rather it should be used for identity verification. Responders to a survey conducted by the Human Genetics Commission in 2008 tended to agree with him. Indeed, a person's DNA is one of the few things that cannot be abstracted from him, in that respect being unlike, for example credit cards, pin numbers, driving licences, and teeth. Its informative nature is the ultimate safeguard against identity theft.[14] DNA databases are also suggested as a barrier against other types of fraud - it has been estimated that there are 80 million national insurance numbers in

13   Foster, C 'Current issues in the law of genetics' [2003] *New Law Journal* vol 29, at p 76.
14   There is a very full exploration of identity theft in the *Newsweek* issue of September 5th, 2005

Table 2-1 DNA Databanks and Databases: the Pervasiveness of Legal Issues*

General area	Issues Involved	Page ref
Criminal law-identity theft	Banking all citizen's DNA to protect identity	44
Criminal law- retention of DNA by police or by other body	Retention from arrestees only, or those charged but released or acquitted; autrefois acquit	45
Criminal law- rehabilitation of offenders	Permanent retention of DNA overriding Rehabilitation of Offenders Act	47
Privacy as right; breach as a tort	Fundamental concepts of personal privacy	131
International law - 'biocolonialism'	Genetic and other integrity of ethnic groups	253
Property and ownership – 'the commons'	Ownership of genetic material in general	176
Intellectual property law	Propriety of patenting genes; genetic information as confidential information	163

* Largely in respect of English law

UK, whereas the total population is not more than 60 million, indicating a substantial amount of double or even triple claims on the welfare services.[15] The construction and use of DNA databases is going to crop up repeatedly as a subject of legal debate (Box 2-1), and constitutes a battleground for those with 'the will to know' against those cherishing the protection of the individual. The polarisation between the two is not new – in nineteenth century France a hospital physician wanted to establish a complete medical and social listing for each patient, but the superintendent objected to what he regarded as modern version of the religious inquisition. It is not too far fetched either, surely, to see an analogy between retaining DNA for some unspecified purpose and the erosion of the time-honoured prohibition of the general warrant, *Entick* v *Carrington* of 1765 recalled.

In the US federal funding has allowed the FBI to construct a database of convicted felons under the DNA Identification Act of 1994. States however vary considerably in the degree to which they retain the DNA of their citizens. Virginia was the first state to construct a DNA bank from convicted

15 <www.parliament.uk/commons/lib/research/rp2001/rp01-010.pdf>.

felons and arrestees, in 1989. It was criticised as being contrary to the Fourth Amendment (the 'right of the people to be secure in their persons [etc] against unreasonable searches and seizures...')

At the moment all the databases are constructed on the knowledge of STR alleles; it has been suggested that SNPs would be more suitable for the databases, as there are thousands of them distributed randomly throughout the genome, but here there is a snag. After DNA samples are sequenced, the physical sample is thrown away (illustrating for the nth time the preponderance of information over substance); if the UK database of three million individuals were to be reconstituted with SNPs, the samples would have to be gathered in all over again, an impossibility from the organisational and financial points of view.[16]

Another ramification of the thrust towards DNA databases is this: on arrest and particularly after charge, the police can take away one's physical possessions, but if proceedings are stayed for some reason or there is an acquittal the person is released his effects are returned. But what if the police take a DNA sample and then refuse to return it? Of course, yet again, it is not the physical DNA in which their real interest lies, but its base sequence. It can be matched against the databases now being widely held, and possibly used in the future to score 'cold hits' (Chapter 2.4 herein). The former suspect cannot maintain he should have his DNA sequence information returned to him, for he never had it in the first place. The progress of the database compilers in England is illustrated by the case of *R (on the application of Marper and Another)* v *Chief Constable of South Yorkshire and Another* (2004).[17] Prior to the Lords' decision, the Court of Appeal (Civil Division) including the Lord Chief Justice Lord Woolf held that the Chief Constable could retain the DNA from former suspects, invoking the principle of proportionality. The two appellants had had DNA samples and fingerprints taken prior to the acquittal of one and the release without charge of another. The police

16   It was reported in the media in April 2006 that the UK database now represents some three million individuals , about 5% of the total population; the corresponding figure for USA is 0.99%. (*The Guardian*, 14 th April, 2006). A survey of databases on the European continent, with details of retention times, anonymisation, and other aspects is provided by Schneider, PM and Martin, PD 'Criminal DNA databases: the European situation' [2001] *Forensic Science International* vol 119, at p 232. Rudin and Inman (note 4) in their Appendix J list the 'DNA' statutes in force in all the US states.
17   [2004] UKHL 39. This was a consolidated appeal with the full title: *R v Chief Constable of South Yorkshire Police (respondent) ex parte LS (by his mother and litigation friend JB)(FC)(Appellant) and R v Chief Constable of South Yorkshire Police (Respondent) ex parte Marper (FC)(Appellant)*. The appeal to the ECHR was heard in mid-2008, and found in favour of Marper.

wished to hold the fingerprints and the DNA under the provisions of s 82 of the Criminal Justice and Police Act 2001. The DNA era, as it were, can be seen to have commenced with this Act, in that under s 82 fingerprints and 'samples' (for this read DNA) can be kept and used later if necessary for criminal proceedings - equivalent to facilitating the 'cold hit'. According to the section, there is no obligation to destroy a sample if the suspect is cleared or not prosecuted. Retained samples, though, can only be used for 'purposes related to the presentation and detection of crime, the investigation of any offence or the conduct of any prosecution.' Use is to include 'speculative searches.' Also, a non-suspect, for example an individual donating DNA or the purposes of elimination, can give consent to retention. The appeal to the House of Lords was based on arts 8 and 14 of the European Convention on Human Rights, incorporated into UK law by the Human Rights Act 1998. The two articles affirm respect for private and family life, and the prohibition of discrimination, respectively. The majority judgement was that although the samples were personal to the individual and prime facie contrary to art 8(1), the interference was not significant and the adverse consequences to the individual were not out of proportion to the benefit to the public. The fight against serious crime outweighed any minimal interference with the individual, and moreover the information was kept secret. In a dissenting judgement Lord Sedley maintained that the Chief Constable should exercise his discretion not to retain the material where he was satisfied that the individual concerned was free of any taint of suspicion. It appears that the Court of Appeal allows the police to regard individuals as bad hats whether they have been convicted or not, which is against all previous doctrine in common law. In that light the judgement has attracted much criticism. There was also vigorous dissent by Lady Hale, who maintained that it was an unacceptable invasion of personal privacy to retain information about a person even if it was not used. This scenario also relates to Question 2 in Box 2.1 in that most certainly I cannot retain the ownership of my DNA sequence acquired by the state, in any manner it chooses, if I live in England. Nominally, the *Marper* case was civil, but that raises an anomaly - it rides roughshod over the Rehabilitation of Offenders Act (1974), for example.

However, any libertarian scruples tend to be quelled by the horror of specific cases. In 1984 a person variously described in the reports as George, B or D, raped and robbed an old lady, then locked her in a cupboard and left her, where she could have died. In 1998 he was arrested for burglary and had a sample of DNA taken but was acquitted. The sample should have been destroyed under s 64(1) of the Police and Criminal Evidence Act (1984), but for some reason this was not done. Later in 1998 the biological material found on the old lady was matched with George's DNA; at his trial for rape the judge ruled that the match evidence was inadmissible by virtue of s 64

(1) and he was again acquitted. On an Attorney General's reference to the House of Lords subsequent to the Court of Appeal's agreement with the decision,[18] Lord Steyn stated that privacy considerations for a defendant were far outweighed by public policy considerations in dealing with serious crime. It is unacceptable to most of us that this criminal got away with such villainy: 'The austere interpretation which the Court of Appeal has adopted was not only in conflict with the plain words of the statute [Section 64(3B) (b) of the Police and Criminal Evidence Act 1984] but produced results which were contrary to good sense.' In the face of a possible challenge to the admissibility of' DNA under the circumstances at hand under arts 6 or 8 of the European Convention on Human Rights, Lord Steyn also made the interesting point that the question of admissibility of evidence was matter for regulation under national law. In any event the Criminal Justice and Police Act 2001 was brought into force without delay, in May of that year, and settled the matter.

The fortitude of the House of Lords in the *Marper* case and the outrage resulting from the B/D case has driven, via DNA, changes in the law in many respects. ('Theft' of DNA is considered below.)A major result of the new technology has been the abandonment of the ancient doctrine of *autrefois acquit* in England although seemingly not yet in any state in the US at the time of writing. (Of course, there were always exceptions to the doctrine.)[19] It was forcibly argued that that if a defendant has been acquitted and he is later shown by DNA evidence gathered *ex post facto* to be the perpetrator of the crime beyond reasonable doubt, it is plainly in the interests of justice that he become accountable again. Additionally, *autrefois acquit* has been held by many to be in any case jurisprudentially redundant – it was formulated at a time when powerful magnates or officials might otherwise play cat and mouse with the disadvantaged peasants. The result has been ss 76-78 of the Criminal Justice Act (2003). The retrial must be allowed by the Court of Appeal. The relevant sections in the act do not mention DNA specifically, only that the new evidence must be compelling, substantive and probative (these conjunctively).

18   *Attorney General's Reference no 3 of 1999.* For a view opposing that of Lord Steyn see Noble, AA 'DNA fingerprints and civil liberties' [2006] *Journal of Law and Medical Ethics* vol 34, at p 149.
19   There was always the possibility of a second trial, for example when there was a so-called tainted acquittal, in which the jury had been 'nobbled'. For a full discussion see James, A Taylor, N et al. 'The reform of double Jeopardy' *Web Journal of Current Legal Issues*, No. 5. Notably, not all the jurisdictions which imported common law also adopted autrefois acquit. In Singapore, for example, whose criminal code is directly derived from the Indian code, the prosecution has always been able to appeal against a not guilty verdict.

The desire for a sea change was also driven by the Stephen Lawrence and Damilola murders.[20] The former was the subject of the MacPherson Report, in which the police were accused of 'institutional racism' and incompetence (such as neglecting to look for bloodstains which might have turned out to be probative). Until now, no person has been convicted. DNA emerged belatedly in the Damilola case. Damilola, a 10-year old Nigerian boy living in London was left to bleed to death in 2001 after being slashed with a broken bottle, and with its racial undertones (as assumed at the time) the case caused uproar. After three trials the DNA evidence, obtained years later from the clothing of the assailants, was decisive in securing a conviction. The original forensic search for bloodstains had been sloppy. In the light of these cases, it was thought scandalous that criminals who secured acquittal due to lack of, or faulty, evidence, should stay free in the face of later more stringent or up-to-date laboratory investigation.

A minor DNA-driven change in the law was an amendment to the Police and Criminal Evidence Act (1984) which distinguished intimate from non-intimate samples. The definition of these was changed by the Criminal Justice and Public Order Act 1994, s65, to allow buccal smears to be considered non-intimate, and the only possible purpose, of course, for taking buccal smears is to obtain DNA.

The legal and ethical circumstances surrounding the acquisition of DNA databanks, sometimes termed 'biobanks' crop up in an number of contexts, and some of these are listed in Table 2-1.

Summary of 2.2

- Presumably a person 'owns' the DNA residing in his own living tissues.

- Physical unsequenced DNA in saliva or other detritus can be considerd to be legally abandoned.

- There may be discernable property rights in genetic material by a tribe or group even if its nature is revealed by a member.

---

20 *The Stephen Lawrence Inquiry – Report of an Inquiry by Sir William MacPherson of Cluny* (Cm 4262, Stationary Office, London, 1999). For an account of the Damilola trials see the Guardian article: <http://www.guardian.co.uk/crime/article/0,,1840590,00. html?gusrc=rss&feed=1>; the findings of the independent enquiry, which is partially concerned with DNA evidence, is on <homeoffice.gov.uk/documents/damilola-taylor-review-2007?view=Binary. The suspects were again acquitted of murder in March 2006 but convicted of manslaughter in August.

- An individual's DNA may be regarded as one resource among many.

- DNA databases are being established by the authorities in all countries, generating varying quantities of unease.

- In UK the police may retain the DNA of arrestees, not just the convicted.

- In the US policy on retention of DNA varies with state; the FBI collects from convicted felons.

- By the Criminal Justice Act (2003) the age-old doctrine of *autrefois acquit* is abandoned.

- The definition of an intimate sample is modified to accommodate DNA in the Criminal Justice and Public Order Act (1994).

2.3 Theft of DNA and its Base Sequences

In the UK, an offence of 'DNA theft' was proposed by the Human Genetics Commission, the body set up in 1999 to advise the government on the novel ethical and legal issues which were arising; its proposal this was incorporated as Section 45 of the Human Tissue Act (2004). Baroness Kennedy, the chairperson of the Human Genetics Commission, is reported to have said: 'Further, this sort of activity is a gross intrusion into another's privacy, and there is not sufficient legal protection to prevent this at the moment.' Presumably it was thought that obtaining property by deception and obtaining pecuniary advantage by deception under the Theft Act (1968, ss 15 and 16) surely possible motives for stealing DNA, would stand as too remote for successful prosecutions under any conceivable circumstances. It is difficult at the moment to imagine DNA being purloined and sequenced out of pure curiosity but there is a view that even if a DNA sample taken is not 'tested', the knowledge that it has been obtained may cause anxiety or distress. The obvious analogies are to computer hacking and stalking, both of which have been extensively criminalised. The legislation is curiously in accordance with the dissenting comments of Lady Hale's comments in the *Marper* case, that it is unacceptable to obtain information about somebody even if it not used.[21] It represents entry into law of a specific offence of breach of privacy.

---

21   On 4th Dec 2008 The European Court of Human Rights held for the plaintiffs in *S. and Marper v The U.K.*, in that the British Government had violated Article 8, but it declined to adjudicate on Article 14. In effect it agreed with Lady Hale's dissent in the House of Lords. Early signs are that the government may ignore the ruling.

The Act repealed the Human Tissue Act (1961), the Anatomy Act (1984) and the Human Organ Transplants Act (1989) (among others) at one sweep.

The wording of the new Act (s 45 - 'Non-consensual analysis of DNA') is:

A person commits an offence if (a) he has any bodily material intending

(i) that any human DNA in the material be analysed without qualifying consent and

(ii) that the results of the analysis be used other than for an excepted purpose.'

Obviously the term 'qualifying consent' has to be interpreted. This is spelt out by Schedule 4, s 2(1). It means consent by oneself for one's own DNA, or for one's child, alive or deceased. Exceptions, not needing consent at all, are made for the DNA of embryos outside the body (to allow for preimplantation genetic diagnosis) and for circumstances in which the holder of the DNA has no personal information about the donor (to allow pre-existing DNA banks to conduct medical research). Others are predictable, for example use in the prevention of crime and for the conduct of a prosecution. As a gesture to commonsense, sequencing the DNA of those who have been dead for over 100 years is not actionable. There is a full list in Schedule 4, Part 2. There is also a defence of reasonable belief in consent. The Act, which applies to all of UK, came into force in 2006 and no prosecutions are as yet discernable. Much of it is concerned with licencing, by the Human Tissue Authority, for exhibiting anatomical specimens, for example (this in response to an EU directive).

It seems though that in future biomedical scientists will have to be doubly careful about sequencing DNA samples obtained in the course of their work, even if they are anonymised and the sequencing is done in the interests of disinterested research. The issues will impinge upon the meaning and import of 'informed consent' in medical law. The wording of the Act will no doubt be subject to extensive interpretation, as and when prosecutions are brought. It would seem not to be an offence to take abandoned DNA with or without consent and keep it as long as it is not sequenced. Of course, without being sequenced it is no good to anybody, except for purposes of blackmail. (In this respect it is a metamorphosis of the compromising photograph of hallowed tradition, so solicitously preserved, for example, by Mrs Adler in *Scandal in Bohemia*.) The wording is specific for human DNA, that is, if somebody takes and sequences DNA from my colonic bacteria apparently it will not be an offence. Nor will it apply to dogs, for example, which may have some repercussions on the pet trade. It has been pointed out that there are three elements involved – (a) obtaining the DNA, (b) 'testing' (sequencing) it and (c) using the results, and presumably these would have to be proved conjunctively.[22]

This special citation of DNA as such in the Act, as opposed to the retention of the term 'samples' in the Criminal Justice and Police Act (2001) suggests that DNA is becoming *sui generis* in law. Its specific entry into the criminal law as a separate entity was perhaps prompted less by altruistic notions of privacy than by the bizarre media reports in 2002 about a conspiracy to steal some hairs from Prince Harry, the second son of the heir to the British throne. There was said to be a plot by a certain newspaper to use an attractive woman to become sufficiently intimate with the young man to pluck one or more hairs from his person. A plucked hair, if it contains the root or follicle, incorporates enough DNA for the determination of paternity, should a sample of the DNA of a putative father also be available. Presumably the issue here was whether somebody could make a lot of money by selling the information to the highest bidder among newspaper editors. The story petered out, but the said prince will have to look after his DNA very carefully for the rest of his life, and not only the DNA in his hair. The smear of saliva left on a wine glass at cocktail party will be of equal import, and if he ever goes for a surgical operation there will necessarily have to be a most conscientious audit of his tissues. It is reasonable to assume that the genomes most susceptible to outright thievery are those belonging to potential victims of blackmail, like politicians. Any benefit derived from purloining the genes of those who are thought to have desirable characteristics, like media and sports stars, so that they can be copied, remains for the moment in the realms of science fiction.

Despite the criminalising of DNA appropriation, and proposed moves against husbands wishing to establish truth about the true parentage of their children, advances in technology are likely to make any enforcement difficult. At the moment samples have to be sent to a laboratory once they are properly collected, but at some point it will all be done with a home kit. The identification of Saddam Hussein, by means of his DNA, was accomplished in Baghdad in December 2003 within 17 hours. The US army undoubtedly had a laboratory standing by, but its achievement will be overreached in future by even more rapid devices. The buccal scrapings will be extracted, amplified in the cold by use of a helicase enzyme (at the moment there is necessarily

22   Skene, L 'Theft of DNA: do we need a new criminal offence?' <File://A:\Prof Loane Skene - DNA Theft-CCLS Publication May 2003.htm> (Cardiff Centre for Ethics, Law and Society).

a heating stage for the PCR, whereas the helicase unwinds the double helix using energy from a substance known as ATP); it will then be digested and the fragments run through a capillary column to give a computerized printout in a few minutes. If this seems far fetched, who would have thought, 30 years ago, that a definitive pregnancy testing kit could sit on a woman's bathroom shelf, and signal its result by the change of colour on a small panel set in plastic?

Summary of 2.3

- A new offence of DNA theft is on the books in UK (Human Tissue Act, 2004).

- New aspects of blackmail based on a knowledge of an individual's DNA can be envisaged.

- The usage ' DNA' rather than 'sample' is now embedded in criminal legislation (Criminal Justice and Police Act,2001).

- New legal principles and issues will be tested when advances in technology allow hand-held 'profilers' to be used by all and sundry.

- DNA is becoming *sui generis* in law.

2.4   DNA, Rape and Murder

The rape and murder cases which first entrained DNA profiling are only about twenty years old, but have already become classics in the area of identification evidence. Some of them are listed in Table 2.2. In that sense molecular biology is contributing a modern extension not only of the Locard principle, but also of *Bertillonage*, that is the use of physical characteristics to establish the uniqueness, or rarity of a particular individual.[23] Of course all such evidence entrains its own perils - it has been maintained that historically '... possibly the most notorious source of miscarriages of justice is identification evidence.'[24] Also, it may come as something of a surprise

---

23   Rhodes, H *Alphonse Bertillon: Father of Scientific Detection* (Abelard –Schuman, 1956); Bertillon concluded that any individual could be uniquely identified by six or seven skeletal measurements; this is well and good, but of course criminals do not leave their skeletal measurements at the scene of the crime, they leave their DNA. For an up to date discussion on Locard, see Chisum, WJ and Turbey, BE *'Evidence dynamics: Locard's exchange principle and crime reconstruction' [2000] Journal of Behavioural Profiling* vol 1, at p 1.
24   Zander, M *The English Legal System* (Butterworths, 8th edn, 1999) p 378.

to some to find that DNA evidence, like fingerprint evidence, is regarded as circumstantial, but authorities on the law of evidence are at pains to assure us that 'circumstantial' does not mean 'weak'.[25]

Keynote cases (UK)

Subsequent to the establishment of the identity of an immigrant in England, Dr Jeffreys' laboratory was involved in a number of pioneer cases. At that time his technique involved many different alleles in the genome simultaneously (technically, the use of multilocus probes, now called *multiplex* methods) and a complex pattern of bands on an autoradiograph was the result. It was readily conceived as being analagous to a fingerprint. Jeffreys maintains that the term 'DNA fingerprinting' should be confined to multilocus methods but notes that it is now applied to all DNA typing. Looking at a single locus is more readily described as 'profiling' but it seems that in practice the two terms are used interchangeably.[26]

Despite sporadic protests here and there that the word 'fingerprint' strictly refers to an idiotype, that is something unique to an individual, whereas a pattern of alleles is usually to some extent shared, if only by very few individuals (and also identical twins), the usage is unlikely now to change.

The first use of DNA fingerprinting to identify a murderer was the Pitchfork case. Two girls had been raped and murdered in Leicestershire in 1983 and 1986. A local boy seemed to know something about the circumstances and eventually confessed to one of the murders. The police wanted to link him to the other and had heard of Jeffreys' work in Leicester University. His laboratory established that the semen found on the victims came from the same man but not from Richard Buckland, the suspect. The trail went cold but the police decided to take blood samples from all adult men in the village, some 5,000 in all. An important point here is that the older serological techniques were still relevant, in that it was known that the murderer was blood type A, so the DNA of only the subgroup with type A was examined. This took the scientists six months at the rate of 2-3 per day. However, none of them matched the materials found on the bodies. Only when the person who had fraudulently supplied his own blood as a substitute for Pitchfork's

25   The nature of circumstantial evidence is of course discussed in the standard evidence texts. See for example Tapper C. *Cross on Evidence* (Butterworths, 7th ed, 1990) p 39. As Sherlock Holmes said, quoting Thoreau : 'Circumstantial evidence is occasionally very convincing, as when you find a trout in the milk.' (*The Adventure of the Noble Bachelor*) .
26   Jeffreys, A J '1992 William Allen award address' [1993] *American Journal of Human Genetics* vol 53 at p 1.

Box 2-2 A Sample UK Criminal case

One is unlikely, of course, to find a single case which comprehensively illustrates the impact of DNA technology on law, however *Kelly* (2004) covers several important issues. It was a reference by the Scottish Criminal Cases Review Commission to the High Court of Justiciary (the equivalent of the English Court of Appeal). The appellant had been convicted of rape in 1989 and in view of possible injustice a referral to the Commission proceeded according to the Criminal Procedures Act (Scotland) of 1995. Albeit that the hearing could be considered as an enquiry of sorts, it is noteworthy in that formally it remained strictly adversarial, with counsel for both Crown and Appellant, backed by their own witnesses, before three Lords Justices.

The victim awoke to find a man kneeling beside her bed. He engaged her in conversation on a number of matters, many of them enquires about the house address, her children and money. He then raped her after having produced a knife. He took her downstairs and left after having taken some money from her. The victim checked that her children were unharmed then went to a neighbour's house for help, the rapist having cut the wires of the telephone. Kelly was not a suspect, but volunteered a sample expecting to be cleared. At the trial there were several items of evidence which might have gone to his acquittal:

(1) The victim did not pick out the accused at two identity parade, one of them 'voice only.'

(2) The victim described the voice as throaty, unlike that of the accused.

(3) The accused was a neighbour and knew the victim well, but yet the assailant had asked questions about the address and other matters .

(4) There was an alibi, although not wholly satisfactory.

(5) The victim described the rapist as smelling 'clean', but when interviewed by the police an hour after the outrage, the accused smelled strongly of alcohol.

(6) The Home Office Laboratory had failed to match the accused's DNA with a semen stain on the victim's dressing gown.

(7) The population database for the (alternative) Cellmark matching comprised 200 individuals from the Chester area (whereas the crime took place in Ayrshire and the name Kelly suggest an Irish, possible Celtic origin).

As against the appellant/accused:

(1) There was shoeprint in the house somewhat similar to the sole on a training shoe of the accused.

(2) The semen stain was of the same blood group of the accused – in common with 39.5% of the population.

(3) The DNA on the stain according to Cellmark showed that the 'chances of a match of six bands in two unrelated parsons was less that one in one hundred thousand.'

Several points are notable. First, the prominent role of the commercial arm in the form of Cellmark; the commercial sector, has remained prominent in DNA jurisprudence from the beginning of the ' DNA era.' Secondly, its findings were given in the odds form, which the jury presumably found decisive, though the quantum is nothing like the billions to one against innocence which are habitually quoted in other cases. (As a probability, this was $P = 0.99999$, which seems equally probative.) Thirdly, the DNA evidence is described by the Lords Justices as being 'circumstantial', which technically of course it is.

At the 2004 referral appeal both Crown and appellant led further evidence on the DNA matching technique, each producing three expert witnesses. In 1988 the single locus probe technique was employed - this was before the advent of PCR. This technique examines one site at a time and an individual yields two bands if a heterozygote and one if a homozygote . The Crown witnesses described the electrophoresis and blotting procedure in detail, emphasising that they followed 'standard operating procedures.' One probe showed two bands from the stain, one of which corresponded to a sample from the victim and one from the accused. Crucially, however, the sample from the victim and the accused has been put in adjacent lanes to allow for side-by-side comparisons. The witnesses for the appellant maintained that there was therefore a real danger of leakage from the appellant sample to the stain sample during the loading stage. The band on the stain sample matching that of appellant was less intense than that of the band matching the victim, suggesting that the former had contaminated the stain sample. The Lords Justices appear to have accepted that had this been adduced at the trial then the jury might have taken it into consideration. From the transcript it is obvious that they made every effort to understand the technicalities of the procedures. Even the use of the pipettes, the force with which their contents should be expelled, and the possible presence of small bubbles was discussed.

A highly technical argument devolved around a band of high molecular DNA in the accused's sample. This was assumed to be an artifact, probably DNA remaining uncut by the restriction endonuclease. A Crown witness maintained that if there had been cross contamination then this artifact would have appeared in the stain sample as well as the accused sample. The defence countered by stating ' .....
this thing is an artifact... something we don't know why it is there... it seems flawed reasoning to use something we don't know anything about..... to explain something else.' Wherever the flawed reasoning lies, it has to be said that in this detail the prosecution argument seems to make more sense than that of the defence.

The judges were satisfied that the new evidence on possible contamination was relevant was relevant, and significant in the sense that it might have been of assistance to the jury. Here we have a point habitually misunderstood by the public, and indeed those who are released after an appeal process claiming they have been declared innocent. Courts of appeal seldom if ever use these word, rather that the original verdict might now be considered to be 'unsafe.' (Or, as

Lord Goddard famously said after a successful appeal in 1954: 'Do not think we are doing this because we think you are an innocent man. We do not. We think you are a scoundrel.') In the Kelly case, the words used were that the 'the existence of evidence [was of] such significance that fact that it was not heard by the jury constituted a miscarriage of justice.' Due to improvements in technology, laboratories stopped running crime scene and suspect samples in adjacent lanes. This solved one problem, but others of a similarly technical nature will inevitably arise. The newer techniques such as capillary electrophoresis may not be susceptible to the type of contamination in the instant case, they are susceptible to other types of contamination. Bafflingly, it seems likely that the accused was innocent but that the DNA test was performed correctly.

was heard boasting about this, was the culprit revealed. Pitchfork was given two life sentences in 1988. Thus this case illustrated the analysis of DNA for both conviction and exoneration.[27] After these initial successes came a period of consolidation and incremental advances in the relevant technology and there was seen the first conviction for a rape per se, that of one Robert Melias. However disputes soon arose about the presentation of the evidence in court and about the performance of the techniques themselves, the latter more particularly in the US. The English courts, lacking a Frye-type procedure,[28]evaluated the scientific evidence on a case by case basis, but of course a *voir dire* is always possible. Notably, as with all evidence, the jury is not bound to accept the opinion of an expert.

In *R* v *Deen*, in the English Court of Appeal in 1994, the Lord Chief Justice Lord Taylor first drew attention of the jury to the 'prosecutor's fallacy'.[29] This was a rape case which the Court of Appeal sent down again to the Crown Court for retrial. The prosecution quoted a RPM (see Box 1.1) of one in three million - that is, that the chance of a member of the public,

27   Naturally this case has been extensively cited: There is an extensive description in Wall, W J. *The DNA Detectives* (Robert Hale, 2005) p 55; also <http://www.forensic.gov. uk/forensic_t/inside/news/list_casefiles.php?case=1> and <http://en. wikipedia/org/wiki/ Colin_Pitchfork>.

28   See p 31, Chapter 1.

29   *R* v *Deen The Times* 10th Jan 1994. The term 'prosecutor's fallacy' was apparently first coined by Thompson, WC and Schumann, E 'Interpretation of evidence in criminal trials; the prosecutor's fallacy and the defence attorney's' *Law and Human Behaviour* [1987] vol 11, at p 167; see also Balding DJ and Donnelly P 'How convincing is DNA evidence?' [1994] *Science* vol 368, at p 285. Leung, WC. 'The prosecutor's fallacy – a pitfall in interpreting probabilities in forensic medicine' Medicine, Science and the Law [2002] vol 42, at p 44. For a concise discussion see: Goodwin, W Linacre A et al *An Introduction to Forensic Genetics* (John Wiley, 2007) p 93.

selected at random, of having the same DNA profile as the suspect, was evidently negligible. There are approximately sixty million people in UK, however, so arguably there was a one in twenty chance of innocence; if this is a fallacy it is the 'defender's fallacy.' (As a side issue, the defence queried the nature of one of the bands on the electropherogram and stated that the RMP should instead have been one in 700,000.) The LCJ stated that there were two distinct questions:

(1) What was the probability that an individual would match the DNA profile from the crime *given that he was innocent*? This accords with the match probability. (The match probability was given as 1 in 3 million or, more correctly 0.000033%, where probability (in fact certainty) of innocence obviously was 100%.)

(2) What was the probability that an individual was innocent, *given that his DNA matched the crime sample*? (This is given as 1 in 20 - a probability of 5%.)

The prosecution was held to have confused the first with the second. The fact that the evidence was not led that there was a probability of one in 20 in 21 (the last figure includes the defendant) or alternatively 80 in 81, that the defendant was innocent, might have mislead the jury. Implicitly, these two items, or calculations, should be considered in conjunction with each other (and also in conjunction with the other evidence).

Curiously, the commentaries seem not to appreciate that in a rape case only men would be suspects so that the true probability of innocence here in terms of the UK population would be 10 in 11 rather than 20 or 21. An even better calculation would include only all men between 15 and 70, say, assuming that the demographic data are available. There was much more room for the prosecution to adjust the figures. What was omitted too was the fact that not all the men in the UK could have committed the crime. A very large proportion for one reason or another could not possibly have been at the scene of the crime at the relevant time (in jail perhaps or overseas if the statistics had been extracted) and if the evidence depends on the examination of the DNA in semen, the statistics of erectile dysfunction might well be taken into account. This is not to be flippant - both the defence and prosecution have to understand the statistics and the nature of sampling procedures.

Deen had considerable fallout. In the Sally Clark case, DNA evidence was not in itself involved, but the prosecutors' fallacy again was an issue. The second *Clark* appeal elicited the declaration that the judge at first instance had failed to warn the jury of the prosecutor's fallacy as set out in *Deen*.[30]

Deen was followed by the two trials of *R* v *Dennis John Adams*, (1996)[31] both of which went to appeal. Therein a RMP of one in 200 million was quoted. In the first appeal, an expert witness used Bayes' theorem (see below 2.5), unusually, as a defence strategy, but the defendant was convicted. The Court of Appeal sent him for retrial and he was again found guilty and appealed. The LCJ, who had not sat on the previous appeal, allowed the conviction to stand, but observed that the separate probabilities of the kind cited above (in *Deen*) required, as items of evidence, to be assessed separately, and that such an approach is too rigid for a jury, being inappropriately theoretical and complex. This was confirmed in *R* v *Doheny and Adams* (a different Adams from the foregoing). It was however confirmed that the judge should explain to the jury the relevance of the RMP and draw its attention to the extraneous evidence which provides the context which gives that 'ratio' its significance.

The judge should explain to the jury the relevance of the random occurrence ratio in arriving at their verdict and draw attention to the extraneous evidence which provides the context which gives that ratio its significance, and that which conflicts with the conclusion that the defendant was responsible for the crime stain. In so far as the random occurrence ratio is concerned, a direction along these lines may be appropriate, although any direction must be tailored to the facts of that particular case.....

Members of the jury, if you accept the scientific evidence called by the Crown, his indicates that there are probably only four or five white males in the United Kingdom from whom that stain could have come. The defendant is one of them. If that is the position, the decision you have to reach, on all the evidence, is whether you are sure that it was the defendant who left that stain or whether it is possible that it

30   See Chapter 1, note 35. The Court of Appeal deprecated the use of the term 'prosecutor's fallacy'. Sally Clark had been convicted on two counts of murder of her young children, with the paediatrician Sir Roy Meadow quoting the odds against them both having died of sudden infant death as one in 73 million. This would only have held good had the two deaths been independent of each other, as pointed out by the Royal Statistical Society in a memorandum after the conviction. The defence counsel was criticised for not pointing this out. The citation is *R* v *Clark* [2003] EWCA Crim 1020. Among extensive discussions of the case see Montgomery, C. 'Forensic science in the trial of Sally Clark' [2004] *Medicine, Science and the Law* vol 44, at p 185.

31   *R v Dennis Adams* [1998] 1 Cr App. R. 377. There is a good account on Redmayne's site: <file://A:\The Evidence Site Mike Redmayne on the Adams Case and DNA.htm>

was one of the other small group of men who share the same DNA characteristics.[32]

The judge has been criticised for describing the RMP as a 'ratio', whereas it is a probability, the denominator in the likelihood ratio, as explained below. (This looseness of language is a constant pain to the scientists - the newspapers continually report that a DNA test has, say, an 'accuracy' of 99.99% - again, actually a probability.) One must note, perhaps to the point of tedium, that the above quotation seems to be yet another statement that the jury should consider *all* the evidence, no more than a reformulation of the venerable rule in *Belhaven and Stenton Peerage* (1875) that the jury should consider

'... the weight which is to be given to the united force of all the circumstances together.'[33]

This area is dealt with in a slightly more mathematical fashion in the next section, but in terms of recorded cases the ones just cited are important in laying down a policy for statistics. Like *Deen*, *Doheny and Adams* was quoted in the *Sally Clark* case [29] which was possible the most statistically contentious case in modern times in England. It has also been influential in Australia - the interest lies in the different ways the judges try to explain the concepts to the jury. In *R* v *Wakefield,* in the New South Wales Court of Criminal Appeal, an aggravated assault case, a judge stated that:

... the statistical probability within the relevant population does not translate to the same statistical probability for a given member of the population. Put another way, the statistical probability of the profile occurring within the general population is not the same as the statistical probability of the appellant's DNA occurring at the crime scene.[34]

This is hardly an advance. The first sentence is impenetrable and the second is otiose. If the defendant is guilty the probability that the DNA at the crime scene is his is 100%, if he is not guilty then the probability is zero, whatever the population statistics.

In the Australian case of *R* v *Karger*[35] the English decisions such as *Deen* and *Doheny and Adams* were considered very carefully and adopted. The defendant was accused of murdering a woman in 1998. Material on the body

32   *R v Doheny and Adams* [1997] 1 Cr App R. 369 (a conjoined appeal).
33   *In re Bellhaven Peerage* [1875] 1 App Cas 278 at 279.
34   *R v Wakefield* [2004] NSWCCA 288.
35   *R v Karger* [2002] 88, SASR 135.

(small bloodstains, fingernail scrapings and hairs) were tested and did not exclude the accused. Three methods were used including the commercially available Profiler Plus system which examined ten loci. Combining the methods, the court was told that the chance of a second person yielding the same results was 1 in 90 billion, one of the smallest RMP ever quoted.

Recently the Soham murders involved an alternative use of DNA forensics.[36] The bodies of the two girls, abducted and murdered in 2002, were badly decomposed and identification evidence was needed. This was accomplished by swabbing a bookmark used by one girl and a musical instrument used by the other, and mtDNA was profiled, presumably because it offered the high copy number necessary in such meager samples. The conviction itself was probably largely based on non-DNA evidence. (The case, of course, led to changes in employment law for those wishing to take up posts involving the care of young children.)

DNA evidence can also deal with situation where the body of a murder victim cannot be found. In the case of the disappearance of Helen McCourt in 1988, the suspect Ian Simms was convicted largely because blood was found on clothing belonging to him. This could not be matched to Helen's blood under the circumstances. However it could be matched to her parents. Appropriate use of the statistics gave a RMP (as odds) of one in 126,000.[37] The body itself has never been found.

Recently a new identification technique has emerged, or been rediscovered, which is in some sense the converse of the McCourt case, that is when there was a victim but no immediate suspect. In 2004 in Frimley, Surrey, a brick was thrown from a footbridge on to the M3 motorway. It went through the windscreen of a lorry and hit the driver in chest. He died of a heart attack. A car had been vandalised the same night and blood on the car matched that on the brick. A search of the National DNA Database produced no hits, but the scientists were able to infer that he was a white male. It could also be inferred from the circumstances that he was under 35. The police selected 350 males under 35 in the immediate area and invited them to give samples, again with no match. The Database was searched again for profiles which were similar, if not identical, to the crime sample. One of

---

36   Khalail, KS 'The science of the Soham murders' [2005] *Medicine, Science and the Law* vol 48, at p 187.

37   The facts of the case are given on the House of Lords website – they were specifically considering the matter of press access to Simms, who continues to protest his innocence. <http://www.parliament.the-stationary-office.co.uk/pa/ld199899/ljudgmt/   jd990708/ obrien01.htm>.

the 350 stood out in this respect, and after the individual was identified his relatives were invited also to provide samples. One of the relatives, Craig Harman, provided a match to the sample on the brick. In April 2006 he was handed down six years for manslaughter. This procedure has now entered the lexicon as 'familial searching.' In fact, a similar technique was used some five years previously in the Lynette White case in South Wales, in which a relative actually led the police to the culprit while finally exonerating three men who had been convicted. The murder occurred in 1988 and the police recovered numerous blood samples, none from the victim, but they could not be matched to any database. Using the newer more effective techniques in 2000, it was found that some of the bands (not a full profile) matched those from a 14 year old boy who had not been born at the time of the murder. Thus it was likely that a relative of the boy had committed the crime. Taking samples from the relatives finally established the identity of the perpetrator. Like every other advance, familial searching has attracted criticism. In the US it may potentially entrap a disproportionate number of African Americans into databases, wherein they are already said to constitute about 40%. It has also been pointed out that familial searching may cause problems outside the criminal process. Individuals who believe that they are related to each other may find otherwise, and others who volunteer samples may not be aware that relatives are already in the database for misdemeanors previously concealed.[38]

Keynote cases (US)

With its much larger population, the USA has seen proportionately more 'DNA cases'.[39] The first, according to general consensus was that of *State v Tommy Lee Andrews* (1987),[40] which at that time involved the RFLP/VNTR technique. The test was done by the private laboratory Lifecodes

---

38   Information on the Harman case is on the Forensic Science Service site <www.forensic.gov.uk/foresnic_t/inside/news/list_casefiles.php?case=24> And on the Lynette White case <http://lideloom.com/I2Sekar.htm>. Familial searching may take diverse forms. In a case in the US, an individual entered on the database had DNA which yielded 16 of the 26 alleles in the crime sample. This pointed to a relative, and his brother yielded a perfect match. For a critique see Noble, AA 'Fingerprints and civil liberties' [2006] Journal of Law, Medicine and Ethics vol 34, at p 149.

39   These are listed by Rudin and Inman, note 4, p 273. The list extends to the year 2000 for STR and mtDNA cases. Appendices in this book include 'Quality assurance standards for forensic DNA testing laboratories' with further details cited as < http:www.for-swg.org/swgdamin.htm> 'DNA statutes' (state by state), 'Summary statistics for STR and mtDNA decisions in the US, and 'Forensic science internet resources.'

40   533 So. 2nd 841 (Fla. 5th Dist. Ct. App.) [1987].

Corporation, which had put out advertisements regarding its expertise, and its conclusions were accepted as evidence, although they were not sufficient to ensure conviction at the actual trial. Thus at this point the DNA testing procedure was accepted after a brief pre-trial hearing by the Florida court. However the first formal Frye hearing regarding the admissibility of DNA profiling appears to have occurred soon afterwards, in the Joseph Castro case in New York. The evidence was a blood spot on Castro's watch, suspected to come from the victim, and the RMP was given as one in 190 million, but was immediately challenged. The Frye hearing thereafter was bitterly adversarial but the judge ruled that in general DNA evidence is admissible. The defence attorney Peter Neufeld may have been one of the first to call for laboratory accreditation, certification and licensing in respect of the molecular biology techniques, as well as a system of quality control. Along with the other defence team he pointed out several anomalies in the evaluation of the scientific evidence:

(1) some bands on the electropherogram were ignored

(2) there was no objectivity in matching the bands

(3) a Hispanic group might not be in Hardy-Weinberg equilibrium

Subsequently the defence and prosecution scientists issued a joint statement that Lifecodes data were not sufficiently reliable to support the assertion that the samples matched. In fact, the judge only accepted that the blood on the wrist watch of the suspect did not come from the defendant; he did not accept that it came from the victim, who in any case later confessed.[41]

An early exculpatory result of DNA technology in the US was the *Woodall* case, in which initially the West Virginia supreme court accepted the DNA technology but did not consider that it exonerated the suspect in terms of the technology at that time, since conventional markers (ABO blood groups, phosphoglucomutase and glyoxylase) appeared to incriminate him. Later however he was retested after the forensic scientist had been shown to

---

41   The Castro case is cited as 144 Misc.2d 956,545 N.Y.S. 2nd 1985 Sup. Ct. See also, among the massive literature on it: Sheard, B. 'DNA Profiling' [1990] *Medico-legal Journal* vol 58, at p 189 ; Anderson, A 'A judge backs technique' [1989] *Nature* vol 340, at p 582 ; Thompson, W C and Ford, S 'Is DNA fingerprinting ready for the courts?' *New Scientist* 31st March 1990, p 38; Neufeld, PJ and Colman, N 'When science takes the witness stand'. [1990] *Scientific American* vol 262, at p 18. Not much later than Castro Lifecodes' procedures were again called into question, in *State v McLeod* (1989). Here the scientists had pronounced a match between suspect and crime scene. The bands on the electropherogram were shifted relative to each other, although the pattern/distribution was the same. This was fatal to the prosecution.

be fraudulent, and he was released after his many years in prison. There may be a record in the case of Michael Anthony Williams, sentenced to life in 1981, exonerated in 2005, that is a wait of 24 years. There has been at least one case of a post-execution exoneration, that of Roger Keith Coleman.[42]

The US cases seem to have been generally less preoccupied with interpretive statistics than those in England, and more with the techniques. However the issue came to a head in the case of *US* v *Jenkins* (2005).[43] Jenkins had been arraigned for murder on the basis of a cold hit in the Virginia Department of Criminal Justice's database of previously profiled offenders. The trial judge held an evidentiary hearing on the issue whether the 'rarity statistic' (the RPM) is a procedure generally accepted by the scientific community. The defence maintained that there was, therein, 'a raging debate' which in itself justified exclusion under the Frye provisions, and the judge agreed. The Appeal Court admitted that as jurists they were '...not in always in a position to determine what is good science and what is bad science,' and had to be guided by experts in the field. It held that the trial court erred only in subjecting a debate on relevancy to the exacting Frye standard of general acceptance in the relevant scientific community. There was no debate in the scientific community and the case was remitted for trial with the DNA evidence admissible.

It emerges that some states allow interpretation of the DNA autoradiographs to be led in evidence, but do not allow any statistical calculations to go to the jury. In the mid-nineties, in *People* v *Miller* (1996) in Illinois, the product rule was accepted, overturning an earlier decision to the contrary.[44] The dissociation of the analysis from the statistics is also illustrated in the *Venegas* (1989) case in California. A woman had been raped in a hotel and thought that her attacker looked Hispanic, but she could not identify the suspect at a live lineup (as the identity parade is called in the US). Based on DNA in vaginal swabs, the odds against an unrelated individual selected at random from the Hispanic population being the culprit was put at 65,000 to one. The Supreme Court of California held that the analytical DNA evidence was admissible but refused to accept the prosecution's statistics. On a retrial in 1999, however, Venegas was convicted.[45] In *State* v *Almighty Four Hundred*

---

42   These cases are documented by the Innocence Project See for example < file://A: The Innocence Project Michael Anthony Williams.htm>.

43   *US (appellant) v Jenkins* (Appeal from the Supreme Court of the District of Columbia) (F-320-00). See note 33 of Chapter 1 and for an earlier perspective, Rudin and Inman note 4 at p 190.

44   *People v Miller* [1996] 173 Ill.2nd 167, 670 N.E. 2nd 721.

45   *State v Venegas* [1989] Sup Ct Calif Ct App 5 F019294. Also <http://cl.bna.com/

(1997) (apparently this is a personal name) the prosecution, unusually, gave both unadjusted and conservative estimates of the RMP, one in 3 to 4 million, and one in 1.2 million, respectively.[46] The defendant maintained that this demonstrated disagreement among experts as to the mode of calculating the statistics, but the appeal court was not moved by this argument and the conviction was affirmed.

United States v *Yee* (1990) was the first case in which the FBI, as the national anti-crime agency, on its own account supplied evidence based on RFLP techniques. The victim had been shot in his own vehicle but there appeared to be another's person's blood in it, possibly due to an attacker's ricocheting bullet. The match with the suspect was confirmed, to the FBI's satisfaction, and the magistrate accepted the evidence on the Frye standard. The District Court however disallowed the evidence. It was over the *Yee* case that groups of scientists became bitterly adversarial in respect of the FBI analysis, because of possible population substructure, an episode now of historical interest.[47] The FBI prevailed again in *United States* v *Jakobetz* (1990), a kidnap and rape case in which the DNA obtained from the victim matched the suspect. The defence challenged on the reliability of the FBI method, as well as the population statistics used to calculate the RMP. The method was generally accepted by the court, as well as the FBI's conservative use of the statistic of one in 3 million for the RMP.[48]

In the US there was much discussion, some of it acrimonious, of the two reports of the National Research Council (1992 and 1996) which despite its name is an arm of the US Academy of Sciences, 'a private, non-profit, self-perpetuating society of distinguished scholars.' However subsequent policy has largely been guided by it.

Cold hits and John Doe warrants

In the absence of a suspect, but with the possession of a tissue or stain which can yield DNA, a database can be surveyed to find a match. (For more on databases, see Chapter 2.2. above.) Alternatively, a population of individuals not *prime facie* connected with the crime, but coming in one way or another

---

cl/19980527/44870.htm>.

46 [1997] 92 CR 8536 3rd Div Ill Interestingly, in this case the court agreed that, whereas the prosecution's citing of a review of the database by an independent medical geneticist (who was not called) constituted hearsay, it could be admitted under the 'business records' exception.

47 *US* v *Yee* 134 F.R.D. 161 (N.D. Ohio 1991). See Sylvester, JT and Stafford, JH. 'Judicial acceptance of DNA profiling', on website <Blackhouses.textfiles.com/law>.

48 US v Jacobetz 747 F. Supp.250 (D.Vt. 1990).

within its catchment area, can be tested for a match. This population can consist of village males, as in the Pitchfork case, or it can be convicted criminals. (In statistics a *population* is the set of all measurements in which the investigator is interested; a *sample* is a subset of measurements selected from the population. As usual the day to day usage tends to ignore the technical definitions.) In the future, the way things are going, the population might even consist of everybody in the country, maybe in the whole world! The finding of a match in the surveyed population is known colloquially as a 'cold hit', sometimes a 'dragnet' in the US. A more formal term is the 'speculative search.' There are various and highly technical views on how the calculation of the RMP for a cold hit should be handled, discussed for example by the National Research Council (NRC). [49] There are several opposing views. One of these is that the procedure should involve two phases. The first search should identify a suspect but that RMPs should not be calculated at that point. Instead, the suspect should be tested by means of a completely different group of genetic markers and if there is a match, these latter probabilities should be used in court. A second view, held by the NRC, is that when a suspect is found by searching the database, the RMP should be multiplied by the number of persons in the database, that is, the larger the database the less probable it is that the suspect is the culprit. (See Box 1-2.) A third view is that if a database is large and a match is made, then the suspect is more likely to be guilty because so many others (in the large database) do not match. Evidently the second and third approaches are opposed to each other and offer great scope to the adversarial nature of criminal trials.[50]

There have been several other cold hits in England after the seminal *Pitchfork* case. Anthony Diedrick was accused of murdering Dr Joan Francisco in 1994, by way of civil proceedings brought by the family in 1998, after the Director of Public Prosecutions declined to prosecute. Their success in that action led the police to reexamine their evidence, and in the meantime there had been advances in the DNA technology, presumably the

---

49 *The Evaluation of Forensic DNA Evidence* (1996) National Research Council. National Academy Press, Washington DC. 1996. There is an informative discussion of cold hits by Krane, DE on <http://www.bioforensics.com>, in connection with the Jaidyn Leskie case in Victoria, Australia. This identifies the names and credentials of the various experts involved in the controversy. See also: Budowle, B Chakraborty, R et al. 'Source attribution of a forensic DNA profile' [2000] *Forensic Science Communications* vol 2, at p 23; also < http://fbi.gov/hq/lab/fsc/backissu/july2000/index.htm> and <file://A:\ Significance of -cold hits.htm>. The defence in *US v Jenkins* (note 43 above) was an attempt to exploit the divergences in views as described.
50 [1999] *State v Pappas* Np CRIO-24688 (Conn Super Ct July 21) furnishes a cogent example.

use of PCR, although it is difficult to identify this specifically in the reports. The victim's tee shirt had minute droplets of blood which matched those of Diedrick and he was convicted in 1999. There was a similar scenario in the conviction of John Taft for the murder of Cynthia Bolshaw, the so-called 'Beauty in the Bath'.[51] Another cold hit was that of B/D, discussed above (p 48) in conjunction with the demise of autrefois acquit.

A lengthy period between a crime and its solution by DNA forensics is evident in the case of Mary Gallacher[52] who was raped and murdered in Glasgow in 1978. Combing the prison populations for a suspect some 23 years later, the police were able to match a the DNA on a hair found in her body with that of one Angus Sinclair, who was serving a life sentence for three rapes. (Unusually, this sentence was indeterminate - presumably he was considered to be a permanent public danger.) The chance that the match could have been derived from a random individual from the population (the RMP) was said to be a billion to one against. Defence counsel urged the jury not to have 'blind faith 'in the conclusions of the expert scientists and that there were doubts about the 'accuracy' of the DNA tests. ('Accuracy' is again discussed below, but it is wearisome to note again that it is a misnomer here - counsel could have done more research on the terms to be used; anyway, reading the case, the defence seems to have been half-hearted, and no wonder, in view of the obvious infamy of his client.) The judge told the jury that the evidence was sufficient 'as a matter of law' for the conviction, presumably meaning that the validity of its technicalities had been accepted in other trials and by higher courts. The last had not been heard of this most unsavoury of criminals, however, see Box 2-4.

Nora Trott was raped and killed in 1978. In 2004 the Essex police carried out a cold case review. A semen sample DNA was put into the National DNA Database but did not produce a hit. However a man was arrested for drink driving in Cambridge and his DNA matched that of the semen sample. He eventually received a life sentence. This a 26 year gap, which may be a record in this context, and indicates too that the Database contains profiles not only from those convicted and from suspects and former suspects, but also from crime scene samples.[53]

51   These cases are discussed in: James, A Taylor, N et al 'The reform of double jeopardy' [2000] *Web Journal of Current Legal Issues* at site <http://webjcli.ncl.ac.uk/2000/issue5/james5.html>.
52   <http://news.bbc.co.uk/1/low/uk/Scotland/1385060> .
53   <forensic.gov.uk/forensic_t/inside/news/int_press_release.php>.

A 23-year gap was closed in the case of Mary Gregson, killed in 1977 on the towpath of the Leeds Liverpool canal. Semen stains found on her clothing were subjected to the blood grouping tests available at the time but did not advance the enquiry. A cold case review in the light of the newer DNA technologies was conducted in 1997 and sperm heads were found. They were sent to a specialist DNA low copy number laboratory. Samples were taken from the men originally involved in the enquiry and a match was obtained from one Lowther. In 2000 he received a life sentence.[54]

Wasting police time when they are hunting a serial killer is rightly regarded as a very grave offence. In the late seventies the Yorkshire police were frantically trying to obtain a lead on the serial rapist/killer who was later identified as Peter Sutcliffe. The investigations were much disrupted by a hoaxer (known as Wearside Jack) who in 1978 sent three letters and a tape to the police, claiming to be the culprit. The investigation was shifted to Sunderland, the source of the letters, and meanwhile Sutcliffe murdered another three women in the Leeds area. Early in 2006 a man called John Humble was arrested for a motoring offence and a DNA sample from him was matched with one taken from saliva on the gum of the offending envelopes. Presumably the police had put the latter on the national database. Humble was sentenced to six years in prison for perverting the course of justice.[55] This represents a 26 year cold hit.

According to the Innocence Project, Brian Kelly was the first person in Scotland to be convicted on the basis of DNA evidence alone;[56] however there were other items of evidence (Box 2-2). It was an example of a cold hit on a sample from a population rather than from a database.

The first cold hit in the US is said to have been that of one Martin Perez, convicted of a murder in Minneapolis in 1991, detected while in prison for other offences. The *Dabney* case is an example of the later so-called ' John Doe' hit.[57] In this Wisconsin case a mixture of semen and saliva was tested

---

54 Indignation over this case is expressed on <file://A:\Legally Scientific (Cold Hits vs Hard Facts).htm>.

55 < http://en.wikipaedia.org/wiki/Peter_Sutcliffe> (with links).

56 A full transcript of the Kelly appeal is on <http://www.bailii.org/scot/cases/ ScotHC/2004/47.html>.
See also < http://www.scotcourts.gov.uk/opinions/Xc458.html>.

57 The Dabney case is cited as Wisconsin CA Div 1 29/4/03; also see <file://A:\DNA_ John Doe_warrants.htm> A textbook discussion is to be found in Butler, note 4, p 446. The Denver District Attorney helpfully provides a model John Doe Warrant on site <www. denverda.org/DNA/John_Doe_DNA_Warrants.htm>. Potential (educated) arrestees by cold hits will recall King Lear's words: ' Tremble thou wretch/ Thou hast within thee

and a charge was filed in December 2000, before the expiry of the six year statute of limitations, against John Doe #12 (unknown male) with a profile derived from thirteen allelic locations. This was run against the convicted offender index of the Wisconsin DNA bank, but no match was found. Then it was to run on a monthly basis as uploaded to the FBI files. On Feb 27th 2001 however the Wisconsin authorities reported a cold hit. In England there is no statute of limitations for criminal charges and so the John Doe issue in its US sense does not arise. The importance of the process in US is that the DNA profile is accepted as a 'description' of the suspect for the purposes of a warrant.

The all-time record for time lapse in a cold hit might well be the case of Fletcher Anderson Worrell. In 2005 he tried to buy a gun in Atlanta and a background check revealed that he was wanted for bail jumping in New York in 1978. Previously he had been arraigned on charges of rapes perpetrated in both Manhattan and Queens in 1973. The Queens trial ended in a hung jury, and the he was released on bail pending the Manhattan trial, when he disappeared. The police checked DNA from the files of the 1973 cases and a sample from Worrell and they matched. Thus a 32 year gap was bridged by DNA technology.[58]

Of course there are glitches/caveats. In the UK in 1999 a man with Parkinson's disease, unable to drive or even dress himself, was linked by speculative search to a burglary which was perpetrated 200 miles from his home. In spite of his protestations and an alibi he was arrested because of the match and only on retesting was the mistake rectified. But contrarily, a cold hit can of course be exclusionary; Stephen Cowans served six years in Massachusetts on the basis of fingerprint evidence before being released by DNA evidence.[59] The record for incarceration before exculpation on the basis of DNA evidence is continually being broken.

Summary of 2.4

* DNA evidence is a particular type of (circumstantial) identification evidence.

* It is useful for both incrimination and exoneration.

---

undivulged crimes/ Unwhipped to justice.'
58 < file:///A:Pacers%20Digest%20-%20Gun%20Background%20Check> An even lengthier time scale, not exactly describable as a cold hit, has been claimed for the (supposed) DNA of Jack the Ripper by the crime writer Patricia Cornwell.
59 Coghlan, A 'How far should DNA fingerprints be trusted?' *New Scientist* 17th Sept 2005, p 6.

Box 2.3 A Sample US Criminal Case

This is not a particularly famous case * but it belongs to the modern (PCR-STR era) and throws up some interesting points . It was a first degree murder in the course of rape, the evidentiary material coming from semen stain on the victim's pajamas. After attempts by the defence to have the judge recuse herself and to argue that there was no such offence as rape on the statute book, it went on to challenge the DNA evidence and along the way accused the scientists for the State of being biased. (There could be no better illustration here than of the attorney's ethical imperative to adduce, for his client, every possible avenue of defence, however far-fetched.) In respect of the DNA evidence, the trial court decided to apply the *Frye* procedure rather than *Daubert* (Chap 1, p 31) for unstated reasons, presumably because it was thought that in terms of admissibility the former, conducted in the absence of the jury, was more apposite to the complexities of DNA technology.

The appeal court firmly disposed of the first two objections, the motions to recuse and to expunge the charge of rape, but not without going to some length in quoting precedent and interpreting statute. When it came to review the DNA evidence it stated, in the habitual manner of appeal tribunals, that it would only reverse the trial court decision on evidentiary matters should its discretion prove to have been unsustainable. But: 'When the reliability or general acceptance of novel scientific evidence is not likely to vary according to the circumstances of the a particular case, we review that evidence independently.' In other words, although each case hinges on its own facts, there may be principles which apply to all. The appellate judges then reviewed the scientific evidence in detail. After extraction the DNA is stated to be 'split in half' which is roughly correct but is an unusual mode of expression. The DNA polymerase is described as an enzyme used to copy specific DNA locations in the course of the PRC amplification so that they can be 'typed and compared to DNA of a known sample.' It is stated that ' STR testing, which involves the testing of DNA at three or more genetic markers, is a subtype of the PCR method.' This is inaccurate - STR testing is a technology designed to utilise microsatellite variation in the interests of matching DNA samples, and PCR is a subsidiary technique to facilitate this technology in the face of a meager sample mass. It is then stated that thirteen (not three) loci were compared to those in the CODIS system. The work was apparently evidently contracted out to Cellmark, which used the Profiler Plus (Perkin Elmer) and the Cofiler (Applied Biosystems) protocols. (Here we see the continuing role of the big biotechnology companies) The application of the PRC fragments to an electropherogram, to produce peaks (i.e. capillary electrophoresis) is then described:

'If the pattern of repeats of the known DNA strand matches the pattern in the questioned strand, the analyst reports that the donor of the known sample cannot be conclusively eliminated as the source of the questioned sample. Similar to RFLP testing [which the appeal court had reviewed in a previous case] the analyst performs a statistical calculation [actually the product rule] to quantify the significance of the similarity between the known and the questioned samples.'

The 'questioned' sample of course means the sample from the crime scene.

The defence had argued that Cellmark's techniques had not undergone sufficient validation studies, and that they could not adequately deal with stutter (see p 20) and other artifacts. The appeal court admitted that it had not yet addressed the reliability of PCR-based STR DNA testing but noted its wide reception by other states, with citations, and that it is used by the FBI. At the *Frye* hearing the defence had argued that the commercial kits used by Cellmark had not been properly validated, but the appeal court ruled that "questions of reliability" went to the weight of evidence, not admissibility. It agreed with the trial court that the defence argument, that Cellmark failed to conduct sufficient validation studies before raising the minimum relative fluorescence unit (RFU) level at which it would consider a peak on the electropherogram an allele from forty RFUs to sixty [this refers of course to capillary electrophoresis] goes to the weight of evidence rather than admissibility under *Frye*. Thus it was pointed out to be 'well settled' that after admissibility the trier of fact is in the best position to assess the credibility of the witnesses, who can be subject to cross-examination. The prosecution witnesses had satisfied the trial court of their credibility.

The defence expert witnesses had criticized the sufficiency of the validation studies (that is, evidently they recognised that validation as such had taken place) but the appeal court pointed out that scientific unanimity is not necessary for admissibility under *Frye*, only a general consensus. On the challenge that the technique could be negated by stutter, as an artifact, the appeal court defined an artefact as "a result that does not come from things one actually intends to test." This is slightly obscure. An artifact is a fortuitous entity that arises incidentally to the main thrust of the analysis. However it was accepted that there were procedures in place to deal with artefacts and stutter. Finally the defence had challenged the product rule, although it is not stated on what grounds. Perhaps there were none, and defence counsel was scraping the barrel by then. Considering the obvious turpitude of the defendant (the victim was described as an 81-year old woman) one must admire his fortitude. The appeal court again shot that objection down.

And so the conviction was upheld.

* *State of New Hampshire* v *Whittey* (2003) No 2001-427; www.denverda.org/ DNA_Documents/WhitteyAP.pdf

- DNA identification evidence lies heavily on the interpretation of the RMP.

- Misuse of the RMP has been held to generate the 'prosecutor's fallacy'.

- New techniques (LCN, familial searching) have increased the sensitivity of testing.

- Recent years have seen the burgeoning of 'cold hits' as databases have expanded.

- Cold hits can also be exclusionary.

2.5 DNA and Forensic Mathematics

The term *forensic mathematics* is a neologism but sufficiently broad to describe the contents of this section.[60] Mathematics might seem a tedious diversion for a lawyer, but it is interesting that two of the most notable UK judges of modern times, Lord Denning and Lord Mackay, started off their careers as mathematicians. If it does exists as a separate discipline, forensic mathematics (or statistics) can be seen as a subspecies of quantitative genetics, which has existed for more than a century.[61] Quantitative genetics allows *inter alia* the counting of genes in a population and one of its main tenets is the Hardy-Weinberg equilibrium (Box 1-2). It is a legitimate defence manoevre to suggest that a population, used for calculating gene frequencies, either is not random mating, or has exhibited selection or mutation or migration (plus any combination of these) in that these nullify the Hardy-Weinberg assumptions. This was indeed an issue in the US case of *State v Yee,* for example.[62] In fact the mathematics of DNA analysis are an extension of those used in the more traditional identification techniques involving blood groups and enzyme/ protein polymorphisms. At the lowest level of discrimination, it could be recorded that a blood stain was type A, say, the same as that of the suspect. But by typing a variety of markers and proteins, it is possible to say that there is only small probability that a blood sample from a suspect could have come from a random member of the reference population. However in samples

60   The descriptive may have been coined by Dr Charles Brenner who appears to publish entirely by interactive website: < http://dna-view.com/ideas/wiptitle.htm>. In some ways his calculations are even more interesting in the context of family law, see Chapter 3.
61   Falconer, D S *Introduction to Quantitative Genetics* (Longman Scientific and Technical, 1989).
62   *United States v Yee*, 134 F.R.D. 161 (N.D. Ohio 1991).

from crime scenes, there is often not enough material for such extensive investigation, and in any case the relevant proteins, as pointed out at the beginning of this chapter, have limited stability outside a freezer. Notably '... the major difference with DNA profiling is the smallness of the frequencies of the occurrence of specific haplotypes habitually quoted, perhaps 1 in 100 million, 1 in 10 billion or even smaller. It is these frequencies which have attracted a measure of incredulity, particularly as they are based on relatively small population samples – perhaps two or three hundred people.'[63] To rephrase this quotation by experts in the field, it is very often stated by the expert witness for the prosecution that the probability of the defendant's DNA matching that of a random member of the population (the RMP) is so small that not a single person in the whole world (current population about 6.5 billion) could provide that match. In cases mentioned above, in *Karger* the RMP was put at one in 90 billion, and in *Miller* no less than 446 billion!

There is much lamenting that legal and scientific minds do not understand each other, but a presumptive point of contact is the concept of probability. Scientists commonly accept a 95% probability of a difference between two groups as being proof of the reality of that difference (technically, $P < 0.05$) whereas the prosecution's burden of 'beyond reasonable doubt is' often thought to go to 95% certainty of guilt. though whether any quantitative estimate can be applied to it is highly controversial.[64]

In mathematics and statistics, P stands for the probability of some event. It is assigned any value between 0 and 1, the former denoting absolute impossibility and the latter complete certainty. It is unusual to assign either of these extreme values to any particular event - we must always consider that we are usually very far from having the ability to attribute absolutes. (This is sometimes called the Cromwell principle.[65] However surely for one event, my death, $P = 1$.) Alternatively it is expressed in percentage terms, for example $P = 0.95$ corresponds to a 95% probability.

63   Evett, IW 'An efficient statistical procedure for interpreting DNA single locus profiling data in crime cases' [1992] *Journal of the Forensic Science Society* vol 32, at p 307. See also Butler note 3 at p 504 and Koblinsky et al, note 4, p 158.
64   Meeran, R 'Scientific and legal standards of proof in environmental personal injury' [1992] *Lancet* vol 339, at p 671; Finney, DJ. 'Between medicine and law' [1983] *Statistics in Medicine* vol 2 at p 113. For a survey of standards of proof in US courts see generally Jasanof S. *Science at the Bar* (Harvard University Press, 1997).
65   'I beseech ye in the bowels of Christ, to think it possible that you are mistaken.' Of course the retort must be: 'Consider that you might be mistaken yourself !' If Cromwell had been a Bayesian, he would have maintained that P(G/M) is near zero.

Two events or states can be either mutually exclusive – examples are male or female, diseased or non-diseased, sane or insane, guilty (G) or not guilty (nG). (These, if counted, are termed *category variables*.) The sum of two mutually exclusive probabilities is unity. This is the *addition rule* and for these last two mutually exclusive events or states it can be written as:

$$P(G) + P(nG) = 1$$

For two events, let us say the gaining of pieces of evidence E1 and E2, which occur completely independent of each other, the probability of them both occurring is the product of their individual probabilities. Formally:

$$P \text{ (E1 and E2)} = P(E1) \times P(E2)$$

This is the *multiplication rule*. It can be derived in formal logic but we know intuitively that it must be correct - if P(E1) = 0.9 and P(E2) = 0.9 and E1 and E2 are independent of each other then the probability of E1 *and* E2 together cannot be additive, this would give P = 1.8 which is impossible. Rather P (E1 and E2) = 0.9 x 0.9 = 0.81. The multiplication rule is forensically important and received its most celebrated airing, or notoriety, in the US case *People* v *Collins* (1968).[66] Whether two events are in reality independent of each other depends on the facts, a point well illustrated in that case.

The concept of odds (O) is often used concurrently with, or as an alternative to, probability. The two are often used interchangeably in normal conversation, and even in the forensic literature. The form of words: 'there is one in a million chance of the suspect being innocent' is an odds statement, but is often described as a probability. Thus it is always open to counsel to ask a witness exactly what he is talking about. By definition:

$$O = P/(1-P)$$

---

66   This was the famous case in California whereby the prosecution led evidence that the perpetrators of a robbery were a black male with a beard and a moustache, in a yellow car, accompanied by a blonde white woman with a pony tail. The probabilities of these characteristics being present at the same time (one in ten, one in four, etc) were multiplied to give a one in 12,000 odds on that the defendants were the robbers. On appeal it was pointed out that the separate probabilities were not necessarily independent of each other, for example men with moustaches often have beards. The citation is: 438 P.2d 33 (68 Cal.2nd 319 1968). It is mentioned in all the textbooks – see Tupper, C *Cross on Evidence* (Butterworths, 7th edn 1990) p 158. The artificial separation of probabilities when they are in fact interdependent has been noticed in medicine and called Kouska's fallacy – if a patient has one disease he is quite likely to have another which is only superficially unrelated. See: Lubinsky, MS. 'Kouska's fallacy : the error in the divided denominator' [1986] *Lancet* Dec 20, at p 1449.

Reciprocally, and here we are reminded that P must be less than unity - if somebody quotes P = 1.2, say, statistical illiteracy is indicated. Conversely:

$$P = O/(1+O)$$

If we refer to the probability of a specific event or state, guilt (G) existing, and the probability of it not existing (nG) then expression for *odds on* of being guilty is P(G)/P (nG). The reciprocal is of course the *odds against*.

If for event E, P = 0.2 (or 20%), the odds calculation is 0.2/ (1-0.2) = 4, or in words, the odds are four to one against E occurring. A French bookmaker (of course these matters my be considered by some more apposite to the turf than to the trial) would say five to one (the original stake to be returned.) In US racetracks it would be given as - 400, the gain from a stake of 100. An event of P = 1 has odds *on* of infinity, and event P = 0 has odds *against* of infinity.

In the context of a DNA match, and to make a link between the odds on of a suspect being guilty, and the RMP, consider first the *law of conditional probabilities*, expressed below in both words and symbols. When two events coincide or intersect, the mathematical symbol to express this is an inverted U, thus: ∩

Probability of guilt given   =   Probability that the match and the guilt coincide [P(M∩G)]
the DNA match [P(G/M)]   Probability of finding the match itself [P(M)]

This relationship is intuitive - we are reducing the probability of guilt and the match occurring simultaneously by factoring in as denominator the probability of finding the match under any circumstances whatsoever. (To put it another way, if P(G/M) is less than one, which it must be, then P(M), probability of finding the match under any circumstances is greater than P (M ∩ G), the coincidence of match and guilt.)

By the product rule, which is again intuitive, recalling that the probabilities of two independent events occurring together are multiplied.

Probability that the DNA match   =   probability of the   probability
and guilt coincide   match given that the suspect x   of guilt *per se*
[P (G ∩ M)]   is guilty [P (M/G)]   [P(G)]

Factor the right hand side of this equation into the law of conditional probabilities just above, and (reverting to symbols) we obtain.

$$P(G/M) \quad = \quad \frac{P(M/G)\ P(G)}{P(M)} \dots\dots\dots\dots\dots\dots 1$$

It is easy to work out the reverse, that is a corresponding equation for the probability of the suspect being not guilty (nG)

$$P(nG/M) = \frac{P(M/nG)\ P(nG)}{P(M)} \quad \text{......................2}$$

Divide equation 2 into equation 1. We obtain:

$$\frac{P(G/M)}{P(nG/M)} = \frac{P(G)}{P(nG)} \times \frac{P(M/G)}{P(M/nG)} \quad \text{.................3}$$

This is the odds form of the Bayes' theorem /equation. It links the prior odds on of guilt P(G) /P(nG) to the evidence gathered from the DNA analysis, known as the likelihood ratio (LR), that is P(M/G)/ P(M/nG). As demonstrated, it is not a probability but an odds expression, however much these two are confused in the literature. The denominator P(M/nG) is of course the RMP.

The *odds ratio* (OR) can also turn up here and there. In words this is "the ratio of odds on the suspect being guilty, given the match, to the odds on the suspect being innocent, given the match. It is formulated as:

$$OR = \frac{P(M/G)\ /\ [1-P(M/G)]}{P\ (M/nG)/[1-P(M/nG)]}$$

Rearranging
$$= \frac{P(M/G)\ [1-P(M/nG)]}{P(M/nG)\ [1-P(M/G)]}$$

The reason for discussing them both at this point is that one must be clear about which is being referred to. Forensic opinion at the moment favours the LR but in medical statistics (which can equally be an issue in court) a case is often made for the use of the OR, technically a dichotomous classification, here P(M/G) versus P(M/nG)

Suppose P(M/G) = 0.5 and P(M/nG) = 0.5. This would be a *reductio ad absurdum*, but it would make both OR and LR calculate to unity and have no probative value. Formally, they can both partake of any value between zero and infinity.

Using the odds version of Bayes' one can do a quick sample calculation to see how he mathematics work out in actual practice. If the non-DNA evidence for guilt is finely balanced then we could put P(G) = 0.5. Since P(G) + P(nG) = 1 the odds expression P(G) /P(nG) = 1. This is the prior odds, excluding the DNA evidence. P(M/G), logically, is usually taken as unity, in that if the DNA from the scene of the crime truly matches the DNA of the suspect, then he is certainly the culprit. However if the probability of a random member of the community showing the same DNA alleles is measurable, it might be put at 0.01. Then the left hand side of equation 3 calculates to 100. Thus, posteriorly, the odds of guilt are 100 to one on. Since probability equals odds divided by odds plus one, the corresponding probability (of guilt) is 100/101 or 0.99. In practice, P(M/nG) is usually given as a very small number indeed, making the LR ratio very large and the posterior probability proportionately so.

It can be appreciated then that the LR is intrinsic in Bayes' theorem, the bone of contention in *R v Deen* and *R v Doheny and Adams* mentioned above. The theorem states that a prior probability (of guilt in this context) can be modified in terms of a probability function generated by new evidence. Put like that, it is little more than common sense, although of course it is to be expressed in quantitative terms. In the simplest statement, in terms of probability rather than odds:

Revised probability = Prior probability x Some probability function based on new evidence

Bayes' theorem of course is of universal applicability, and there is some evidence that it has been used intuitively.[67] It can be used to calculate the probability of having a disease or not or more prosaically the outcome of a football match (with new evidence on players' injuries factored into the prior probability) but more importantly it violates the hallowed statistical principle that chance has no memory. Every treatment of it in the literature however seems to give a different formulation and use a different notation and the mode adopted herein seems most suitable.

The probability version can be worked out on the same principles as the odds version. As before, by the law of conditional probabilities:

---

67   The intuitive use of Bayes' theorem has been discerned, for example, in the Howland Will forgery trial, in which the issue was the probability of seeing patterns of descending loops on a signature – see <File://A:Howland Will forgery trial.htm> For the intrepid student there is an extensive literature on the legal applications of the LR and Bayes' theorem. A classic, now, is Robertson, B and Vigneaux, GA [1993] *Oxford Journal of Legal Studies* vol 13, at p 475. Also see Jowett, C. 'Lies, damned lies, and DNA Statistics: DNA match testing, Bayes' theorem, and the criminal courts' [2001] *Medicine, Science and the Law* vol 41, at p 194 who advocates a species of reasoning which is so arcane that few lawyers have a chance of understanding it, never mind juries, and whose detailed treatment is impressive but who switches back and forward between probabilities and odds in manner which seems unnecessarily complex. See also Redmayne, M 'Science, evidence and logic' [1996] *Modern Law Review* vol 59, at p 747; Koehler, J J Chia, A et al 'The random match probability in DNA evidence: irrelevant and prejudicial?' [1995] *Jurimetrics Journal* vol 35 at p 201.

$$P (M \cap G) = P (M/G) \ p(G) \text{ and } P (M \cap nG) = P (M/nG) \ P(nG)$$

So $P(G/M) \ P(M) = P(M/G) \ P(G)$

Rearranging, $P (G/M) = \dfrac{P(G) \times P(M/G)}{P(M)}$

P(M) is the total probability of a match, that is the probability of the match coinciding with the suspect being guilty, plus the probability of a match coinciding with non-guilt, or:

$$\begin{aligned} P (M) \ &= P(M \cap G) + P (M \cap nG) \\ &= P(G/M) \ P(M) + P(nG/M) \ P(nG) \end{aligned}$$

Substituting this in equation we obtain

$$P(G/M) = P(G) \quad \times \quad \dfrac{P(M/G)}{P(M/G) \ P(G) + P(M/nG)P(nG)}$$

The right hand side of the relationship, the prior probability of guilt, (nG) is factored by the probability of a match given that the suspect is guilty, P(M/G), divided by the whole of the evidence. Taking the numerical values as before, the right hand side calculates to:

$$= 0.5 \quad \times \quad \dfrac{1}{(1 \times 0.5) + (0.01 \times 0.5)}$$

$$= 0.99$$

Thus the same result is obtained as for the odds form.

It seems that the Bayesian formulation has not been considered by the US courts.[68] It was specifically discounted by the National Research Council Second Report (1996): 'Some have proposed a Bayesian approach but this does not avoid the kinds of population genetic problems and no lab has used it … in USA.'[69] Of course the English courts have followed suit subsequent to the *Dean* and *Dohoney* cases. The view is that what is needed is a formulation of the LR that need not resort to Bayesian analysis, so statistics *per se* are not disdained. The LR is based of course on the product rule, and is now generally accepted in evidence, despite doubts which in origin can be traced back to the *Collins* case. Thus in *People v Miller* (1996)[70]a triple murder case in Illinois, blood of victim was found on a napkin and pillow in the home of the defendant and using the RFLP technique the prosecution expert witness

---

68 Rudin and Inman, note 4, p 251.
69 See note 49.
70 *People v Miller* [1996] 173 Ill.2nd 167, 670 N.E. 2nd 721.

calculated the RMP as one in 466 billion Caucasians. Despite the magnitude of these odds both the trial and appeal court specifically affirmed the use of the product rule to calculate it, so that logically a LR of very large magnitude is generated.

The (O J) *Simpson* case (1995) of immense public interest, did not proceed as far as the issue of the LR in that the defence managed to circumvent the DNA evidence entirely by suggesting that the blood had been planted by the police. This has not deterred some post-hoc mathematical comment. Thus it was maintained by the defence that although Simpson had battered his wives, only 0.1% of such husbands kill them. A Bayesian analysis of this statistic, using also the figures for the murder rate in US, indicates that the probability that Simpson murdered his wife is over 50% (which would obviously have been good enough for the civil case, although presumably it was not required).[71]

A cogent objection to the use of Bayes' theorem, apart from the fact that few non-statisticians can understand it, is that the inclusion of prior probability, being largely subjective, logically renders what seems like an objective mathematical calculation into a subjective one. It would be different could an objective assessment of prior probability be made, but that is of course an absurdity, with so many other factors like character and motive being laid before the jury. In the *Kelly* case for example (Box 2-2) the suspect was known personally to the victim but could not be picked out by her in an identity parade. The prior probability of guilt then must have seemed very small, but it was completely overwhelmed by a LR of many thousands. In any case the use of the prior probability has been criticized in that it is flies in the face of the presumption of innocence.

Another difficulty, sporadically discussed in the literature, lies in the inability of the human mind to grasp the reality of very large numbers, as when the RMP is expressed as one in three million, for example. If a scientist says that the RMP is one in 466 billion, even a minimally astute juror will

---

71   Good, I J ' When batterer turns to murderer' [1995] *Nature* vol 375, at p 541. Of course the literature on the OJ Simpson case is immense. See Rudin and Inman, note 4, p 101. Dr Charles Brenner provides a sardonic analysis of the DNA aspects of the OJ Simpson defense. Here the complication was that the prosecution had been alleged to plant the potentially incriminating blood, and Brenner points out that this makes the LR equal to 1. (In the notation used herein P(G/M) remains unity, but P(nG/M) then also becomes unity.) A LR of unity of course is devoid of probative value. The prosecution had put the LR at 200, that is the hypothesis of guilt was favoured over the hypothesis of non-guilt by 200 to one (without taking into account the prior probability). The relevant Brenner site is <http://dna-view.com/assump.htm>.

know that there are only about 6 billion people in the world. What then does the figure mean? Does it imply that another 460 billion people will have to be born before a profile like that of the accused turns up? Or does it mean that, since only probabilities are cited, there could be a match already, maybe several, but that there might have to be 100 or perhaps 1000 billion more births before substantially more matches turn up? These are perverse considerations indeed.

And then again, the posterior probability (usually in fact an odds expression, as has been shown above) can be criticised as a reification of the complex question of human guilt or innocence - it is odd by any standards to express guilt as a number, even if the number is very respectably derived. Here the word 'reification', which has a number of meanings[72] is applied to the logical fallacy of reducing a tissue of complexities and subtleties to a mere number. The best example outside law remains the so-called intelligence quotient (IQ).

Ceilings, confidence intervals and bins.

The ceiling principle is largely of historical interest in that it was a means to modify the product rule, criticised for not taking into account the possible non-independence of two estimates of allele frequencies, and for not accommodating the paucity of databases in the early 1990s.[73] In effect it was designed to minimize the type I error, the occurrence of false positives. It did not appear to arise as an issue in English law, possibly because it was thought unlikely to influence the jury's reading of the figures. Thus, suppose seven alleles are examined, and the frequencies are all (for simplicity) one in a hundred. Then if a suspect yields a match, the RMP (to use the correct notation) is 0.1×10^{-7} or (to use the normal [incorrect] mode of expression), one in ten million. By the ceiling principle the RMP is calculated as 0.05×10^{-7} or one in five million. To any trier of fact these would both merely be

72 The term 'reification' is used in the sense of, for example, transforming formerly precious or sacred objects like human eggs into tradable commodities. An alternative usage, as adopted here, is explained by Gould SJ *The Mismeasure of Man* (Penguin Books, 1984) p 238. Yet another way of describing it devolves on the 'numerical supremacy syndrome' (in that audiences, including juries, pay more attention to numerical than to other data). This is discussed by Iedema, R Braithwaite, J et al 'The reification of numbers: statistics and the distance between self, work and others' [2003] *British Medical Journal* vol 326 at p 771.

73 It is thoroughly described by Connelly PM. 'Reference Guide on Forensic DNA Evidence' [1996] *Jurimetrics* vol 36 at p 193 ; it is also of historical interest in being the basis of a ferocious dispute between leading DNA scientists, some of whom were later involved in the OJ Simpson trial.

very large numbers. Ceilings were an issue in the Venegas case in the US, when the concept as presented by counsel was not accepted.[44]

Confidence levels also relate to an adjustment of the raw figures to make them more conservative. In calculating the frequency of an allele in a population, a sample of that population has to be surveyed. If a different sample from the same population is also surveyed, a different answer is invariably obtained. This is 'sampling variation', a universal phenomenon. In science, this difficulty is dealt with by making an estimate of the range over which the true measurement is likely to lie, usually at a 95% probability. The range is known as the *confidence interval*. Thus for example the RMP could be said (as odds) to lie between one in 50,000 and one in 60,000. The calculation is fairly technical, and not universally agreed upon.[74] Indeed, it is rare to see confidence intervals quoted in the case reports; the expert witness appears almost always to be be presenting point estimates.

With respect to bins, observation of the practicalities of separating DNA fragments on gels, or by capillary electrophoresis, reveals that they do not always appear in the same physical space (a manifestation of random error, see below). The bands, or peaks, are also very close together. Thus a DNA band on an electropherogram containing 20 STR repeats can readily be distinguished from a band with 10, but not so easily with one with 21. So, measurement of bands has been grouped into 'bins'. Wider bins increase the likelihood that two distinct bands fall with the same bin and would be thought to be identical, creating false positives. (This makes a type Type 1 error more likely; alternatively it can be said to decrease sensitivity.) If the bin is too small, the laboratory may decide on a mismatch and so a type II error is introduced, decreasing specificity. At the moment it appears that bin sizing is the responsibility of individual laboratories.[75] It is therefore open to defence counsel to query the choice of bin size.

From the evidentiary point of view, it is important to note that all the adjustments noted above are conservative, that is, they operate in the interests of the defendant.

The problem of mutation rates

Supposing that a match is not found between a DNA sample at the scene of the crime and the DNA in a suspect's cells, how do you know that the

---

74   DNA Advisory Board Recommendations. *Forensic Science Communications* 2, July 2000. <http://www.fbi.gov/hq/lab/fsc/backissu/july2000/dnastat.htm>.
75   For 'binning' see NRC, note 48, p 142, and Connelly note 70.

suspect's DNA has not mutated in the interim so that the potential match is undetected ? This would lead to a type II error (statistically speaking) that is, where a real match should be detected but is not. The answer is that mutation is never so fast as to cause such difficulties. In Jeffreys' words: ' The novel population-genetic behaviour of minisatellites, with their....... demonstrable propensity towards convergent allele length evolution, sets them aside from conventional loci and can make them especially refractive to genetic drift processes.'[76] The mutation rate can however be measured by the application of MVR-PCR (Chap 1.1). In a paternity case Jeffrey's team picked up a slippage mutation (an increase or decrease of one repeat in a minisatellite/ microsatellite) in an alleged father, so a son was incorrectly excluded from the relationship. However he was shown to be compatible in allele pattern to the grandparents.[77] SNPs have lower mutation rates than STRs and so if rates in the latter should turn out to be a problem, SNPs may be examined as an alternative.

The problem of subpopulations

Databases of diverse ethnic groups are being constantly created and published, but even so, there is suspicion that subpopulations within them may create linkage disequilibrium and failure to obey the Hardy-Weinburg law. In the *Kelly* case, discussed below under 'contamination', the database was derived from 200 individuals in the Chester area, whereas the comparison suspect was from Edinburgh. As far as one can tell ethnicity was not an issue in the case, but the name suggests Irish ancestry at least in part, so did the inhabitants of Chester conform to an overall Caucasian database? This sort of question is legitimately posed. One might think that subpopulation considerations would be most acute in large, cosmopolitan cities like New York and London wherein there is bound to be substantial interethnic mating. However such considerations might apply almost anywhere. In *Springfield v the State* (1993) the defendant's DNA was referred to the native American database, which was compiled from Navajos, Cherokees and Cheyennes.

---

76   Jeffrey's investigations of mutations are described by him in note 26 above and in May, CA Jeffreys, AJ et al 'Mutation rate heterogeneity and the generation of allele diversity at the human minisatellite MS205' [1996] *Human Molecular Genetics* vol 12, at p 1823. Textbook treatments are : Duncan GT, Tracey, ML et al 'Techniques of DNA analysis' In: James, S H and,Nordby, J (eds) *Forensic Science* (CRC Press, 2003) p 239 and Butler, note 3, p 269.
77   Yamamoto, T Tamaki K, et al. 'The application of minisatellite repeat mapping by PCR in a paternity case showing false exclusion due to STR mutation ' [2001] *Journal of Forensic Sciences* vol 46, at p 374.

The defendant himself was a Crow.[78]

In *People* v *Pizarro* (2003) prosecutors presented the jury with the statistical frequency of the killer's genetic profile within the Hispanic community, but no independent proof of the killer's ethnicity was available.[79] The court maintained that the scientists should have employed a multiethnic pool. Obviously a suspect's ethnicity should always be factually established, in relation to the database used, rather than just making an assumption from his name. Thus defence counsel may feel the need for vigilance in enquiring about the database from when the RMP has been calculated. The consensus is that if a suspect is from a group which has not at that point been used to generate a reliable database, the RMP should be calculated from all groups in the neighbourhood, area or even country.

Nonetheless the problem is being overcome in two ways, first of all by constructing databases for ever more and ever particularized ethnic groups, secondly by introducing a correction factor θ (theta) which is factored into the allele frequency such that it operates conservatively.[80]

The problem of mixed samples

Obviously, a stain or other sample from a crime scene is potentially a mixture from two or more individuals. This situation does not make it unsuitable for DNA profiling, as long as certain considerations are taken into account. Thus, a sample may be adjudged a mixture of major and minor contributions if there is a distinct contrast in signal intensities among the alleles. Nonetheless investigating mixtures with multilocus probes can cause difficulties in interpretation, as can be imagined - there can be a substantial increase in the number of bands to be assessed. It could be better in such cases to use single locus probes, thus producing only one band for homozygotes and two for heterozygotes.[81] If there is a known contributor to a mixed sample, however, then subtraction of the alleles of the interloper is generally feasible. In cases where there is a relatively large amount of female DNA and a relatively small amount of male DNA, the former can mask the profile of the latter. Then, STR regions on the Y-chromosome (from the male, of course) can be investigated and interference is thus avoided. Another difficulty is the enormous number

---

78   *Springfield v the State* [1993] 860 P.2nd 435, Wyo.
79   *People v Pizarro* [2003] No F030754 Calif. App. 5th Dist.
80   See Rudin and Inman, note 4, p 144.
81   For mixtures see NRC, note 48 p 129, Butler note 3, p 158 and Rudin and Inman note 4, p 248.

of comparisons to be made. The informatics staff of the FSS have addressed this and are promoting a software called DNAboost, patent pending.

The problem of relatives

The discussion above assumes that there is no relative who is also a suspect; the closer a relative who is indeed a suspect, the more alleles identical to those of the prime suspect will be found. It is quite possible that a suspect is eliminated at the same time as a relative is implicated. Of course, a suspected relative may or may not available for DNA typing. In *Her Majesty's Advocate General* v *Aslam* (1992) (a Scottish case) the forensic scientist reported a RMP of 1 in 50,000 for unrelated individuals. (It will be noticed that these are unusually small odds, but here only three single locus probes were used.) The suspect had five brothers. If the other evidence did not distinguish between all six brothers, the expert witness put the odds against the defendant's innocence at the exceptionally low figure of one in five.[82]

In an even more recent English case *R* v *Watters* (2000) there was a successful appeal against the presentation of the DNA statistics.[83] It was a case involving five burglaries, there being similar features to each of these. The prosecution however relied solely on the DNA evidence taken from cigarette butts found at them. The expert witness testified that she had done STR profiling at seven sites, giving a RMP, in the absence of close relatives, of one in 86 million. In other words, nobody else in the United kingdom could credibly have been the source of the DNA. If the appellant had two brothers, then the RMP would reduce to one in 267. The suspect indeed had two brothers, from neither whom was a DNA sample available. The accused maintained that the RMP of one in 267 (called a 'margin of error' by the Court of Appeal, to further complicate the nomenclature) was large enough to engender reasonable doubt. The judge in his summing up indicated that if the jury could not exclude a brother, the 1 in 267 'probability ratio' should be considered by them. This was held by the Court of Appeal to be a misdirection – if the jury could not exclude a brother, then they had to acquit. (The forensic scientist here stated under cross examination that her results did not mean that the DNA had actually come from the suspect, that they should not be used in isolation, and that DNA evidence, in itself, was not proof. - presumably the emphasis here is on 'in itself.' Nonetheless, as

---

82 <www.scotscourts.gov.uk/opinions/c716_99.html>; also discussed by Balding, DJ. and Donnelly P 'How convincing is DNA evidence?' [1994] *Nature* vol 285, at p 369.
83 *R* v *Watters* [2000] CA (Criminal Division) Oct 19 Relevant website is <www. forensic-evidence.com/site/EVID/DNA_Watters.html>.

the discussion on 'cold hits' above makes clear, it is very much being used 'in itself.').

The main point however, as the figures cited in these cases show, the participation of a relative can drastically affect the RMP - in the *Watters* case, a reduction of no less than 700,000-fold. The mathematical treatments are given in a series of specialist papers, starting with a pre-DNA (1954) statistical treatment.[84]

Contamination

Because the word contamination is widely coopted to describe so many situations, no widely accepted definition of it exists. In testing for the drugs of abuse, it refers to the deliberate addition of a substance to a urine sample to mask the substance to be analysed. In terms of forensic DNA testing it means the addition of biological material to a sample after it has been removed from the crime scene. This can occur from the time when the sample is placed in container to the time it is placed on a gel for electrophoresis.[85] In the converse situation of taking DNA samples for matching to a crime scene, deliberate contamination is unlikely to be less of a problem than drug testing, for buccal smears or blood are not necessarily taken in conditions of individual privacy. Any contamination thereafter must be the responsibility of someone along the chain of custody.[86]

An odd form of contamination consists of criminals contriving to spread blood and semen samples from others around the locales wherein they operate. Also, one Turner smuggled his semen sample from his prison cell and paid a woman to simulate a rape whereby this was found on her person.

---

84   Li, CC and Sacks, L 'The derivation of joint distribution and correlation between relatives by the use of stochastic matrices ' [1954] *Biometrics* vol 10, at p 347 ; Li, CC, Weeks DE et al. 'Similarity of DNA fingerprints due to chance and relatedness' [1993] *Human Heredity* vol 43, at p 45 ; Buckleton, J and Riggs, CM 'Relatedness and DNA: are we taking it seriously enough?' [2005] *Forensic Science International* vol 152, at p 115; Belin, TR Gjertson, DW et al 'Summarising DNA evidence when relatives are possible suspects' [1997] *American Statistical Association Journal* vol 92, at p 706 ; Paoletti, DR Doom TE et al 'Assessing the implications for close relatives in the event of similar but non-matching DNA profiles' [2006] *Jurimetrics* vol 46, at p 161.
85   The companies supplying PCR kits provide guidance on avoiding contamination. See e.g. Applied Biosystem's site < http://www.ambion.com/techlib/tb/tb_176.html>.
86   Edwards, K. ' Ten things about contamination that lawyers should know' [2005] *Criminal Law Journal* vol 29 at p 71. The writer makes the point that if the RMP is less than 360 million the profile is not complete, either mixed, partial, or derived. This is worth investigating for the defence.

Of course the match would have rendered his previous conviction untenable. Fortunately he did not get away with it.[87]

James Hanratty was convicted of murder and rape in 1962 and subsequently hanged. In 1999 the Criminal Cases Review Commission entertained representations by the convicted man's brother that there had been, at the trial, non-disclosure of relevant evidence by the prosecution, and flaws (by present day standards) in the summing up. However - and this is said to be unusual in a criminal case - the prosecution also adduced fresh evidence, namely the DNA profiles of the convicted man (extracted from the teeth) and the stains found on the rape victim's underwear. The Court of Appeal accepted that the profiles showed a match and dismissed as groundless the family's contention that the samples had been contaminated. Had they been contaminated, which is not the same thing as being replaced, the bands of the victim's and murderer's profiles would still have appeared on the electropherogram, and there would merely have been extra bands from the putative contaminants(s).[88] The case shows the (here, misplaced) lengths which families will go to establish the presumed innocence of their members, and is also another illustration of (a) the robustness of the DNA technology - in this case there was an interval of 37 years - and (b) the necessity for the police to store and preserve, in good condition and in perpetuity, all evidence relating to a crime. The Kelly case in Scotland is troublingly illustrative of the way in which DNA evidence can be challenged on the grounds of contamination (Box 2-2).

As a general point, the more sensitive an analysis becomes, that is, the more able it is to quantitate smaller and smaller quantities of the substance being analysed (in more appropriate language, if 'detectability' is enhanced), the more susceptible it becomes to contamination. At the present time mtDNA matching is one of the most sensitive procedures in service, and so especially stringent precautions have to be taken when handling it to prevent contamination by detritus on container vessels, skin cells from laboratory workers, and the like.[89] (See also Box 2-3)

Summary of 2.5

- Matching of DNA profiles can be formulated as either probabilities or odds.

87   Scoville, D. 'Tales of the double helix'. *Police Magazine* (US), Feb 2003.

88   <file://A:\Hanratty (deceased). htm> .

89   Isenberg, AR. 'Forensic mitochondrial DNA analysis' In Saferstein, R (ed) *Forensic Science Handbook*, vol II (2nd edn). (Prentice Hall, New Jersey, 2004) p 297.

- The calculations rest basically upon the multiplication rule.

- The probability of, or odds on of, a suspect being guilty can be calculated by Bayes' theorem.

- Bayes' theorem employs an estimate of prior probability (arguably subjective) and the RMP, calculated from the frequency of alleles in a population.

- The calculations should be adjusted to yield confidence intervals.

- Problems arise due to:

  - mutations

  - subpopulations,

  - mixtures,

  - contamination,

  - relatives who are suspects.

2.6 Challenges to Forensic Laboratory Practice

The Jeffreys DNA fingerprinting technique was patented and licenced to Imperial Chemical Industries (ICI) which set up subsidiaries in USA (Lifecodes) and in UK (Cellmark). Thus there has been a marked commercial input into forensic DNA testing from the start. No working scientist would deny a debt of gratitude to the manufacturers of laboratory equipment and chemicals; their products save time, they are innovative, and are supplied along with a vast amount of useful information. (The corporations also support conferences, found scholarships, and devise other benefits.) Inevitably, however, their basic strategy must be assumed to be to generate profit. In this respect they do not attract quite the obloquy of the Big Pharma (drug) corporations, but none the less they have been criticised in respect of their policy vis-a-vis DNA profiling kits. They are perceived to wish to withhold information about the details of their kits in the interests of patenting and trade secrets, whereas from the legal point of view, the nub of the matter is that defendants should have as much information as possible during the discovery process.[90] In the *State v Schwartz* (1989) the Supreme Court of Minnesota was the first appellate court to reject DNA evidence because of non-disclosure of population data, while criticising the associated secrecy

90   Mellon, J. ' Manufacturing convictions: why defendants are entitled to the data underlying forensic DNA kits' [2001] *Duke Law Journal* vol 51, at p 1097.

surrounding the laboratory procedures and the lack of independent audit of their operations.[91] After other cases along the same lines the manufacturers have had no choice but to offer more disclosure. In any case the emphasis has now shifted from private testing laboratories to private companies supplying the testing kits, which are used by the FBI in the US and by the Forensic Science Service in the UK, and whose procedures are audited both internally and externally. Nonetheless in the modern era it appears that challenge to the competence of DNA laboratories remains a constant threat to the prosecution. One thing is clear - nowadays evidentiary material cannot be mysteriously hidden away in the niceties of scientific practice. In England the bunglings in the seventies in connection with the Birmingham Six, Maguires, the Guildford Four and Judith Ward put an end to that type of legal lacuna and lead to the formation of the Criminal Cases Review Commission.[92] In the US the assiduity of Neufeld and Shreck in the *Castro* case (see above) and founding the Innocence Project,[93] have been equally salutary.

Before advances in DNA forensics, in the sixties, there was a burgeoning of laboratory practice in connection with healthcare. Many new tests became available, and sometimes the results they produced did not seem to the health carers to correspond to what might reasonably be expected. Some concerned individuals, the forerunners of today's whistleblowers, divided blood samples into aliquots and sent them separately to clinical laboratories. When the results came back, the spread of purported values was staggering. Ultimately quality control/ assurance schemes, both internal and external, were introduced, as well as the accreditation of laboratories. Since some of this activity was legislated, one can see here the further entrée of administrative law, which has been said to be the fastest growing legal arm for the last century. There was, in effect, a rerun of all this when DNA profiling/fingerprinting was introduced. The first cases were investigated in laboratories not designed for forensic practice, indeed they were done in Jeffreys' university department. Gradually, as defence lawyers managed to raise the spectre of defects in the technology, regulation was introduced and is now on a par with the traditional clinical laboratory. It could be argued that in forensic laboratories, where the liberty and indeed the life of an individual

---

91   *State v Schwartz* [1989] 447 N.W. 2nd.422 (Minn).

92   These miscarriages of justice were thoroughly explored in the media at the time but are now more soberly treated in standard texts on the English legal system. See Slapper, G and,Kelly, D *The English Legal System* (Cavendish, 5th edn, 1998 p 151. Zander, M *Cases and Materials on the English Legal System* (Butterworths, 8th edn 1999) p 254. The Judith Ward case is particularly instructive on forensic science. Its citation is [1993] 1 WLR 619.

93   See note 41.

is often at stake, there is special need for rigour. If this cannot be consistently demonstrated, then as part of the adversarial system, defence counsel should quite legitimately attack lack of rigour where it can be detected, and even when it cannot. In UK the legislature too became equally concerned about laboratory standards. In the committee stage of the Criminal Justice and Police Bill in 2001, according to Hansard, one MP said:

> I am concerned about the conduct of science in criminal trials. It is always an issue when scientific evidence is presented to non-scientists. Juries are largely composed of non-scientists, yet they are often told that the scientific evidence is unarguable. This my worry about DNA profiling. We do not yet know how testable DNA is, or how reliable databases are. It raises all the issues about the reliability of forensic laboratories, ensuring that the right sample is attached to the right name....[94]

This presents a strictly lay cast of language (for example what does 'testable' mean?) and for forensic purposes a definable set of terms is necessary. Any counsel wishing to impugn laboratory practice had better get them right. The following are some points. Admittedly, however, all of them must lead in the direction of 'reliability', (used above), which like 'guilty' is not a technical term and is assumed to be readily understood. All the scientific language, and indeed the legal language, must in the end be reduced to a concept assimilable by (one ventures to suggest) the man in the Clapham omnibus, who has now, it appears, become more of a contributor to the statistics of the RMP.

Errors, mistakes and blunders

All scientific measurements are subject to error, meaning that they are apt to stray from the true result, for various reasons. The easiest source of error to understand is random error, analogous to electronic noise, in that perturbations in environmental conditions affect the results both positively and negatively in a random fashion. In other words, there is scatter about the true value. *Error* cannot be avoided - thus, the exact position of a DNA fragment on a gel will depend on small fluctuations in temperature, electric current, and others. *Blunder* (or perhaps 'mistake' or even 'glitch') on the other hand is human-based. (Admittedly, the term human 'error' seems universally acceptable in relation to air and rail disasters.) The misidentification of samples is one example, that is putting the wrong name on a sample, or otherwise mixing samples up; another, in the context of DNA

94   See note 15.

testing, would be miscalculation of the RMP by pressing the wrong key on a calculator. Unfortunately, in the legal literature especially, no distinction is made between error and blunder, all modes being described as error, although some writers distinguish between different varieties of the latter.[95] The confusion can be almost amusing - in the Australian case of *Karger* (2002) a defence expert witness claimed that DNA technology was prone to 'errors' but he could not describe them quantitatively, because ' .....we are talking about errors we don't know about.' His language was so vague that his evidence was disallowed.[96] Presumably he meant that 'blunders', randomly occurring due to human failures, by their very nature, either go undetected or are covered up. The authors of one authoritative text[97] blandly describe error as a false inclusions or matches, and suggest that they cannot be measured. It would be better to describe this category as false positives, and of course they can be measured - samples of known provenance can be sent to laboratories and false matches can be counted.[98] It is well established that non-forensic laboratories can quantitate error/blunder rates if adequate records are kept.[99] The US NRC report dropped the idea of giving error (blunder) rates to the jury, presumably to avoid making an already complex matter completely impenetrable, so one assumes that they accepted, at least, that they were capable of being quantitated.

Controls

Controls are intrinsic to the scientific method, and rest on the general principle that there are few if any absolutes. In decision making about a set of bands on a gel, interpretation is made more confident by setting them against a set of bands of known properties. (Due to its appearance on the electropherogram, this is often referred to as the "ladder".) Related to controlling is *blinding*, whereby the analyst is not informed of the source of a specimen of pre-established properties, so that there is no chance of personal preconceptions

95   Berger, MA 'Laboratory error see through the lens of science and policy' [1997] *University of California Davis Law Review* vol 30, at p 1081. Reason, J *Human Error* (Cambridge University Press, 1990) p 9 offers a taxonomy of the topic but this pertains more to 'blunder' than the type of error intrinsic in scientific measurements as such.

96   *R v Karger* [2002] SASC 294 at para 141. This is eerily reminiscent of Donald Rumsfeld's assertion that '....there are also unknown unknowns - the one's we don't know we don't know.'

97   Rudin and Inman, note 4, p 147.

98   Thomson, WC Taroni, F et al. 'How the probability of a false positive affects the value of DNA evidence' [2003] *Journal of Forensic Sciences* vol 48, at p 92.

99   Morling, N 'Forensic genetics' [2004] *Lancet* vol 364 (Supplement: Medicine, Crime and Punishment) p 1202.

influencing the report. Incidentally such procedures fly in the face of the (former) public perception of the scientist as an objective, dispassionate servant of society.

Accuracy and precision

The former relates to how near the result is to the true result. Precision however refers to repeatability – that is, will the same answer be produced every time a specific sample is examined by the same method? A test can be both accurate and precise (in which case it will be described as having validity), but it can exhibit neither of those, or possibly one or the other. In terms of DNA sizing, an accurate procedure will make sure that electrophoretic bands or peaks are situated in the *correct place*; a precise procedure will ensure that they are always in the *same place*. Obviously it is greatly desired that a procedure exhibits both qualities. They will be assessed by quality control/ assurance programmes.

Precision, or repeatability, is related to an aspect of numeracy often misunderstood, even by mature scientists; this is the concept of significant figures. When, in *R v Deen* (p 57) the RMP was expressed as one in 70,000 the analyst was making an estimate of precision by the choice of one significant figure - the implication is that in a series of repeats the value will always lie between 65,000 and 75,000. If the figure is given as 75,000 (two significant figures), say, the claim is that in a series of runs the values will lie between 74,500 and 75,500. The validity of the choice of significant figures is among the many aspects susceptible to challenge.

Sensitivity and specificity

Sensitivity relates to a test's *inclusionary* properties, or, in the present context how often it detects a real match; P (M/G) should be maximal. Specificity is an *exclusionary* index – it minimises false positives – that is, P(M/nG) should be minimal. Alternatively, in the language of statistics (and returning to the word 'error') Type I and II errors respectively are false inclusions and false exclusions, although this language has apparently been little used in the courts. In terms of DNA gels, the high specificity implies refusing to declare that bands match each other when in reality they do not match. Poor specificity will be demonstrated by declaring that bands match when in reality they do not. It is held that multilocus (multiplex) methods enhance sensitivity (more bands to make matches with), whereas single locus probes go more towards specificity (for it is easy to see when bands do not match).[100]

---

100   Zumwalt, RE 'Application of molecular biology to forensic pathology' [1989]

Language problems constantly arise, however. When a witness uses the word 'sensitive', one has to determine what he actually means. Forensic scientists regard sensitivity as being enhanced when less DNA is needed for profiling. This meaning takes heed neither of inclusionary or exclusionary results, just the ease of obtaining them.

Validation

Validation is the process of demonstrating that a test can be relied upon. It can alternatively be described as achieving certain criteria. It can be conducted by a manufacturer or a laboratory. It should be accompanied by stringent documentation, which of course could be demanded during discovery. It must address the factors immediately above.[101]

Robustness

Robustness refers to the quality of producing reproducible results combined with ease of operation and lack of sensitivity to, say, the room temperature or the skill of the technician. Here 'sensitivity' has its normal plain language meaning, that is liability to be disturbed or perturbed by a change in the environment. 'Deskilling ' as an aspect of robustness is a primary aim of all method development – the less human skill needed the more reliable are the results (obviously less prone to human error) and the cheaper they are to operate.

Laboratory competence

There are a number of interlocking terms related to what one might describe in its most general way as the reputation of a laboratory. *Certification* is the recognition of the competence of an individual analyst. In the US it is offered by the American Board of Criminalistics. In the UK a Council for the Registration of Forensic Practitioners is being set up - this will provide registers of competent expert witnesses. *Licencing* refers to the recognition, usually by a governmental agency, that a laboratory is qualified to do the work it purports to do, and it cannot continue if the licence is revoked. *Accreditation* is the recognition of analytical merit by some other body, sometimes a learned society or association. In the US this is voluntary and done by the Laboratory Accreditation Board of the American Society

---

Human Pathology vol 20, at p 303.

101   A list of references for validation procedures is helpfully provided by Dr John Butler on <file://A:ValidationHomepage.htm>. It lists 46 commercial kits for DNA analysis. Also Butler's book, note 4, p 98.

of Crime Laboratory Directors. (ASCLD). In the UK accreditation of the Forensic Science Service is essentially bestowed by the government via their UK Accreditation Service (UKAS) In 1989 most of the relevant bodies in European countries agreed to standardise their techniques after modalities led by the UK Forensic Science Service.

The laboratories so accredited will be able to show *standard operating procedures* including *chain of custody* records, as well as *quality assurance procedures*. Some authorities distinguish between quality assurance and *quality control*, but from the legal point of view the difference would not seem to have any significance. Sometimes the two are subsumed to the term 'proficiency testing'. The FBI set up its quality assurance programme in 1987, to supercede the monopoly of the commercial laboratories like Cellmark and Lifecodes. It is based on the recommendations of the Technical Working Group for DNA Analysis Methods (TWGDAM), put out in 1989. Some laboratories have achieved ISO 17025, which refers to laboratory standards and which is recommended by the International Society of Forensic Genetics.[102]

Personal challenges to scientists

There is of course a difference between attacking a laboratory, which might have a separate legal personality as limited company, and attacking a scientist as an individual employee. (Independent consultants working for the defence would appear to have the status of agents.) Bearing *Castro* in mind, there appear to have been fewer challenges to the competence of scientists in the English courts than in the US, at least after the prominent miscarriages of justice instrumental in setting up the Criminal Cases Review Commission. Thus: 'The process of crime reconstruction is often built on the assumption that evidence left behind at a crime scene, which has been recognised, documented, collected, identified, compared, individuated, and reconstructed is pristine.....this assumption is not always accurate'.[103] This is the view of an academic. In Judith Ward's successful appeal after the reference by

---

102   For the FBI view see: Quality assurance standards for forensic DNA testing laboratories on website <http://www.fbi.gov/hq/lab/fsc/backissu/july2000/codispre. htm>. Also, Kubic, TA and Buscaglia, JA 'Quality assurance in the forensic laboratory' In Aitken, C and Stoney, DA (eds) *The Use of Statistics in Forensic Science* (Ellis Horwood, 1991) p 221. The revised SWGDAM guidelines (successor to TWGDAM) were published in Forensic Science Communications in July 2004. See also: Cormier, K Calandro, L et al 'Evaluation of quality assurance documents for DNA labs' *Forensic Magazine*, Feb/March 2005, p 67.
103   Chisum and Turbey, note 23.

Table 2-2 Landmark Cases Involving DNA Technology*

Case	Jurisdiction	Issues arising/significance	Page ref
Pitchfork (1987)	England	First population sampled for cold hit; first elimination of innocent suspect; first murder conviction	54
Andrews (1987)	Florida	First 'DNA' case in US	63
Castro (1988)	New York	Frye hearing on admissibility of DNA evidence; agreement by defense and prosecution on test validity; genesis of Innocence Project	63
Woodall (1989)	West Virginia	DNA evidence accepted as potentially exculpatory	64
MacLeod (1989)	Maine	Reliability of DNA challenged in respect of gel correction factors	63
Simpson (1995)	California	Allegation of planting of DNA evidence	79
Watters (1989)	England	Challenge to DNA evidence when relative might have been involved	84
Jacobetz (1992)	Vermont	Statistics (RMP) accepted by Federal Court on appeal	48
Yee (1991)	Ohio	RFLP evidence accepted; attack by defense on basis of possible population substructure	72
Deen (1994)	England	Appeal on use of 'prosecutor's fallacy' successful	57
Schwartz (1989)	Minnesota	Court refused to admit results from private laboratory, and defendant should have been given sample	88
Adams (1996)	England	DNA evidence overcoming alibi; appeal court states that Bayes' is inappropriate for jury	59
Miller (1996)	Illinois	Product rule affirmed	79
Venegas (1998)	California	Acquittal due to lack of compliance with NRC (1992) recommendations	64
Doheny & Adams (1997)	England	Ultimate issue rule applied; reiteration of 'prosecutor's fallacy'	59

Perez (1994)	Minneapolis	Probably first conviction based entirely on cold hit in US	68
Marper (2004)	England	Decision of HL that retention of DNA of acquitted persons is illegal	46
Dabney (2001)	Wisconsin	Probably first John Doe warrant	68
Karger (2002)	Australia	No general duty to warn juries that statistical evidence can be misused; LR affirmed	61
Harman (2004)	England	One of first examples of 'familial searching' and of low copy number technology	61

The items are in approximate chronological order. The first state by state applications of DNA technology in the US can be found on <file://A:\ Genetx The Paternity DNA Testing Site.htm

---

Box   2-4   The Special Position of Low   Copy Number (LCN) Technology

Low copy number technology was developed by the UK Forensic Science Service (FSS) in 1999. As the name implies, it utilises very small amounts of DNA and is sometimes termed 'touch DNA' since it can be based on, say, a fingerprint or a smear of sweat. The DNA is extensively amplified in an extension of the Second Generation Multiplex Plus (SGM Plus) technology. It has not had an easy ride, however, and at the time of writing it is still not in use in the US.

In 2007, during the trial of Sean Hoey in connection with the IRA Omagh outrage in Northern Ireland, the judge, Mr Justice Weir, accepted that the technique lacked external validation - external, that is, to the FSS.[1] It was suspended at the end of 2007 and reviewed by the Crown Prosecution Service (CPS) which pronounced itself satisfied as to its probative value.[2] The CPS emphasised, though, that it should still be considered as one item only within the totality of the evidence. A further review by the University of Strathclyde endorsed the technique but made some suggestions, such as the provision of very clean (i.e. DNA free) collection kits for, obviously, LCN DNA is particularly susceptible to contamination. One of the defence expert witnesses in the Omagh case was Professor Allan Jamieson, who regarded (at that point in time at any rate) the LCN technology as being unsafe, mainly because of the danger of contamination. This is said to have made him many enemies, including those in the FSS who regard him as a witness inferior to those who have actually worked on the samples in the laboratory.[3] They make the point, interesting in the context of the law of evidence, that not all expert witnesses should be accorded the same status by the court. (And see 'Personal challenges to scientists', Section 2.7 herein.)

Its evidentiary status was an issue in a notorious case in Scotland, also starting in 2007. Back in 1977 two young women had been murdered and raped. Importantly, as became apparent later, they had been bound and gagged by their own underwear. The forensic samples were carefully preserved for the next 30 years, during which time police investigation was unfruitful. However by 2005, following speculation in the media, it was decided there was enough evidence to indict one Angus Sinclair. At that time he was serving a life sentence for the murder of Mary Gallagher (and incidentally he was convicted for that crime largely also by DNA evidence, see p 67). His DNA was sampled along with stored forensic material on the underwear. The DNA from the underwear however could not be matched to any in the national database, which of course included Sinclair. A further search of clothing revealed a stain on a coat which one of the girls had been wearing at the time she was killed. This second sample matched Sinclair. It happened that Sinclair had had a crony, his brother-in-law Hamilton, and though this individual was deceased, the police took DNA from Hamilton's brother. This DNA (not tested by LCN, of course, there was ample sample) showed that there was only a one in 20×10^6 chance [4] that the DNA on the underwear did not come from the brother-in-law. The ligatures used to tie up the girls were re-examined, and skin cells were found, the DNA of which partly matched that of Sinclair, but more exactly matched that of Hamilton. This phase of the investigation of course used LCN technology. This evidence was not presented by prosecuting counsel, however, leading the judge to dismiss the case against Sinclair without it going to the jury. He stated that no evidence had been adduced to show that Sinclair was the murderer, although Hamilton might have been, while allowing that there must have been sexual intercourse. The judge's decision caused general outrage, and much criticism was levelled at the prosecution for failing to bring forward the evidence from the skin cells. Sections of the press took the opportunity to demean the LCN technique. [5] The Lord Advocate (the equivalent of the Attorney General) was forced to offer an explanation in parliament. Curiously, she made the point that a difficulty had arisen in that the DNA in question was 'cellular' (i.e. skin) as opposed, presumably, to bodily fluids such as semen, as though that made any difference, the DNA in the semen of course also deriving from cells. She stated that the ligature evidence was withheld for fear that it might confuse the jury, but it seems that LCN technology was operating at the limit of its efficacy and that the RMP for Sinclair, rather than the brother-in-law, was low, in other words considered weakly probative by the prosecution. Sinclair went back to jail, then, without the families of the murdered girls being able to put a finality on their ordeal.

1   R v Hoey [2001] NICC 49

2   http://www.cps.gov.uk/news/pressreleases/101_08.html

3   Anon ' Court drama proves DNA cases aren't as simple as TV shows' *The Guardian* 16 Aug 2007; Linklater, M 'We're not fools – DNA evidence is

far from foolproof' *The Times* 10 Aug, 2007;   McKie, R. ' Did a killer evade justice due to withheld evidence?' *The Observe* , 16 Sept, 2007.

4 It is preferable to use exponents rather than strings of noughts for the RMP; however this seems never to be done in court, presumably once again to avoid confusing the much-maligned jury.

5 Anon   *The Scotsman*, 18 May 2008

the Criminal Cases Review Commission Lord Justice Glidewell was more explicit: ' For lawyers, jurors and judges a forensic scientist conjures up the image of a man in a white coat working in a laboratory, approaching his task with cold neutrality, and dedicated only to the pursuit of scientific truth. It is a sombre thought that the reality is somewhat different. Forensic scientists employed by the government may come to see their function as helping the police. They may lose their objectivity.'[104]

There is, or was, a prevailing view that if blunders are made then every attempt is made to cover them up, and some writers put these blunders as high in one out of every hundred samples. It appears that at the present day proficiency testing is not blinded - the staff know which samples are coming in under the quality assurance schemes and are naturally more careful with them. In a lengthy article the director of the University of Technology Sydney Innocence Project states that the most common cause of DNA contamination is cross-contamination (that is one sample becoming mixed up with another during the laboratory procedures, not contamination by some extraneous material.). She provides a checklist, some of which relates to police procedure, but under a section headed 'laboratory protocols and standards', there is a sixteen point sub-list which defence counsel can consult.[105] One of its most important points is: has the laboratory been audited or evaluated by an outside agency? She states that if the people giving the evidence are not the same as those who actually conducted the tests, this can be grounds for appeal. A further (and novel) point is that to a degree, results are predictable, and if inconsistent with the circumstances, can be challenged. For example, DNA from a vaginal swab should have alleles from the X-chromosome. She also suggests subpoena of biodata to check a technician's credentials. Dividing the sample and sending the fractions to two different laboratories is another possible safeguard. This was recommended by the 1996 NAS report but was criticised on the grounds that public defendants do not have sufficient funds to contemplate it.

104   See note 92.
105   Edwards, note 86.

The point about reporting being done by somebody who has not actually conducted the test was specifically addressed in a Scottish case, *Bermingham* in 2004.[106] This was a case of assault and attempted rape. Swabs from inside a glove found at the crime scene had allowed the profiling of DNA which appeared to come from more than one person. However the major bands matched the DNA of the suspect. DNA from outside the glove also had multiple origins but the major component matched that of the victim. There was other evidence from a stain. At the end of the Crown submissions the counsel for the defence submitted that there was no case to answer on the grounds that the analysis of the DNA could not properly be spoken to by the forensic scientist who was called, since he had not personally extracted the DNA (This was done by a technician not normally identified, stated to be normal laboratory practice.) There had been a break, it was alleged, in the evidential chain between the submission of items to the laboratory and the analysis of the results by the scientists. An earlier case was quoted in which a judge had opined that results should not be presented to the court by scientists who had not taken part in the analysis themselves. An analysis in itself could have been carried out by anyone and would be evidence as long as two authorized scientists had adhibited [attached] their signatures. "On that view, the evidence of either signatory …….. would be sufficient even if the analysis had been done by an unqualified person while the signatories were abroad. That cannot be right." However neither the trial court nor the High Court would have truck of this. The forensic scientist was recalled to give evidence as to reception of the sample, logging, numbering, storage, electrophoretic technique, and interpretation. Further precedents were adduced to the effect that an expert witness could present evidence gained by a subordinate if the court was satisfied that standard laboratory procedures had been carried out. Effectively, the scientists assume responsibility for the complete process. (It might be noted in passing that in these circumstances hearsay evidence may be presented.)

The implication in defence arguments about laboratory practice, of course, is that the technician has blundered. No doubt blunders do occur. Supposing the blunder rate is such as to cause false attribution of a match (false positives) in 5 % of submissions to a laboratory. What are the implications? Referring to P(M/G), the numerator in the LR, should it become 0.95 rather than unity? This would make very little difference to the numerical value of the LR if the RPM (the denominator) is a very small number, as is usually the case when a prosecution is being mounted. It is also not logical. If there is a blunder in a

106 *Bermingham v Her Majesty's Advocate* [2004] Scot HC 26 ; also available on <http://alpha.bailii.org/scot/cases/ScotHC/2004/26.html>.

specific instance, then P(M/nG) (the RMP) is unity and P(M/G) is zero. Thus the probabilities cannot be used to construct any meaningful LR. It would be more sensible to maintain that if there is a one in twenty chance that a blunder has been made then this breaches the conventional 95% probability and the corresponding cut-off point for deciding on guilt beyond reasonable doubt. Statistically speaking, one would only accept data from a laboratory which can demonstrate that it has a blunder/error rate of less than 5%. This however might be of scant comfort to those wrongfully accused.

By general consensus the most frequent failing on the part of the individual scientists is contaminating the sample by introducing traces of unrelated biological material, usually derived from themselves, and due to talking, sneezing or coughing while the processing is being conducted.

Ultimate issue

It is established on authority that the purpose of the expert is to provide the court with information which is outside the experience of the jury, or whatsoever tribunal is the adjudicator of guilt or innocence.[107] Historically the rule was important in disallowing a psychiatrist to infer that because an accused was insane he was not guilty as charged. In recent cases attacks have been made by defence counsel on forensic scientists for similarly 'usurping the role of the jury': 'The scientist should not be asked his opinion on the likelihood that it was the defendant who left the crime stain, nor while giving evidence should he use terminology which may lead the jury to believe that he is expressing such an opinion.'[108]

The issue arose in the *Doheny* trial discussed above, where the expert witness was invited to state whether he was satisfied beyond reasonable doubt the defendant was guilty. The conviction was accordingly quashed. The expert was not allowed, also, to give an opinion as to whether the evidence was very strong, strong, or weak, only that the RMP, by his calculation, was one in 55 million.

In England the ultimate issue rule in civil cases was abolished by ss 3(1) and 3(3) of the Civil Evidence Act, 1972 (so presumably it does not apply to evidence ascribing paternity) but has never been overruled in criminal courts. Some writers argue that the rule is necessary to distinguish between the LR and the prior odds, and this must surely be the truth of the matter. The

107   *R v Turner* [1975] 1 QB 834. An earlier authority lies in *Haynes v Dowman* [1889] 2 Ch 13.
108   McSherry, B 'Psychological and psychiatric testimony and the ultimate issue rule [1999] *Journal of Law and Medicine* vol 7, at p 9.

DNA expert can only go as far as the LR. If he attempts to factor in the prior probability, in other words go to the full Bayes' approach, he is going beyond his competence – this is a matter for the prosecution per se.[109] The point was well put in the Australian case of *Karger* a rape and murder case devolving on DNA evidence:

> Counsel for the appellant [accused] submitted that the judge should have excluded the evidence of the match probability and the likelihood ratio. It was said that this evidence was part of Bayes' theorem and as a result was inadmissible. However the court's rejection of the use of Bayes' theorem [after *Doheny and Adams*, see above] is not based on the fact that it is a statistical equation. The rejection arises because Bayes' theorem involves subjectively attaching numerical value to evidence and usurps the role of the jury.[110]

One of the most extensive of recent discussions of the ultimate issue rule occurred in *R v Mohan* (1994) in the Supreme Court of Canada.[111] In this case a paediatrician had allegedly molested four of his teenage patients. A psychiatrist wished to testify that the actions of the perpetrator were characteristic of person who could not be the defendant. (Read for this, in the context of DNA: 'the stain found at the crime scene does not sufficiently match that of the defendant.') One of the judges asked: " Is the jury likely to be overwhelmed by the 'mystic infallibility' of the evidence, or will the jury be able to keep an open mind and objectively assess the worth of the evidence?" Although the arguments in this case were based on psychiatric evidence, an analogy to DNA evidence was drawn by the judge. There was thought to be danger that the jury would regard DNA evidence in isolation as a measure of the probability of the accused's guilt or innocence and thereby undermine the presumption of innocence, and erode the value served by the reasonable doubt standard. The expert witness could use phraseology such as 'rare' or 'extremely rare' but should not cite such overwhelmingly large statistical probabilities that they would immediately be identified with the ultimate issue.

In the US, testimony in the form of an opinion or inference otherwise admissible is not objectionable because it embraces an ultimate issue to be decided by the trier of fact – Congress enactment of Federal Rule of

---

109   Robertson, BWN and Vigneux, GA 'Probability - the logic of the law' [1993] *Oxford Journal of Legal Studies* vol 13, at p 457.
110   See note 96.
111   *R v Mohan* [1994] 2 SCR. See site < file:///A:R_%20v_Mohan.htm>.

Evidence 702 (1975). This was modified to make it applicable specifically to psychiatric testimony and therefore narrows it considerably.

It has often been pointed out that at base the problems in evaluating DNA evidence, like other scientific evidence, stem from dichotomous attitudes: judges and juries (like the general public) prefer black and white, 'yes' or 'no' classifications; scientists go in for probabilistic classifications as a guide to decision making – the data they produce set the bounds of probabilities, not absolutes. They believe that they do careful work on this basis and are appalled to see it ridiculed by defence lawyers who do not understand probabilistic reasoning.[112]

Summary of 2.6

- Discoveries in DNA technology were quickly adopted by commercial laboratories companies who provided convenient kits for forensic use.

- The reluctance of private companies to exhibit complete technical transparency has largely been overcome.

- There is much concern over the effect on justice of possible laboratory mispractice.

- Errors and blunders must be distinguished one from another.

- Laboratories necessarily must adopt standard practice in respect of controls.

- Validation of methods is a prerequisite to practice and should lead to their robustness.

- Competence is assessed by certification, accreditation, licencing, and quality assurance.

- Challenges to the personal competence of scientists by defence attorneys are not rare.

- Expert witnesses are precluded from opining on the ultimate issue.

- Scientists have difficulty in explaining the probabilistic nature of their evidence.

---

112 Freckelton, I and Selby, H. *Expert Evidence: Law, Practice, Procedure and Advocacy* (Thomson Lawbooks, 2002); <www.lawlink.nsw.gov.au/lawlink/lrc/ll_lrc.nsf/pages/LRC_ r109chp01>.

2.7 Criminal Responsibility and Molecular Biology

This section is much more jurisprudential than what has gone before, and its biomedical input is also greater. In addition it cannot escape a whiff of philosophy. Philosophers define *determinism* as the theory that all events, including human actions and choices, are without exception, totally determined, in the sense that any event is caused by what has occurred prior to it, whether the causes are attributable to scientific laws (were they to be known) or by the preordination of God. Of course if the latter view is taken then it will naturally assume that scientific laws are formulated by God.[113] The relationship between modern molecular biology and genetics and their laws, in so far as the latter can be identified, and criminal behaviour, has its origins in a venerable debate.[114] Genetics, of course, has a profound influence on the course all human lives, including in many instances their behavioural patterns, and it would be trite to cite examples.[115] Similarly, environment early in life is a known determinant of later human behaviour, so that it is a determinist view that criminal tendency is totally ascribable to heredity and environment combined, these being preordained. A tangential view is that human behaviour is random, or at least driven by random events, such as accidents, natural disasters and illness. However this is no answer to a determinist, because what might seem to be randomness to our no doubt puny intelligences might well constitute a plan or predetermination by either scientific forces/laws, or by God, which comes down to the same thing.[116]

113   Study and assessment of the attitudes of all the religions to the free will/determinist dilemma would consume a career in itself and it trusted that it is not an oversimplification to state that, broadly, and with many internal dissensions, the Islamic and Protestant Christian faiths adhere to determinism, whereas free will is favoured by the Judaic, Roman Catholic, Buddhist and Hindu faiths.

114   The debate on free will versus determinism goes back at least to Aristotle (in the Nicomachean Ethics, in which he identifies lack of coercion and sufficient information as the prerequisites of choice) and no doubt even before him. The debate has been enjoined by virtually every philosopher and theologian in history. In the end, it tends to a *reductio ad absurdum*. As Woody Allen wrote: 'Professor Needleman had always been obsessed by the problem of evil and argued quite eloquently that evil was only possible if its perpetrator was named Blackie or Pete.'

115   Just to take a simple example, the Lesch-Nyhan syndrome, which is due to a defect in the gene for the enzyme hypoxanthine guanine phosphoribosyl transferase, and in which there is characteristic self- mutilation and aggression against others.

116   Chaos theory and quantum mechanics are sometimes imported into arguments for free will but prove to be equally if not more controversial. If complexity theory (to use another, related term) sees consequences in random quantum events, and these quantum events are parts of a causal chain leading to decisions, then this may be some sort of free will, but not the sort of free will that we want. The above is a paraphrase from part

Philosophers however paradoxically appear also to recognise that human beings often act in way that seems to demonstrate free will, especially when confronted with choices (and indeed they obviously assume the truth of it in their day-to-day lives). Since the stance that free choice (*indeterminism*) exists is a logical contradiction to determinism, only one of them must be true. A way of resolving the dilemma, in some quarters, has been to adopt *compatibilism*, or soft determinism, which '...according to this theory, if I can do what I choose, I am free only in the sense of free used in ordinary parlance and in ascriptions of responsibility, and it matters not whether my choice was causally determined.' This is a definition by the philosophers Feinberg and Shafer –Landau,[117] and if it is serious it is patently unsatisfactory. Moreover, if we define '.......acts freely done as those whose immediate causes are psychological states in the agent [rather than] those whose immediate causes are states of affairs external to the agent....'[118] we get no further forward. None of these intermediate views seem acceptable, being merely plays on words – for a start, one only has to assume, in respect of the last quotation, that psychological states are predetermined. Philosophers are entitled to argue in circles, but any legal system by necessity must seek an end-point, and traditionally, as a coherent system (of legislators, judges, prosecutors, and juries) it has taken the view of the indeterminists, that is, that in the absence of (for example) insanity or pathological automatism criminals consciously choose, by their own free will, to wreak their maleficence. Even the defence of diminished responsibility assumes choice.[119] However the advances in genetics have been so pervasive, with more and more genes described in terms of the functional proteins they code for, that a new type of determinism has arisen which hopes to ascribe most, if not all, human behaviour to the base sequences in the genome. This puts the indeterminism

of the text of Holm, S. 'Does chaos theory have major implications for the philosophy of medicine?' [2002] *Medical Humanities* vol 28, at p 78. For another discussion see Honderich, T. *How Free Are You?* (Oxford University Press, 1993) p 78. A readable article on this topic is by Merali, Z 'Free will –you only think you have it' *New Scientist* 6th May 2006, p 8.

117   Feinberg, J and Shafer-Landau, R 'Hard determinism: the case for determinism and its incompatibility with any important sense of free will' Editorial in: *Reason and Responsibility* (Thomson Wadworth, 2005) p 385.

118   Stace, WT *Religion and the Modern Mind* (Harper Collins Inc, 1952) p 248.

119   Diminished responsibility (called diminished capacity in the USA) is of course a defence against the *actus reus* of murder recognised in some but not all jurisdictions. The irresistible impulse, successfully pleaded by Lorena Bobbit in the famous dismemberment case in the US, seems to have a determinist flavour, as does the 'instructions from God' defence.

of the legal system in peril. It used to be said that anatomy is destiny; now the catchphrase might be: DNA is destiny.[120]

Genetic theories of human destiny have been around for a long time, of course and are still blithely propagated. As societies developed, the more successful members felt compelled to attribute their positions to an inherited biological superiority. Hence the persistent discrimination against, for example, women and ethnic minorities.[121] Historically there were numerous scientific or pseudoscientific attempts to justify such elitism, so well described, for example, in one of the classic works of Steven Jay Gould.[122] In the context of the prevalent theory that US blacks have a predisposition to crime, it has been written that: 'Genetic theories of social behaviour have abounded since the early 19th century. As each theory crumbled from internal absurdities, a new one was jury rigged to carry the torch of discrimination a little further. None of these scientific theories has stood the test of time.'[123]

It is evident that intellectual battle stations are in the offing.

Genetic determinism

Thus, as more and more is known about gene function, biological determinists hold that correspondingly more of human behaviour and motivation will be explainable in terms of genetics. On an extreme view, it is the 'selfish DNA' which is directing our fates - our bodies are seen as mere throwaway appendages to ensure its propagation.[124] The ideas propagated by enthusiasts for genetic explanations have achieved wide diffusion. One commentator recounts that a judge in a US family court, in all seriousness asked geneticists whether 'divorce is in the genes'![125] Criminality, prostitution, feeblemindedness, laziness, vagrancy and pauperism were candidates as genetic attributes in the past;[126] attributions have become a little more specific in this millenium, but not much - two favourites are

120   Kern, S *Anatomy is Destiny* (Bobbs Merril, 1975).
121   Alper, JS and Natowicz, MR 'The allure of genetic explanations' [1992] *Nature* vol 305, at p 666.
122   Gould, SJ *The Mismeasure of Man* (Norton, 1981).
123   Feit, P 'Crime and genetics' *The Economist* 20th Aug, 1992.
124   Dawkins, R *The Selfish Gene* (Oxford University Press, 1976) (Dawkins himself is by no means a genetic determinist.)
125   Wallerstein, JS Lewis, J et al 'The unexpected legacy of divorce' In : Slife, B (ed) *Taking Sides: Clashing Views on Controversial Psychological Issues* (McGraw Hill, 2004) p 152.
126   Neilkin, D 'A brief history of the political work of genetics' [2002] *Jurimetrics* vol 42, at p 121.

Box 2-5 Reference Matrix for the Determination Problem

Defence arguments for genetic determinism	*Prosecution arguments against genetic determinism*
Many known mutations or chromosomal aberrations cause behavioural changes.	Most aspects of human behaviour cannot be attributed to genetics.
A fortiori, clusters of genes may cause behavioural patterns.	Human behaviour is too complex to complex to ascribe to even a combination of genes.
Criminality demonstrably runs in families.	Criminality in families is a result of poverty, deprivation, stigmatisation, or tradition.
A person cannot control his genes.	'Genetic' does not mean immutable.

---

homosexuality and alcoholism, both of which have numerous connections to forensic science.[127] (Indeed homosexuality remains a criminal offence in most countries to this day.) More than decade ago there was an attempt by some scientists to show that it is due to a single gene.[128] This was said to be on chromosome X (importantly, this predicates that it would be transmitted through the mother), on the basis of a study of forty pairs of homosexual brothers and it had a *lod* score of 4.0.[129] The findings, which were said by

127   Interestingly, there have been strenuous attempts in some quarters to maintain that homosexuality has no relationship to genetics; President Mugabe of Zimbabwe has been widely quoted as saying that it has was introduced into his country by whites.

128   Maddox J ' Is homosexuality hard-wired?' [1992] *Nature* vol 353, at p 187.

129   The lod score represents a mathematical estimation of the distance between the putative gene for some behavioural characteristic, call it H, and the gene for some established genetic marker, call it G. If H does exist and is near G on the chromosome, they are likely to segregate together, that is migrate together in the same chromosome in the course of meiosis. If H and G are far apart on the chromosome, then in the course of the process of recombination they are more likely to end up on different chromosomes in the progeny. Thus in pedigrees in which H and G appear at all, sometimes they will occur together, sometimes there will be only one or the other in an individual. By counting the number of times they appear together, a probability of their proximity can be estimated. In other words, if H is probably close to G, then probably H exists. mlod is an extension of lod to estimate maximum probability of proximity.

the author Dr Hamer to be tentative, were of course sensationalized by the press, and viewed ambivalently by pro-gay groups. On the one hand, if a sexual orientation is predetermined there can be little or no blame attached to it; on the other hand, homosexuality could come to be viewed as a genetic disease in the same way as thalassaemia, for example, and a cure for it could be sought. (Of course the difference is that most owners of the faulty gene for thalassaemia wish to be cured, presumably, whereas most of those possessing a gay gene, if it exists, presumably wish to remain as they are.) Moreover it was pointed out that many gays subsequently go 'straight', so where lies the genetic determinism? In any case, the work was soon discredited and Dr Hamer placed under investigation.[130] Nonetheless, as Gould has pointed out, genetic explanations are quite conceivable – if our ancestors operated in small, closely related groups, and some contained homosexuals, other groups did not, in the former group they, the homosexuals, could have functioned as helpers to their kin (caring for children during hunting expeditions, for example) and could have then given them a survival advantage over the exclusively heterosexual groups. Then homosexuality genes would have been maintained by kin selection. (But Gould writes that there is no evidence for all of this.[131]) It appears that Hamer's views have not recognised their own demise. A recent paper in which he is senior author reports a study to compare, in pairs of homosexual brothers, microsatellite markers (the same stretches of DNA which are used to match blood samples to suspects in criminal investigations), and it found that a high maximum likelihood estimation (*mlod*) was 3.45 at an autosomal position with approximately equal maternal and paternal contributions.[132] Such studies have been criticized on a number of grounds, for example that the brothers were volunteers. A gay man with a gay brother would be more likely to volunteer than a gay man with a straight brother. Also, there was no control group.

Brothers may be useful subjects, but for geneticists, identical (monozygotic) and even dizygotic twins are like gold dust. Studies are based on the theory that when twins are separated at or near birth and brought up in different environments the effects of genes and environment can be dissected one from another. In a recent study some economists indicated that such socio-political traits as, for example, reaction to the death penalty, plus views

130   Wickelgren, I 'Discovery of "gay gene" questioned' [1999] *Science* vol 284 at p 571.
131   Gould, SJ. 'So cleverly kind an animal' In: Bowie, GL, Michaels, M et al *Twenty Questions* (Thomson Wadworth, 5th edn, 1999) p 34.
132   Mustanski, BS, Dupree, MG, et al 'A genomewide scan of male sexual orientation' [2005] *Human Genetics* vol 116, at p 272.

on taxes, abortion, modern art and divorce are genetically determined, based on a study of 8,000 sets of twins.[133] At this point the common man is entitled to wonder at the credulity of scientists.

Alcoholism genes have so far proved elusive but practitioners in the area have no doubt that they will be found.[134] But in reaction against genetic triumphalism researchers in New Zealand have been at pains to point out that attempts to study ethnic differences in something like alcoholism *assume*, a priori, that such have genetic causes.[135] They were prompted by their studies of a gene which protects against alcoholism, the alcohol dehydrogenase-2 gene. This has a higher frequency in Europeans than in Maoris but the prevalence of alcoholism is much higher in Maoris than in Europeans. So where is the genetic imperative? They note that the Pellagra Commission in USA, in the early 20th century assumed that the disease was genetic because it ran in families – nobody realised that poverty and malnutrition ran in families – and in ethnic groups – also.

Even more proximate to criminality is the possible link between the genome and aggression. Monoamine oxidase is an enzyme which degrades neurotransmitters such as serotonin. Serotonin is known to affect mood, being antidepressant and placatory. In 1993 a group of workers in Holland identified a family, across three generations, some of the males of which showed undesirable modes of behaviour, including arson, attempted rape and exhibitionism, and who also shared a variant in the gene for monoamine oxidase.[136] Subsequently the same sort of association was claimed, by other workers, in mice. The monoamine oxidase gene is on the X-chromosome, inherited from the mother, so it seemed reasonable to suppose that aggression generated or at least associated with the male Y-chromosome was gaining ascendancy in the individuals studied. The results were widely quoted as indicating a genetic basis for aggression, but there were those who demurred in that the range of behaviour in the humans was too diverse

133   Alford, JR, Funk, CL et al. 'Are political orientations genetically transmitted?' [2005] *American Political Science Review* vol 99, at p 153. With the persistence of the genetic determinists, this aspect has reemerged recently in an anonymous editorial: 'Voting: in your genes?' [2008] *Science* vol 321, at p 468. ('Heritability of 46% for party loyalty.')

134   Nurnberger, P 'Evidence for a locus to chromosome 1 that influences vulnerability to alcoholism and affective disorder' [2001] *American Journal of Psychology*, vol 114 at p 718.

135   Pearce N, Foliaki, S et al 'Genetics, race, ethnicity and health' [2004] *British Medical Journal* vol 328, at p 1070.

136   Brunner HG, Nelen M, et al 'Abnormal behaviour associated with a point mutation in the structural gene for monoamine oxidase' [1993] *Science* vol 262, at p 578.

to be labelled simply as 'aggression.' In the 1993 Mobley murder case in the US the defence attorneys requested that they be allocated funds for the sequencing of the monoamine oxidase gene in the accused. They believed they had evidence for some sort of hereditary predisposition. The request was denied because the court very sensibly discounted the level of scientific knowledge surrounding the association, but further, it has been pointed out that even that was totally misunderstood by the defence attorneys.[137] The mode of transmission of antisocial behaviour in the Mobley family was grandfather to father to grandson, that is through the paternal line. However the monoxidase gene is on the X-chromosome, so any defect in it could only have been inherited from the mother!

The topic was enlarged by a paper in 2002 which described a study of 442 young men in New Zealand.[138] It was found that there was no link between diminished monoamine oxidase activity and violence as such, but those in the group who had both suffered abuse in childhood, and had low enzyme activity, were four times as likely to have been convicted of a violent crime by the age of 26. The implication is that the calming effect of the X-chromosome is subsumed to the genes for aggression on the male Y-chromosome, for it is established beyond doubt and indeed a matter of common observation that, worldwide, males are responsible for most of it. However the trigger has to be abuse in childhood, and it would be far fetched to reach further back for genetic causes in these scenarios.

One canard can be dismissed summarily if it ever comes up again in court. This is the myth of the XYY genotype, the male who has two Y-chromosomes instead of the normal singleton and who was thought at one time to be overrepresented in prison populations.[139] This genetic argument was used by the defence in the trial of Richard Speck, the psychopath who killed eight student nurses in Chicago in 1966. Since he did not even have the XYY genotype, it remains a case wherein, interestingly, defence lawyers tried to use *fictional* genetics to hoodwink the jury. But if true XYY genotypes could be detected early, could not their owners be segregated and prevented from reproducing? Subsequently two Harvard bioscientists started screening all newborn males for the XYY genotype in the hope of correlating this with any

---

137   Carey, G and Gottesman, II 'Genes and antisocial behavior: perceived versus real threats to jurisprudence' [2006] *Journal of Law, Medicine and Ethics* (Symposium on DNA and Civil Liberties, Summer 2006) at p 342.

138   Crespi, A, McLay, J et al. 'Role of genotype in the cycle of violence in maltreated children' [2002] *Science* vol 297, at p 851.

139   Cook, EB 'Behavioural implications of the XYY genotype' [1973] *Science* vol 179, at p 139 (1973).

subsequent patterns of behaviour. This was roundly criticized in that, *inter alia*, there was a flawed consent procedure (obviously the babies could not in themselves consent) and there was a gratuitous stigmatization procedure in operation. Nothing has been heard of this issue in recent years.

In his legal history text Baker points out that the common law decided on the extent to which moral turpitude was a necessary element in the criminal offence - leading to the concept of *reum non facit nisi mens rea* (or *mens rea*).[140] It is said to reflect canonist teaching, originating in St Augustine. Intent could only rest upon the evidence, and so to the present day (in the absence of strict liability) it is a matter of fact rather than of law. "Fact" might of course include genetic predisposition as well as sheer cupidity and wickedness. One eminent barrister, in the journal *Justice of the Peace* (presumably read by magistrates who pronounce sentences every day of the week) cites the case of one Vernage, convicted of the murder of a policeman and the attempted murder of two others.[141] The sentence handed down, a minimum of 25 years, can be seen both as retribution by society but also, even in the face of determinists who might argue that he was impelled to do what he did, as a measure of safety for the public. The writer states that Vernage's genetic and environmental history does not fully emerge from the reports, but apparently he was brought up in a children's home, and had a long history rapes, robberies and custodial sentences. No doubt the acts committed were bad, it is pointed out, but we must distinguish between passing moral judgements on people and passing judgements on acts people carry out. He asks: ' If suppose we took two people with identical genetic endowments and identical environmental experience, would we expect them to be capable of behaving differently in any particular situation? If the answer is in the affirmative, I would like to know exactly what it is in them which would explain the difference.' The answer to this is that no two people have identical genetic make up, probably not even identical twins (for spontaneous mutations are always occurring) and most definitely no two people have the same environmental experiences, not even identical twins in the same family. The variations surely generate the choices made in life.

Genetic determinists disabused

In 2003 there was a well-publicised offer by Dr Craig Venter, the free lance alternate to the workers in the official Human Genome Project, to supply a

---

140   Baker, JH *Introduction to English Legal History* (Butterworths, 1999) p 434.
141   James, L 'Is the criminal responsible for his actions? [1993] *Justice of the Peace* April 17, at p 247.

complete sequence of a person's genome for \$750,000. Will this enable such a very rich man to predict his future, or even a small part of it? Can it tell him whether he is likely to become an alcoholic in later life? What are his chances of dying of a heart attack rather than colon cancer? Or whether, in the present context, he will fall foul of the law? In many quarters even the possibility of such determinism provokes scepticism, similar to that about cloning – the best view is that a cloned individual if produced, will have nothing like the characteristics expected of him. There are writers on medical law who roundly deprecate triumphalism in molecular biology, genomics and the human genome project, thus:

> Those familiar with medical research funding know the disgraceful campaigns waged in the 70s and 80s by scientists hunting the genes for such diseases as cystic fibrosis. Give us the money, and we'll find the gene then your problems will be solved, was the message. The money was found, the genes were found - then came nothing but a stunned contemplation of the complexity of the problem, which many clinicians had understood all along... the tragedy is that the whole-organism biologists and clinicians who have tried to unravel the complexity have almost all gone, destroyed by the reductionists, those who maintain that everything can be understood at the molecular level.[142]

The Nobel Prize winner Sir Paul Nurse, too, mildly castigates the excessive optimism which the genomic entrepreneurs have generated:

> Genes do not make the man or woman. There are some conditions such as Huntington's disease and cystic fibrosis which are caused by a mutation in a single gene, where a genetic test can determine whether a person will develop a disease later in life. But most genetic tests can only indicate whether.there is an increased risk, and not whether there is a certainty of developing a disease.[143]

Another writer has adduced the example of schizophrenia, which has been frequently[144] put forward as an insanity defence in criminal trials:

---

142   Horrobin, D 'Not in the genes' *The Guardian* 12th Feb 2003.
143   Nurse, P 'Fear of genetic "apartheid"' *The Guardian* 4th March, 2003.
144   Paranoid schizophrenia seems to be a favourite pleading for defence attorneys. It was attempted in the case of Peter Sutcliffe (mentioned in the text). A more recent example was the trial of John McLaughlin in Minnesota, who killed two of his classmates while aged 15 in 2003.

I would like to imagine what may happen if it does turn out that mental health can be shown to have a genetic basis. Let us assume as an example that a gene is isolated which in several mutated forms predisposes for schizophrenia. It will take by then a matter of weeks to determine the complete DNA sequence of such a gene. Will the sequence reveal anything about schizophrenia? Does it mean we will understand schizophrenia if we know that it often occurs in people when a certain ion channel or a certain enzyme is damaged? Many scientists or doctors would answer in the affirmative.... but ... understanding a biochemical defect brings us no nearer to understanding the thoughts and actions of the schizophrenic. Those opposed to my view would argue that knowledge of the gene will allow us to identify which lifestyles are dangerous for such a person. But we do not need any knowledge of the gene of its product to do this....[145]

It will be appreciated that there are many voices raised to bring the genetic determinists down to earth. What these commentators are saying is that however hard we try to understand the genetic basis of disease (and by analogy, criminality) we must face the fact that any genetic knowledge is peripheral to the context of a shifting external environment. Factors external to genetics include among many others the demands of growth, of other pathologies, of psychological stresses. Turning again to disease, it can well be argued that the real breakthrough comes when the biochemical pathway implicated in a disease, is elucidated *before* the gene which causes the defect is detected. A salutary example is phenylketonuria, a derangement of amino acid metabolism. Biochemists identified phenylpyruvic acid in the urine of sufferers from the disease, and worked out that they have a defect in the enzyme phenylalanine hydroxylase, which is necessary for the removal of excess phenylalanine from the system. Thus there is accumulation of the alternative rather neurotoxic product, phenylpyruvic acid. It was then a matter of designing diets with the correct, minimal amounts of phenylalanine, and children who were found to have the defect (by ordinary chemical, non-genetic screening methods subsequently introduced) have had near normal lives and have survived to bring up children of their own. In the same way diabetes became manageable when biochemists learned to measure blood glucose accurately and later learned to fractionate pancreatic tissue for the purification of insulin. The analogy with crime, again, is that once proximate causes have been established (poverty, deprivation, or – to speak plainly -

---

145   Muller-Hill, A 'The shadow of genetic injustice' [1993] *Nature* vol 362, at p 491.

sheer greed and wickedness) measures can be put in hand to reduce these, or at last get them off the streets. Genetic explanations are of no relevance in the context of society's response - retribution, rehabilitation, and ensuring the safety of the public. In particular, genetic determinism in jurisprudence will never prevail in the face of the first of these, which is related, I believe, to a plausible genetic explanation, not for criminality, but to our intrinsic reaction to the worst excesses of it. Karl Jung's theory of the collective unconscious has attracted much criticism, but it cannot be discounted entirely. Our flesh creeps in primaeval revulsion when we read of the most base and horrific crimes. Some crimes are so unnatural, so unconscionable, that their perpetrators have to be expunged from the face of the earth to make it cleaner again, or at least we want them to be locked away in the dark forever. (This goes beyond the *lex talionis* '….an eye for an eye….' which has an element of proportionality about it.) That is why there were vigilante groups poised ready to kill the late child-murderer Myra Hindley should she ever have been released from prison, and why the mass-killer Peter Sutcliffe was not allowed, by the judge, to enter a defence of insanity even although several psychiatrists diagnosed him as schizophrenic, and he was attacked several times while in prison by fellow-inmates. And in terms of archetypal horror, why Adolf Hitler, had he survived, would have been hanged and his execrated ashes thrown to the winds.

One final point in this area: it is intrinsic in genetic theory that there is pressure on adverse genes to disappear because their carriers are presumptively disadvantaged in the struggle for survival and they die out. (Of course, many genes are superficially harmful but have survival value in special circumstances. The gene for sickle cell anaemia produces a severely non functional variety of haemoglobin but it has a survival advantage in malarial areas.) If there is a genetic basis for criminality, how is it related to the persistent high prevalence of criminal behaviour? If the gene or genes confer disadvantage, how can they have persisted ? Or is the other view more tenable – that such genotypes are positively advantageous, and are surviving very well indeed?

Summary of 2. 7

- The age-old debate about free will versus determinism has a direct bearing on criminal culpability.

- Equally venerably, heredity impacts on the concept of mens rea.

- Defence attorneys will more frequently try to excuse the actions of their clients by citing mutations in genes as more becomes known about gene function .

- Attempts have been made to link an extra Y-chromosome to violence, the monoamine oxidase gene to antisocial behaviour, and the alcohol dehydrogenase gene to alcoholism.

- The generality of informed opinion regards such attempts as simplistic.

- Public outrage and desire for retribution in the face of the worst criminality will render any future genetic defences, even if scientifically credible, difficult to sustain.

Chapter 3

Aspects of Civil Law

3.1 Preserving the Bloodline

There are sections of society which believe that there is a certain purity or pristine quality to the blood in their veins; firstly, this must be recognised by all, and secondly, it must not be diluted. Of course for 'blood' one should now substitute 'genes', or alternatively DNA. Such sentiments reach their its apogee in the concept of 'royal blood', the tainting of which can attract a charge of lesé-majesty. 'Tainting' of course means the introduction of lowly DNA into the gene line. It is very curious, though, how rapidly DNA can cease to become lowly, should its female owner marry into the nobility or (traditionally) its male owner kill off any possible rivals to the power and wealth which the top job confers.

In England, until the Inheritance Act 1833 the half blood line deferred to the whole blood line, that is to say, if a tenant died having a half brother and a sister (of his own mother) then the half brother would not inherit, being 'more remote in blood.' The Act inserted the half blood into the chain of inheritance, permanently as it turned out.[1] Of paramount importance when almost all wealth resided in land, the presumption was that a tenant (for theoretically, of course, all landholders were tenants) should be succeeded by close members of his own family, the problem being of course to decide who were, and who were not, in that category. The problem, naturally, was proportional to the importance of the tenancy. There are considerations which might be more important than real estate, however. In the 1990 House of Lords debate on the Human Fertilisation and Embryology Bill, Lady Saltoun ('Chief of the Name of Fraser'), having become aware of new reproductive technologies, expressed fears that chiefs of Scottish clans might have their titles inherited by children who are not blood relatives.[2] She stated that the clan is an extended family, all of whom theoretically are related to the chief. 'If the chief himself is a fraud and not of the blood, it makes nonsense of our system,' she declared. This seems to be a recognition that the wives of clan chiefs might not necessarily be more virtuous than wives in the lower

---

1   Baker, JH. *Introduction to English Legal History* (Butterworths, 3rd edn, 1990) p 307.
2   'Clan chiefs fear for the future of their blood line' *The Times* 14 th Feb 1990. According to Cannadine D. in *The Decline and Fall of the British Aristocracy* (First Vintage Books, 1999), p 524, an ancestral Lord Saltoun, in 1911, was one of the main opponents of the Parliament Acts. He might have declaimed, with Ulysses in Troilus and Cresida: 'Take but degree away, untune that string/And hark, what discord follows!'

echelons. In the same debate the Lord Chancellor of the time, Lord Mackay, put the prevalence of non-paternity in marriage at one birth in twenty.[3]

The main reason for turning down Lady Saltoun's amendment, to which Lord Mackay declared himself in essence sympathetic, was that he was not prepared to contemplate the introduction of any stigma on the birth certificate; this goes to the persistent reluctance of the judiciary to declare bastardy (see Chap 3.2) a sentiment which most commentators believe goes only to their credit, and a theme which will reoccur repeatedly in the jurisprudence of medical genetics. However it is arguable that the ability of DNA testing to establish paternity with virtual certainty is making the principle difficult to sustain in many cases.

To indulge this topic a little further, DNA testing is destined to confer exclusivity on members of ethnic groups and/or clans when it shows that they are related, and to extrude those who were previously presumed to belong to the group. In that sense it may displace language in fostering group identity. It seems that Lady Saltoun's (feudal) 'system' might well be strengthened as the clan members with the correct DNA root out the interlopers. A further result of the new genetics, related to future legal attention, is that the

---

3   There is a considerable and disputatious literature on the prevalence of non-paternity, that is the number of children who are being brought up by men erroneously thinking themselves to be the father. Leaving aside the statistics for the moment, the subject is of great interest to students of sociobiology, for it would appear that women tend to marry (or pair bond with) men whom they think might be stable, good providers/carers, but would rather become pregnant with men who would appear to have the best genes, those genes which elicit physical strength and beauty, perhaps associated with power. Pregnancy appears to be an imperative about the time of ovulation so it is then that straying, if it may be put like that, is most likely to occur. A reliable article on the subject is by Macintyre, S and Sooman, A. 'Non-paternity and prenatal genetic screening' [1991] *Lancet* vol 338, at p 869, who state that the figure of 10% non-paternity which has been traditionally quoted but is no more than folklore; also often cited is a specific figure of 30%, resting on an unpublished and non-evaluated source. A more recent investigation has put the figure at 4%. See: Meikle, J 'One in 25 fathers is not a biological parent – study' *The Guardian*, Aug 11, 2005. The most recent scholarly evaluation puts the figure at 1.7% when there no *prime facie* suspicion of non-paternity. It is pointed out that the quantum is bound to be higher in the face of suspicion. Anderson, K. 'How well does paternity confidence match actual paternity?' *Current Anthropology* [2006] vol 47, at p 515. The website <childsupportanalysis.co.uk/…/misattributed_paternity.htm> constitutes a database of research on this topic worldwide and indeed again quotes Dr Elliott Philipp, the purely verbal source of the original 30%, at the Ciba Symposium in 1972. There is much debate among male pressure groups as to what should be done – see for example website <home. earthlink.net/~elnnes/pir.htm> and <file://A:KingHell.htm> for very strident *cris de coeur*.

'science' of ancestry tracing by means of DNA profiling is attracting its share of charlatans and fraudsters. It is reported in the media that a well-respected institute in China will now perform DNA profiling to ascertain if a testee is in the direct line of descent from Confucius (551 – 479 BC)! Slightly tangentially, but in the context of sharp practice, one company claims to operate a social introduction service based on 'using' DNA to find partners with a compatible body fragrance – a matching of 'physical chemistry' [*sic*].

3.2 Paternity and Maternity

The very first application of the VNTR fingerprinting technique was in an immigration-cum-paternity case, the Ghanaian boy suspected not to be the son of the mother who claimed him. Sir Alec Jeffreys pays tribute to the perspicacity of the solicitor Sheona York involved in the case, for it seems that at that point he himself had not thought of such an application for his techniques.[4] Of course the law takes as its starting point the principle enunciated by Lord Mansfield[5] that a husband is presumed to be the father of any child born to a wife during a valid marriage, or alternatively *pater est quam nuptiae (matrimonium) demonstrant* for those who still like to use Latin tags to baffle the general public. (The idea was of course derived from Roman Law. The corresponding maxim for motherhood is sometimes quoted as *mater est quam gestatio demonstrat.* It is interesting that the plural [*nuptiae*] is used for males; this presumably reflects a historical perception of roles. Also current, formerly, was the maxim *mater certus est.* In the days of in vitro fertilization and surrogacy the truth of this last one must be in some doubt.) In terms of the law of evidence these are all rebuttable presumptions.

In England *Pater est* is now statutory by the Human Fertilisation and Embryology Act, s 28 (5) (a), but specifically in relation to in vitro fertilisation. The common law principle could always be overridden by the impossibility of physical contact and by proven physical incapacity. Before the DNA era, husbands who were victims of paternal discrepancy (as it has

---

4   Jeffreys, AJ. '1992 William Allen Award Address ' [1993].*American Journal of Human Genetics* vol 53, at p 1. DNA changed the process of immigration clearance in that in 1989 the Home Secretary announced a 'Concession' (it is usually capitalised) which enables a person whose application for entry clearance was refused when that person was under 18 on the basis that relationship could not be verified to have the case given special consideration in the light of DNA testing. A relevant case can be read on <http://alpha. bailii.org/uk/cases/UKIAT/2004/UD180.html>.
5   Lord Mansfield's rule is quoted in almost every referred case involving a paternity dispute. Its citation is 98 Eng. Rep. 1257 [1777] at 1258. For a full discussion see Hirczy, W 'Protecting the father-child bond against non-paternity actions: legislative judicial and constitutional approaches' [1995] *Murdoch eLaw Journal* vol 2, no 3.

been called) faced extreme difficulty even when these two probative factors were pleaded. In the case of *Gaskill* v *Gaskill* (1921) a gestation period of 331 days (over 11 months) was not ruled out as impossible.[6] However in 1951 the House of Lords ruled that if it could be proved that a child had been born 360 days after the last possible contact with his wife then non-paternity was established. There was however an important rider to this, the *Preston-Jones* v *Preston-Jones* (1950) case – it was also held that adultery had to be proved beyond reasonable doubt, that is, beyond the normal standard in civil law.[7] (Since this once again goes to the reluctance to declare bastardy and is to that extent protective of wives, it must give pause to those feminists who argue that, as was patently not the case here, an all-male bench is always prejudiced against them.) However the standard of proof was lowered by the Family Law Reform Act, 1969 (as amended in 1987) s 26, to a balance of probabilities although this is said not to be a drastic lowering of the burden.[8] In terms of the power of DNA tests the issue in any case becomes irrelevant, as we can see from the numerical values of the paternity index to be explained below.

In the UK the Child Support Agency will refund maintenance on non-paternity being proved, at public expense. With the advent of DNA testing, however, there was still reluctance to disturb a family triad. In the case of *In re F (Blood Tests: Parental Rights* (1993)[9] the Court of Appeal refused to direct a blood test on the application of a man with whom the mother had had

6   This case is cited by Barton, C and Douglas, G *Law and Parenthood* (Butterworths, 1995) p 58.

7   A statistical discussion of the Preston-Jones case is provided by Altman DG. ' Statistics and ethics in medical research' [1980] *British Medical Journal* vol 281, at p 1182. Its legal citation is 1 All E.R. 124; 49 LGR. 417 [HL 1950]. Lord Jauncey in *In re Moynihan* [2002] 1FLR 113 stated that the standard of proof of paternity although not so high as that of beyond reasonable doubt is more stringent than the mere tipping of the scales in favour of probability – unnecessary in the DNA era.

8   Barton and Douglas, (note 6 above) (quoting *Serio v Serio*) at p 58. *In re F (DNA Evidence)* [2007] EWHC 3235 (Fam) the judge gave procedural directions for obtaining DNA evidence in family court proceedings. These were to be in accordance with the Family Law Reform Act (1969). *Inter alia*, the company doing the testing should be named and come from an accredited list; the reports prepared for the court by DNA experts should be couched in clear language for lay people; the use of the LR ('a concept which had uncertainty inherent within it') should be explained. See *New Law Journal*, 1 Feb 2008, at p 183.

9   [1993] 1 FLR 598. On the other hand, in *Re H (a Minor) (Blood Tests: Parental Rights)* [1997] Fam 89 the court ordered a blood test on a child largely on the grounds that it is public policy to have open questions (paternity) resolved.

a relationship on the application of that man – the social role of the father was held to be preeminent. In their standard text Barton and Douglas write that:

> ... the legal position in the 1990s therefore appears to be that while DNA testing can effectively provide positive proof of a genetic relationship and the stigma of illegitimacy carries little if any weight, courts will still hesitate to direct a test which would not affect the outcome of legal proceedings, but which might disrupt the stability of an intact family (but have been criticised in that they take no account of a child's necessity to know its genetic identity).[10]

However we are now in the 21st century. In the case of *P v B (Paternity: Damages for Deceit)* (2001)[11] the Queen's Bench judge ruled affirmatively on the preliminary issue of whether the tort of deceit was applicable to a cohabitation situation. The man in question claimed that his partner, with whom he had had a long-standing conjugal relationship, had fraudulently misrepresented to him that he was the father of her child. (DNA testing established that this was in fact the case.) He claimed 90,000 pounds sterling as special damages and also damages for indignity, mental distress and humiliation. The decision raised spectres which have not been resolved, in particular the familiar 'opening the floodgates' argument and the difficulty of recovering such sums were they to be awarded. Counsel for the defendant stated that it was distasteful and morally offensive to equate such monetary sums as a total loss when the plaintiff had experienced, perhaps enjoyed, a nuclear family life for a number of years. Also, it is against public policy to seek monetary restitution for the life of a healthy child, as is well established in law by the *McFarlane v Tayside Health Board* (2000) case.[12]

P v B does not appear to have gone to a substantive hearing, however. In a later case, *A v B* (2007)[13] the Court of Appeal had the opportunity to reconsider such matters. Here, the plaintiff claimed damages for deceit after terminating the relationship with a woman, within which he had been caring for a child he thought was biologically his own. He had applied for a parental responsibility order after the break-up, but the former partner opposed this. The DNA test he requested showed him not to be the father. The court held that the ingredients of the tort of deceit (alternative nomenclature, 'fraudulent misrepresentation') were established. He had suffered 'damage', that is financial loss, and it was not contrary to public policy to compensate him

---

10   Barton and Douglas, note 6 above, p 63.
11   *P v B (Paternity:Damages for Deceit)* [2001] 1 FLR 1041 QBD.
12   *Mcfarlane v Tayside Health Board* [2000] 2 AC 59.
13   *A v B* [2001] 1 FLR 1041.

in special damages (meaning expenses which are quantifiable). However, importantly, the compensation went only to the money spent on the partner, not the child. It is *not* public policy, the *MacFarlane* case considered, to award damages for any sums spent on maintaining a family relationship with a healthy child. There was also, notably, an award for 'distress', 7,500 pounds.

In England it is possible that the recent Fraud Act (2006) will give a platform for the aggrieved in parental discrepancy disputes. Section 1 reads:

A person is in breach of this section if he-

(a) dishonestly makes a false representation –

(i) to make a gain for himself or another, or

(ii) to cause loss to another....

The language seems clear enough. False representation of paternity can be a criminal act but only if it involves loss to the deceived partner. But will the Crown Prosecution Service be willing to take up a case? No damages accrue, this being a criminal statute, so the aggrieved party would presumably wish to shame or humiliate the mother.

Notably, many American states do not recognise DNA evidence as establishing non-paternity if the testee has been acting to all intents and purposes as the father, as in the *Sidi Thiero* case which received much publicity.[14] There have been decisions in the other direction, such as *Cohen v Nudelmann* in Georgia.[15] All states, it is held, adhere *prime facie* to the common law *Pater est* presumption.[16]

The Supreme Court in *Tuan Anh Ngyuen v Immigration and Naturalization Service*[17] considered DNA testing for the proof of paternity at length. This was in essence an immigration case, demonstrating once again how pervasive is modern DNA technology in law. The court held that it is an important 'governmental interest' to assure that a biological parent-child relationship

14   *The Daily Telegraph* 16th April, 2007; <http://www.my daily news.com> In a parallel domestic imbroglio in England, following secret testing of DNA by a man outside the social family, the Family Court on appeal held that a child could have two fathers – the social one and biological one. In practice of course this merely means equal access rights. *The Daily Telegraph* 31st July, 2008.

15   *Cohen v Nudelmann* [2004] Court of Appeals of Georgia No. A04A1444.

16   <http://www.uslegalforms.com/paternity-forms-htm>.

17   *Tan Anh Ngyuen v Immigration and Naturalization Service* [2001] Supreme Court Collection 208 F. 3d 528.

exists. The mother's relation is verifiable from the birth itself, but the presence of the father 'is not incontrovertible proof of fatherhood'. The court points out that legislatively, 8 U.S.C § 1409 (a)(1) (proof of parentage is that: 'a blood relationship between the person [born out of wedlock] and the father is established by clear and convincing evidence.') does not mandate DNA testing, which is what might be implied by the language in this day and age, rather that there has been 'some demonstrated opportunity to develop a relationship that consists of real, everyday ties providing a connection between child and citizen parent and, in turn, the United States.' There are some other relevant cases.[18]

Notably also, US States differ in their standard adopted for the declaration of parentage when DNA testing is performed; some (Alaska, Ohio, etc) will take a combined paternity index (CPI) (for the derivation of this see below) of 0.95 as conclusive, others (for example Louisiana) require 0.999. (This latter figure transposed into words means that every thousandth man in the same ethnic group could also be presumed to be the father on account of his DNA profile.) No doubt in England, the judge or jury will be invited to consider, factually, what is probative to the oft-cited reasonable man. In the US the draft Uniform Parentage Act seeks to standardise parentage law federally, including the specifics of genetic testing, but no state has adopted it verbatim – this is yet another illustration of the geographical diversity of the system (an issue currently being addressed by the National Conference of Commissioners on Uniform State Laws). The Act contains another and commonsense statement of what seems now to have a normative quality.

The revision allows standing to challenge the marital presumption of paternity. If a child has a presumed father (the husband) then complexities arise. The right of an 'outsider' to claim paternity of a child born to a married woman varies considerably among the states. Some states do not allow such actions, while others permit such actions. The revision provides a middle ground. It allows a proceeding which will seek to rebut the presumption of paternity, but the proceeding must be commenced not later than two years after the birth of the child (which follows the pre-existing rule in California). A two-year period allows an adequate time period to resolve the status of the child within the context of an intact family unit; a longer period may have severe consequences for the child.

---

18   Other cases are listed in: <http://www.irvinelaw.com/PATERNIT.HTM>; <http://www.fact.on.ca/newpaper/lw990412.htm and < www.etax.byu.edu/wardle/New_Fam/chapter10.htm>.

One of the most recent cases involving paternity fraud, *Magill* v *Magill* (2008) was heard in the High Court of Australia in Canberra, on appeal from the Supreme Court of Victoria. Here, a wife had declared, on birth certificates, that her husband was the father of her two children, and DNA testing, after a divorce, had subsequently indicated the falsity of this. The ex-husband had succeeded initially in the county court, being awarded damages for anxiety and depression, but this was overturned by the Supreme Court, hence his appeal to the High Court. The headnotes of the Victoria Court are couched in terms of tort and contract:

> Deceit – paternity – whether tort or deceit applies within the matrimonial situation -claim confined during hearing to misrepresentations in birth forms – whether honest belief by representor as to the truth of assertions of paternity – whether representations of fact or opinion – whether representor wife intended husband to rely on the representations – whether husband induced to act on the representations.'[19]

When the higher court came to consider these points, all six judges dismissed the appeal, but on different grounds, without providing majority support for any clear principles. One view was that '......private matters of sexual conduct and a false representation of paternity ... are not amenable to assessment by the established ... elements of deceit.' Slightly more narrowly: 'False representations concerning an extra-marital sexual relationship or its consequences during the course of a marriage are not actionable in deceit.' Some of the judges searched for a misrepresentation (of paternity) by the wife, but could find none (in contrast to the English *A* v *B* case cited above). A specific misrepresentation might have established her liability, but the facts were that the couple just behaved every day as though they were a biological unit. The husband entered his name on the birth certificates, but the court could not find evidence that the wife had induced him to do so. It was the wife's silence on the matter of her affair which constituted the deception; however silence in itself is not a misrepresentation. Even if it was, the judges were unanimous that no spouse has a legal or equitable obligation to disclose sexual infidelity. There are bound to be many more such cases; the facts will almost certainly widely differ from one to another, and the judges will be hard pressed to come to decisions unless guided by legislation.

Interestingly, DNA has even driven a wedge between civil and criminal law. (Of course all the cases mentioned above are civil ones.) In *Lambeth London Borough* v *S,C,V and J (by his Guardian)* (2006) a child was in the

---

19   *Magill v Commonwealth of Australia* [2006] VCC 1395.

care of the local council and it wanted to establish his true paternity. He had been with his mother and her husband, but the mother had been previously been living with another man and the child believed this man to be his father. Unfortunately the husband had stabbed the former partner to death. The authority wanted to place the child with the deceased mother (the putative grandmother), which would be facilitated if her son was indeed the father. When the former partner was in hospital prior to his death, his blood was taken and a sample remained in the possession of the police. The Lambeth authority sought a direction that this sample should be released to determine whether its donor was the father of the child. However the application was refused on the grounds that determination of paternity using a retained sample was not a purpose authorised by s 64 (1A) of the Police and Criminal Evidence Act 1984 (as amended); broadly, the purpose must be related to crime in some way. Interestingly, the court held also that there is no absolute right of access to genetic information and art 8 of the European Convention on Human Rights cannot be interpreted in that direction.[20]

Forcible and secret testing

Before the DNA era, Lord Reid in *S v McC:W and W* (1972)[21] ordered that blood tests be performed (on children in this case, in two separate paternity disputes) because failure to have available the results would amount to a suppression of evidence; the normal criterion for decision, the best interests of the children, was not *a priori* a factor since it was not known whether the results of the tests would go to the best interests of the children or not. At this time the blood tests involved blood grouping and the determination of the presence or absence of genetically transmitted protein and enzyme variants. By knowing the modes of inheritance a probability of paternity could be estimated. In *In Re J (a Minor)* (1988)[22] one of the early cases taking cognisance of the new technology, a mother was prevented from leaving the country until she could provide a blood sample for DNA analysis. This was under s 37 of the Rules of the Supreme Court Act 1981 (now superceded by the Civil Procedure Rules 1998) which allowed the High Court to grant an injunction when such appeared to it to be 'just and convenient.' Here it was held that it was in the interests of the alleged father and the child that the test be carried out and these interests outweighed the mother's freedom to travel. Once again, we see the judiciary trying to do a balancing act with diverse

20 *Lambeth London Borough v S,C, V and J (by his Guardian)* [2006] EWHC 326 (Fam)
21 *S v McC: W v W* [1972] AC 24, 43E.
22 *In re J (a Minor)* [1988] 1 FLR 65.

interests at stake. The Child Support Act 1991, by allowing reduction in the state benefits of uncooperative mothers, puts pressure on them to provide information about a child's father, and this can be regarded as obvious pressure to have DNA testing done. Indubitably the courts have the capacity to order DNA testing, and this must surely be encouraged by the ability of laboratories to achieve results with a few buccal mucosa cells or a hair root rather than blood. (Thus s 23 of the Family Reform Act (1987) substitutes 'scientific tests' for 'blood tests.' but of course the decision to order or not will still depend upon the circumstances of the case. Indeed there is statutory power to order blood tests under Section 20 of the Family Law Reform Act (1969). The early years of the present century saw a number of cases in which DNA became more intrusive than ever In one, a married couple with a fertility problem arranged for the wife to have intercourse with a family friend, but without result. Ten years on, the wife had intercourse with four men, including the family friend, and this time successfully conceived. After the birth the family friend claimed paternal responsibility. This was refused by the family court, which refused to order DNA testing, but he re-applied for this when he was enabled to do so under the Human Rights Act (1998) Sch1 Part 1, art 8 (Right to Respect for Family and Private Life). The second application was allowed on the grounds that the child was entitled to know his true parentage. There was an interesting importation of the doctrine of proportionality, often said to be inherent in the jurisprudence of European human rights. The judge said that any interference with the rights of the mother and the husband in respect of their family rights, as opposed to those of the applicant, was proportionate to the legitimate aim of providing certainty of knowledge to the child. (The circumstances of this case were unusual in that the applicant had gone around the district claiming parentage, so the child was also to be spared rumour and perhaps gossip.) In another case in 2002 there was an application for DNA testing of twins by a man who had had an affair with a married woman. The application was refused because a positive result might have broken up the existing home, the husband having been until the application unaware of the liaison and the wife herself refusing to contemplate testing. However on appeal the test was ordered. The reasoning was that the interests of justice demanded the establishment of the truth especially since the stigma of illegitimacy had been removed. Thus it appears that courts will only refuse to order a DNA test when it clearly against the child's best interests[23]

---

23 *T (Paternity: Ordering blood tests) Re. sub nom T (a Child)(DNA test:Paternity)* [2001] 2 FLR 1190; *H and A (Children) (Paternity:Blood Tests) Re; sub nom.H and A (Children)* [2002] EWCA Civ 383 [2002] 1 FLR 1145. These cases are helpfully discussed

Important in this context is the suggestion by Baroness Kennedy of the UK Human Genetics Commission that it should be made illegal for men to test the DNA of their children without the mother's permission. This would constitute an extension of s 45 of the Human Tissue Act (2004) (referred to also in Chapter 2.3) and has met with much derision by male persons who feel that the anti-discrimination pendulum has swung too far in the other, pro-female, direction. Indeed it would appear that such provision is impossible of enforcement, at least in its laboratory phase. The single hair bulb of a child need only be sent to a laboratory overseas to elicit a result in a week or so by email. Presumably, alternatively, there would have to be provisions to prevent any legal action on the basis of a secret test done on a child, but this extension is difficult to conceptualise. If the secret DNA testing were to lead to the breakdown of a marriage, would the resultant divorce proceedings be accompanied by a custodial sentence or a fine for the non-father? However in addition, a time limit has been proposed, that is the secret test, to be non-culpable, must be sought within a certain time of suspicion of non-paternity being generated. Two years has been suggested, strikingly similar to the limitation period suggested in the draft US Uniform Parentage Act, mentioned above. Students of law will be immediately reminded of the statutes of limitations – the principle of which, applicable here also, is that an aggrieved person should not think he can rest on his claim.

Secret DNA testing of course, is an activity suspected of employers. This is dealt with in Chapter 3.3 and 3.5 since it goes to privacy and risk, but the UK Human Genetics Commission is said to have found no evidence that it occurs.[24]

The paternity report

A representation of paternity using gel electrophoresis is given Fig 3.1 and a sample paternity report in Fig 3-2. Bayesian analysis again is central to the construction of the latter. Various formulations are given in the literature, many of them convoluted. To understand it, a convenient and simple nomenclature for present purposes is:

P(F) the prior probability that a particular man is the father, based on all the evidence prior to DNA profiling.

---

generally by Standley, K *Family Law*. (Palgrave Law Masters, 2004).

24   Postnote (The UK Biobank Newsletter), July 2002. Parliamentary Office of Science and Technology.

P(nF) the prior probability that a man is not the father, again before any DNA evidence

P(M/F) probability that a man is the father given the DNA match

P(M/nF) probability that man is not the father given the DNA match. This is where the DNA analysis comes in. If a an allele is found in both the child and the putative father, but this allele occurs in 10% of the population, then the probability that the man is not the father is 0.1.

P (F/M)/P(nF/M) the calculated posterior odds *on* that the testee is the father

In the odds form the Bayesian formula is as follows. (The derivation with a slightly different notation suitable for criminal evidence is given in Chapter 2.5.)

$$\frac{P(F/M)}{P(nF/M)} = \frac{P(F)}{P(nF)} \times \frac{P(M/F)}{P(M/nF)}$$

Again we identify P(M/F)/ P(M/nF) as the likelihood ratio (LR) but it is sometimes called the paternity index (PI). It can take any value from a very small number up to infinity. The value 0.5 is usually taken for P(F). (The logic here is that the defendant is either the father or not, that is by the addition rule P(F) + P(nF) = 1) Moreover logically P(M/F) must equal unity, for if there is a match the defendant must be the father. Furthermore P (M/nF) must be the same as the frequency of the allele evaluated in the reference population. Substituting these in the formula above (and arbitrarily taking the frequency P(M/nF) as 0.1 merely for the purposes of a sample calculation) it becomes:

$$\frac{P(F/M)}{P(nF/M)} = \frac{0.5}{0.5} \times \frac{1}{0.1}$$

$$= 10$$

That is, the odds are ten to one *on* that the putative father is the biological father. Converted to probabilities, using the formula P = (odds/odds +1) we arrive at P = 0.91. We must bear in mind for a moment that this figure is derived from only a single allele.

In general then, one can understand that if P(M/nF) is very small, in other words, that the probability of a random member of the same ethnic group having the same DNA profile as the alleged father is small, then the left hand term P(F/M)/P(nF/M), the odds *on* of biological fatherhood, become proportionately greater. For many allele (multiplex) testing, P(F/M)/ P(nF/M) for each allele is calculated and these are multiplied, which in

Fig 3-1   An Electrophoresis Pattern to Determine Paternity

Four alleles have been examined here by gel electrophoresis. On the left hand side , clearly the child has obtained four bands from the mother and four from the father. Suppose that each of the four alleles/bands from the father are found in 20% of his ethnic group, the probability by the multiplication rule, that he is not the father, is   0.2x 0.2 x 0.2 x 0.2 = 0.0016, or,   in terms of odds, approximately 600 to one against.

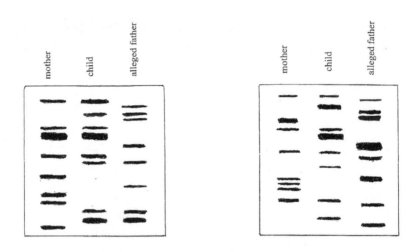

the case of true genetic identity gives a very large odds, in turn yielding a probability very near unity, that is absolute certainty We are accustomed to multiplying probabilities, but multiplying odds or LRs may not at first sight be so transparent. The process can however be regarded as an iterative use of the Bayes theorem. That is, for the first allele, $P(F/M_1)/P(F/nM_1)$ when calculated becomes the prior probability for the second allele so is multiplied by $P(M_2/F)/P(M_2/nF)$ where M_1 and M_2 are matches for the first and second allele respectively. The final figure represents the combined paternity index (CPI). To sum up, the progression is:

Ascertain the frequency of alleles	→	DNA analysis	→	Assume values of P(F), P(nF) & P(M/F)	→	Calculate all PIs	→	Calculate CPI

The assignment of 0.5 for P(F) has been disputed, especially when there is the possibility of diverse men being the father. Obviously, evidence extraneous to the laboratory tests will be important in such instances. In practice however P(F) can be almost any number below unity without affecting the inevitable probability of paternity, CPI/(CPI + 1), approaching unity 1 in multiplex testing when there is indeed paternity. However if the value 0.5 is used in a paternity calculation when its possible falsity is demonstrable it might still be a weapon for the respondent; it would at least allow challenge to the calculation. The reporting of CPI/(CPI +1) has also been criticised. A probability of 0.99 looks impressive but it means that every hundredth man in the same ethnic group will have an allelic composition identical to that of the alleged father. There is a view that the CPI in itself is more informative.

There is an alternative formulation of Bayes theorem, similar to the one given on page 78 (Chapter 2.5) but with a 'parental' notation for clarity, as here. It is the probability, not the odds form, in that it calculates the posterior *probability* that an alleged father is indeed the father of a child, given that their alleles match.

$$P(F/M) = \frac{P(M/F)\, P(F)}{P(M/F)\, P(F) + P(M/nF)\, (PnF)}$$

The top line on the right hand side (the numerator) is the match probability with the prior probability factored into it and the bottom line (the denominator) is the summation of all the available evidence. We can ascribe some values. Usually it is assumed, as noted above, that:

$P(F) = P(nF) = 0.5$ and we may note that mathematically $P(F) + P(nF) = 1$

Logically, $P(M/F) = 1$

$P(M/nF)$, just as logically, must be the frequency of the allele in the reference population. Take this as 1%, that is 0.1 for the purposes of a sample calculation.

$$\text{Then} \quad P(F/M) = \frac{1 \times 0.5}{1 \times 0.5 + 0.1 \times 0.5}$$

$$= 0.91$$

So this is the probability just for one allele. When multiple alleles are taken into account the probability becomes 0.9999 or more. Perhaps the odds result is more user friendly. It may not be immediately obvious that a paternity test with a 99% probability is one hundred times more likely to result in a false attribution than one with a probability of 99.99%.

Some complexities

There are a number of other factors which distort the simple calculation above. What if the putative father and the child have a common ancestry, for example, if he is an uncle of the child ? For a start the prior probability

Fig 3-2   A Sample Paternity Report

This has been performed at nine loci simultaneously, possibly with one of the modern commercially available analysers using capillary electrophoresis. The figure at the end of each row is the likelihood ratio/paternity index. The alleged father is eliminated because, by the multiplication rule, 0 x 0 x 0 x 2.6 x 0 x 2.4 x 0 x 0 x 0 x 0 = zero.

As would be expected, the child has over 50% of alleles in common with the mother.

Alleles	Mother	Child	Alleged Father	Paternity Index
D3S1358	15,17	17,17	16,18	0
vWA	15,16	15,19	14,17	0
FGA	21,22	22,25	20,24	0
D8S1179	11,13	10,13	14,16	0
D21S11	31,32	29,32	28,29	2.4
D18S51	13,16	13,14	18,18	0
D5S818	11,11	11,11	11,11	2.6
D13S317	11,12	10,12	11,12	0
D7S820	12,13	11,12	8,9	0

$P(F) = 0.5$ would most definitely not hold, arguably it might be 0.25. Experts on kinship analysis have however attacked this problem and come out with formulae based on the coancestry coefficient, which is the probability that two homologous alleles are identical due to descent. This is an advanced, mathematical extension.[25] In addition, it would seem at first sight that there might be problems in incest cases; if however one considers father/daughter incest, any child of the liaison would have 75% of the father's genes, indubitably probative of his guilt.

What if the alleged father is dead? Dr Brenner's website provides an entertaining treatment of the real life (and death) case of Larry Hillblom the cofounder of DHL couriers and a serial lecher of young Asian girls.[26] Those

25   See Ayres, KL and Balding, DJ ' Paternity index calculations when some individuals share a common ancestry' [2005] *Forensic Science International* vol 151, at p 101; also the explanation of Dr Charles Brenner on <http://dna-view.com/manyhyp.htm>.

26   <http://dna-view.com/hillblom.htm> This small addendum can be read in conjunction with Chapter 2.3 or one can speculate that it would apply where an alleged father, who is

girls who had become mothers banded together after his death and sought shares of his $600 billion fortune. None of Hillblom's DNA was available, due to the *male fides* of the hospital in which he had been treated some years before. (It too was trying to gain a share of the estate.) Brenner's strategy was to prove that several children from widely different geographical locales had the same allelic compositions. He had four children to evaluate. He started by comparing child one and two via the calculated LR, then one and three and so on pairwise. One and three being similar, he compared them together with two and four, and so on over all the possible combinations. He was able to conclude that three out of the four were related to each other, that is half-siblings, but one was not.

Although it is normal to prepare profiles of mother as well as child and alleged father, there is no particular difficulty if the mother is not available. There is however a potential social difficulty in that if an alleged father is excluded in the absence of a mother, then the possibility is raised of relationships of which the family might previously have been unaware. Leaving aside paternity as such, there may be occasions when grandparents wish to establish relationship with a child in the absence of a mother. In this instance mtDNA testing is favoured; the allelic patterns are transmitted from grandmother to mother to child, male or female. Obviously this concept is equally important in immigration law.

Infidelity testing

This has presumably been a godsend for those suffering from Othello syndrome[27] and perhaps private detectives like Rumpole's Fig Newton, who will be spared long hours of surveillance in cold and/or damp environments. It might also be of interest to those concerned with divorce law, albeit that adultery *per se* must now be such that it leads to irretrievable breakdown of the marriage, in England at least. There is however a lack of decided cases in this context. One company in the US offers its services at $150 per (stained) garment. To quote its prospectus:

> The client knows that their mate is cheating, however they need to know who with. The client has several suspects. The article is sent

---

in fact the real father, manages to supply a random blood sample for the test rather than his own. See <file:///A:Assumptions%20in%20the%20Probability%20of%20Paternity>.
27 Also known as 'delusional jealousy', see <http://www.priory.com/psych/othello. htm>. It would be most invidious to treat with Islamic Law in this context, but it appears that many scholars therein persist in regarding DNA evidence as insufficient to prove adultery. It can only support the evidence of four male witnesses thereto (!) or a confession.

to our laboratory for analysis. Also an oral swab is collected from the client (using a kit sent to the home) and a piece of chewing gum or cigarette used by their partner. The suspect stain(s) are tested and genetic profiles are identified. Genetic profiles of the couple are now known....[28]

Apart from autosomal DNA, tests offered are prostatic acid phosphatase and prostate specific antigen (both enzyme proteins synthesised by the prostate gland), microscopy (for sperm) and (importantly) chromosome Y-DNA. The first three will establish whether the suspected culprit is male or female and the last would be crucial in the same context if the stain is *not* semen. Some of the companies state that if you want to know about such tests you can telephone and talk to a 'scientist'! The present writer cannot express too vehemently what a startling departure this is – that the most arcane and mysterious of professionals, the scientists, like doctors and lawyers, should be considered competent to advise the public. DNA changes everything.

Two final points – firstly, there is a large practical difference between DNA testing in criminology and in family law. At crime scenes the specimen more often than not is degraded, or a mixture, or contaminated in some way, and meagre in quantity. (The same constraints might well apply in infidelity testing, for obvious reasons.) In routine paternity testing (there are always exceptional circumstances) no such challenge exists – the specimens are taken under controlled conditions and the analyst has as much DNA as he wants. Secondly, one misapprehension fostered by the commercial companies and misunderstood by the media is that 'home testing kits' for DNA matching are available. Of course all that is offered is a means of taking a buccal smear and putting it into a plastic bag. The typing itself is still the province of sophisticated laboratories, but there is no doubt that genuine 100% home testing kits will become available at some point.

Summary of 3.2

- DNA matching has completely shifted the evidentiary basis of paternity attribution.

- Even in the face of this the courts are reluctant to disturb the *pater est* presumption.

---

28 Two illustrative (US) sites are <http:infidelitycheck.us/dna_infidelity_test.html> and <file:///H:/Infidelity%20ID%20Testing.htm>. For convenience, the parties smoke and chew gum!

- The courts have no hesitation in ordering DNA testing in the interests of justice.

- The tendency is to order DNA testing so that a child may have certainty in knowing its parentage.

- Paternity testing involves the application of Bayes' theorem to the distribution of alleles in the relevant parties.

- The paternity index remains only a probability, however probative.

- Complications arise due to the possibility of related putative fathers and non-availability of testees – these are susceptible of mathematical solutions.

- There is a burgeoning industry using DNA profiling to detect infidelity.

- In general there are fewer technical problems in parentage testing than in criminal work.

3.3 DNA and Privacy

Classical privacy cases often devolve upon strip searches,[29] unwelcome photography,[30] private diaries,[31] eavesdropping upon telephone conversations,[32] voyeurism,[33] and medical records,[34] but these by no means exhaust the list. In the UK the 1990 Calcutt Committee decided against a

---

29 *Wainwright v The Home Office* [2003] HL 53 For a discussion see: Murdie, A. 'Privacy, searches and bodily integrity – how far can a lawful search go? ' *Justice of the Peace* [2005] vol 169, at p 219. The issue also goes, of course, to powers of entry, which is beyond the scope of this treatment. For a cogent article on this, however see: Paine, S. 'Powers of entry private property' [2000] *Solicitors' Journal* 15 Sept, at p 824.

30 *Douglas v Hello! Ltd and Others* [2005] EWCA Civ 595; *Hellewell v Chief Constable of Derbyshire* [1995] 1 WLR 804.

31 *Argyll v Argyll* [1965] All ER 611.

32 *Malone v Metropolitan Police Commissioner* [1979] 2 WLR 700 leading to the Interception of Communications Act [1985].

33 In a landmark US case, *DeMay v Roberts*, a woman was observed by a non-medical person during childbirth. The alleged tort was 'battery', not 'privacy' but the word privacy was used in the judgement. See discussion in Edge, R and,Krieger, JL *Legal and Ethical Perspectives in Health Care* (Delmar Publishers, 1998) p 91 citation of the case is: 46 Mich 160, 165-166, 9 N.W. 146, 149 [1881].

34 *X v Y (Disclosure of Doctor's HIV Status)* [1988] 2 All ER 648; *W v Edgell* [1990] Ch 359.

tort of privacy principally on the grounds that 'privacy' was impossible of definition.[35] The existence of so many heads, as above, is bewildering until one comes to rationalise that one's personal autonomy has if necessary to be defended against all the world, and that would include one's neighbours, the government, the police, employers, insurance companies, the press, compilers of DNA databases – this list too is endless. It is immediately obvious too that the law of confidential information, as portion of intellectual property law,[36] has an obvious abuttment to privacy considerations, but until recently it has been mainly concerned with purely commercial issues. For example, in a recent case, *Tillery Valley Foods* v *Channel 4* (2004)[37] an application for an injunction preventing publication of a piece about insanitary food production was switched seamlessly by the applicant from breach of confidence to breach of privacy, although neither was successful. Here we are concerned with the extent to which personal genomic or genetic information can be considered to protrude into the law of privacy, with further ramifications to confidentiality and medical law.

First, a few words relating to the US, important because of interest in the interplay of the constitution, the courts and the legislature in such a large and technologically progressive country retaining the common law. The legislators in UK have not yet written a constitution, and the US founding fathers presumably had the opportunity to write something on privacy into theirs, but apparently the word does not appear in it. It has been pointed out that the federal constitutional right to privacy is based on the Fourth (security in the person, house, papers and effects) and Fifth (prohibition of unreasonable search and seizure) Amendments to the Constitution, not the substantive text.[38] The view has also been expressed that the amendments cited are all but nullified by the First Amendment, which lays down the right to free speech and freedom of the press. The press in US is generally

---

35 *Report of the Committee on Privacy and Related Matters*, Cmd 1102 (1990). There had been an earlier report on privacy, in 1972, by the Younger Committee, which also declined to recommend specific legislation – it decided that the existing equitable remedies for breach of confidence were adequate.

36 All commentaries refer to the *loci classici*, namely *Saltman Engineering v Campbell Engineering* [1963] 65 RPC 203 CA (the information must have the necessary quality of confidence about it) and *Coco v A..N. Clark (Engineers) Ltd* [1969] RPC 41 (in addition, the information must have been imparted in circumstances importing an obligation of confidence, plus, there must be unauthorised use of that information.....) Of course the details are to be found in all the intellectual property textbooks.

37 *Tillery Valley Foods v Channel 4* [2004] EWHC 1075 (Ch.).

38 Rothstein, MA. The impact of behavioural genetics on the law and the courts. [1999] *Judicature* vol 83, at p 148.

acknowledged to be the most intrusive on the face of the earth whereas in the UK it is notoriously wary of the libel laws. The American Convention on Human Rights, Article 11 (Privacy) is explicit however, s 2 stating that 'No one may be the object of arbitrary or abusive interference with his private life, his family, his home, or his correspondence, or of unlawful attacks upon his honor or his reputation.' (This echoes the language of art 12 of the UN Universal Declaration on Human Rights.)[39]

In the US the concept of 'privacy' is often deemed to be coterminous with the oft-cited phrase from a paper written by Judges Brandeis and Warren, simply stated as '…..the right to be let alone.'[40] There is an important case, *Griswold* v *Connecticut* (1965) in which the Supreme Court enshrined the right of privacy in relation to the marital bedroom.[41] In addition, *Roe v Wade* (1973), the famous Supreme Court case enabling abortion, is often deemed to be largely a decision in favour of personal privacy.[42] In 1974 came the Privacy Act (1974). This might be expected to be definitive but of course it was enrolled before the DNA era. Its provision 552a(b)8, prohibiting disclosure without consent about the health or safety of an individual, might well cover genetic information, however. The Department of Justice's commentary on the Act merely notes that it refers only to practices conducted by the federal executive branch agencies, that its language is imprecise, and that most cases based on it are unpublished.[43]

The Americans with Disabilities Act 1990 prohibits discrimination against a person who is regarded as having a disability, and this obviously incorporates disabilities based on genetic defects. One can argue that this relates more to medical law than to privacy, but the former is thoroughly infused with the later throughout. Many commentators have interpreted its provisions such that unaffected carriers of genetic diseases or those with late-onset conditions like Huntington's disease are not covered by the Act, that is, they *may* be discriminated against.

---

39 Alderman, E and Kennedy, C *The Right to Privacy.* (Alfred A Knopf, 1995).
40 Brandeis, L and Warren, S 'The right to privacy'. 4 *Harvard Law Review* 193 (1890).
41 381 U.S. 479 [1965]; for an interesting discussion on the case see White, AR *Misleading Cases* (Clarendon, 1991) p 78. Ms Griswold was executive Director of the Planned Parenthood League of Connecticut and was convicted under a state law criminalising counselling on contraception to married couples (this as late as 1965!). The Supreme Court, while admitting that the constitution did not confer a general right to privacy, that the First, Third, Fourth and Ninth Amendments created a 'penumbra' thereof.
42 *Roe v Wade* [1973] 410 U.S. 113.
43 <http://www.usdoj.gov/o4foia/1974intro.htm>.

The Health Insurance Portability and Accountability Act (HIPAA) (1996) applies only to commercially based group insurance. It states that genetic information in the absence of a current diagnosis of illness shall not be considered as a preexisting condition. Regulations attached thereto in 2002 (the Privacy Standards) protect privacy in respect of all medical records, not merely genetic ones. As usual though variation in state practice has to be considered.[44] The commentaries on the Act tend to stress the aspect of genetic discrimination in the workplace but the barring of the use of such is just another aspect of privacy.[45] Further into the DNA era, the DNA Backlog Elimination Act (2000) has been ruled constitutional, and not an invasion of privacy under the Fourth Amendment, by several appeals courts, in requiring parolees, not suspected of additional crimes, to yield blood samples for the FBI's DNA database.[46] In *Whalen* v *Roe* (1977) it was held that pharmaceutical information could be given to the state health department, an earlier erosion of the right to (medical) privacy in the interests of combatting the illegal drug trade since privacy consideration were outweighed by the need to combat the illegal drug trade.[47] In 2000 President Clinton by Executive Order 13145 banned federal and agencies from discriminating against employees on the basis of genetic information and also, the privacy provision, banned the acquisition by employers of genetic information via medical records. Therefore there is some recognition of the privacy of DNA sequences in the US; whether, if a newspaper published a person's genome, he would have a remedy, is difficult to answer. Looking at the total picture, it seems that in the country wherein DNA technology was kick-started and most signally blossomed, privacy is well protected in the civil sphere but as a matter of public policy is non-existent for the actual and potential criminal.

To begin again at source, by general consensus there is no basic right to privacy in common law[48] but that may be a reflection, once again, of the difficulty of knowing just what the word means. It is stated by Baker in his legal history text that privacy can be asserted by local custom.[49] Also,

44   Diverse US state practice can be accessed on: < file:///A:genetics%20Legislation. htm>. A discussion is provided by Hurewitz, B and Schnabel, T 'Genetic privacy in the United States; a patchwork of protection' [2006/2007] *Bioscience Law Review* vol 1, a t p 14.
45   See also Rosati, K B 'Human genetic sampling and the HIPAA privacy standards' [2005] *Jurimetrics* vol 45 at p 251.
46   See website <The PrivacyPlace.Org>..
47   *Whalen v Roe* [1977] 429 US 589.
48   Slapper, G and Kelly, D *The English Legal System* (Cavendish Publishing, 5th edn, 2001) p 389.
49   See note 1, p 488.

Blackstone quotes a 1360 statute which states that: '... such as listen under walls or windows, or the eaves of a house to hearken unto discourse........are a common nuisance, and are punishable by a fine and by finding sureties for their good behaviour.'[50] The provision was used in a 1982 case (*R v Jones*)[51] wherein an 'eavesdropper' had planted a bug (listening device) in the ceiling of a neighbour's bedroom.

With the incorporation of the European Convention of Human Rights into domestic law, the English courts have had to consider its meaning and import in respect of privacy as for all else. The Convention does not specifically mention privacy *simpliciter* but art 8 (Respect for Family and Private Life) in its section 1 states that: "Everyone has the right to respect for his private and family life, his home and his correspondence", the language of which is usually interpreted in a general way to protect privacy. In the Campbell case (discussed more extensively below) art 8 was held up to art 10 (the right of freedom of expression) and Blackbourne J said:

> ... Neither Article (8 and 10) has such precedence over the other. Secondly, where the values under the two articles are in conflict, and intense focus on the comparative importance of the specific rights being claimed in the individual case is necessary. Thirdly, the justifications for interfering with or restricting each right must be taken into account. Finally the proportionality test must be applied to each. For convenience I will call this the ultimate balancing test.

Leaving aside the question of whether the application of 'proportionality' can in fact be used to obviate the principle of Article 8, if the concept at least of privacy can be read into it, then indeed this is now embedded in English law. Nonetheless the House of Lords recently stated in *Wainwright v Home Office* (2004) that to create a separate tort of privacy based on art 8 was 'too bold an undertaking, ' and that any change in the law was best left to parliament.[52] According to Lord Scott: 'The issue .....is whether the infliction of humiliation and distress by conduct calculated to humiliate and cause distress, is without more, tortious at common law. I am in full agreement ...that it is not. Nor, in my opinion, should it be.'

---

50 Blackstone: *Commentaries on the Laws of England* 169 [1769]. This quotation is also recounted by Geoffrey Robertson at p 95 of his *Freedom, the Individual and the Law* (Penguin Books, 6th edn, 1989) Robertson, incidentally believes that the US courts have 'moulded the common law so as to award damages whenever a person's interest in seclusion, or in personal dignity.... is interfered with......' in contradistinction to the English tradition.
51 *R v Jones The Daily Mail* 15th May, 1982.
52 *Wainwright v The Home Office* [2003] HL 53

Could publishing or otherwise casting abroad the knowledge of a person's DNA sequence cause 'humiliation and distress'? Possibly the question would go to a person's fortitude, but a better response surely is that a person is humiliated when he thinks he is humiliated and genetic information tending to show him in a bad light in one way or another would presumably fit the bill. *Wainright* was the culmination of a long series of cases and statutes which have skirted round the concept of privacy. For example the *Malone* case[53] went to the European Court of Human Rights which affirmed a privacy right for telephone calls. However *Kaye* v *Robertson* (1991) (the case of the invasion of the hospital room case by the press) again established that there was no law of privacy in England.[54] What is usually known as the *Brown* case also ended up in the European Court of Human Rights.[55] The sadomasochistic acts in question, conducted in private, were confirmed to be subject to prosecution under ss 20 and 47 of the Offences Against the Person Act 1861; art 8 of the Convention was deemed not to be interpreted too liberally. So there seems to be a swing hither and thither, but the aspects of privacy are so diverse that it is difficult to generalise. Of significant importance jurisprudentially is Baroness Hale's dissenting judgment in *R* v *Chief Constable of South Yorkshire ex parte LS* (2004), referred to in passing in Chapter 2.3, in which the issue was the retention by the police of the DNA of individuals who have not been convicted of any crime: 'Storing information almost inevitably involves someone else knowing it. it is an interference with privacy for someone to have access to private information even if they make no other use of it. The mere fact that some has read my private correspondence ...is an interference with my privacy even that person tells no one else what he has seen....'[56] One wonders if this will be one of the dissenting judgements destined to become more influential than that of the majority, like Lord Atkin's famous proclamation of personal inviolability in *Liversidge* v *Anderson* (1942).[57]

In the statutory arena, the Unsolicited Goods and Services Act (1971) protected privacy in so far as it forbade delivery through the post of items which might be offensive to the recipient; the Protection from Harassment

53 *Malone v Metropolitan Police Commissioner* [1979] 2 WLR 700.
54 *Kaye v Robertson* [1991] FSR 62 (CA).
55 *R v Brown* [1996] 1 All E.R. 545; *Laskey, Jaggard and Brown v United Kingdom* (ECHR 109/1995/615/703-705).
56 *R v Chief Constable of South Yorkshire Police (Respondent) ex parte LS (by his mother and litigation friend JB) (FC) (Appellant:; R v Chief Constable of South Yorkshire Police (Respondent) ex parte Marper (FC) Appellant) Consolidated Appeals.* [2004] UKHL 39.
57 [1942] AC 206.

Act (1997) seeks to prevent a certain category of intrusion into private life. In respect of this legislation, the court has to strike a balance between arts 8 and 10, as in the recent *Howlett* v *Holding* (2006) case, dealing with an application for an injunction against a person who had gone to the extent of flying personally abusive banners from an aircraft; the judges of the Queen's Bench exercised the principle of proportionality in weighing the two articles and came down on the side of the protection of privacy.[58] Probably the most important instrument in this context is the Data Protection Act (1998) which is currently being redrafted.[59] Although it seems that the Act is more orientated around direct marketing, employment and financial services, it does impinge upon DNA databanks. (For discussion of DNA banks, see Chapter 2.3). There are eight principles in the Act, but those most relevant to the present theme are that information must be:

(1) Processed fairly and lawfully

(2) Obtained for specified and lawful purposes.......... [and].

(5) Not kept any longer than necessary

Suppose a company surreptitiously acquires the DNA of an employee because it wishes to ascertain whether he is liable to sickle cell anaemia. It might want to avoid promoting him if it knows it will shortly lose him to this disability, which often requires repeated blood transfusions. It might even – although this might be held to be far-fetched – want to know if he is overwhelmingly genetically similar to a relative who is a known to be an arch embezzler. It might want to store the DNA for many years. These activities would probably be caught under the Act. It is certainly the view of the House of Lords (as a legislature) and the Department of Health that human rights law and the common law, via the interpretation of legislation in the courts, should be brought to bear on the connection between genetic information and the Act. Certainly enquiries under the Act, to the police, require the enquirer to fill in a form which has 'DNA Database' as one of the boxes to be ticked. If the cases cited above seem amorphous in their connection with the present theme, a better analogy to make with the intrusion on the genome, possibly, is the photograph. Photographs are inherently intrusive, invasive of privacy, certainly in proportion to the lack of preparedness of their subject(s), and

---

58 *Howlett v Holding The Daily Telegraph* 9th Feb 2006. Here Queen's bench enunciated the important principle that, in general, it was not appropriate to accord automatic precedence to one Convention right over another.

59 The Data Protection Act (1998) was passed as a result of European Union Directive 95/46/EC and has to be upgraded in accordance with further developments within the Commission.

potentially tortious, and the defamation courts seem to be more incensed by them than by the written word.[60] It is a widely held view that if sneak images attract the weight of the law, then so much more so must the purloining of the sequence of bases in a person's DNA, the key to his or her life, as it were.

There have been several interesting photography cases. Princess Diana had a contretemps with the owner of her gymnasium in 1993, after he took surreptitious but apparently innocuous pictures of her on the treadmill.[61] She obtained an injunction against publication but in the event the case was settled out of court. General opinion is that she succeeded more on the grounds of breach of trust than of breach of privacy or confidence, for her activities were quite open to observation by others in the gym. But if the gym owner had purloined her DNA – he could have mopped up some of her sweat had he been aware of the technology of the polymerase chain reaction – and had it sequenced, instead of taking her photograph, would that have gone more to breach of privacy than breach of trust? Or would it have been actionable at all? Of course it might now be a criminal matter, in terms of the Human Tissue Act 2004. But in civil terms, it would surely have invoked a tort of invasion of privacy.

Later, there was the case in which Michael Douglas and his wife brought an action in breach of confidence (not privacy) against the publishers of the magazine *Hello!* which ran a 'spoiler' by infiltrating their nuptial celebrations and taking photographs claimed by the plaintiffs to be damaging them in diverse ways.[62] (The magazine *O.K!*, which had been commissioned to obtain the fully sanctioned pictures litigated on contract, not tort.) The High Court recognised that an individual had a right to personal privacy based on the equitable principle of breach of confidence. But the desire to maintain confidentiality must be clearly expressed, or at least implied. (In respect of genetic information and medical law generally, this requirement would be transposed to signing a consent form with a confidentiality clause.) It was stated that the law could now recognise privacy as a right deriving from the fundamental value of personal autonomy. (Here we have a harking back to Kantian ethics and a lurch forward into modern medical law.) In

---

60   There is an informative article on the photographic imbroglios by Rizvi, R 'The privacy pendulum'. [2005] *New Law Journal* 28th Oct, p 1622.

61   *HRH Princess of Wales v MGN Newspapers Ltd* [1993] EMLR 443.

62   *Douglas and Others v Hello! Ltd* [2005] ECWA 595, [2005] All ER (D) 280. There were various statements on privacy throughout the complicated course of this litigation; the case started in the High Court on an injunctive action, went to the Court of Appeal, was remitted back to the High Court and then went up to the Court of Appeal again for the substantive hearing.

the Court of Appeal, the privacy judgement was confirmed. According to the Master of the Rolls: "It is quite wrong to suppose that a person who authorizes publication of selected personal photographs taken on a private occasion, will not reasonably feel distress at the publication of unauthorised photographs taken on the same occasion. " Thus by analogy, if you donate your DNA to research unit so that it can show your sequence to a medical convention, and the somebody at the convention copies it and uses it for his own purposes, you may with justification feel legally aggrieved.

In another well-publicized photography case the model Naomi Campbell brought an action against the *Daily Mirror* for invading her privacy by taking pictures of her leaving a drug rehabilitation clinic.[63] The case went all the way up to the House of Lords. There, albeit be a narrow majority, it was ruled that there are limits to the exercise of freedom of information by the press (and impliedly by anyone else), and that an activity related to medical treatment was capable of invoking protection whereas an ordinary day-to-day activity like buying a bottle of milk would not. We seem to be seeing here too, perhaps, the exercise of the principle of proportionality, also expounded (in the other direction) in the *Marper* case[56] although in that context the DNA sequence is not to be published, but retained in police files. So the question is: is viewing or publishing a lady's DNA base sequence equivalent, in law, to the viewing or publishing photographs showing her buying a bottle of milk, or alternatively viewing or publishing photographs showing her leaving a detoxication clinic? One would tend to the latter.

Finally, Princess Grace of Monaco was shopping and was snapped by paparazzi. Her complaint went to the European Court of Human Rights, which held in her favour. It stated that '.... whenever a public figure has a 'legitimate expectation' of being safe from the media his or her right to private life prevails over the right to freedom of expression or the right to be informed.'[64] Here the balancing Act between arts 8 and 10 is extensively tipped in favour of the former.

Dealing specifically with tortious aspects of the acquisition of genetic data in circumstances which might foreseeably breach the law of confidential

---

63   *Campbell v MGN* [2004] HL 22. See Moreham, NA 'Privacy in public places' [2006] *Cambridge Law Journal* vol 65, at p 606.
64   *Von Hannover v Germany* [2005] App No 59320/00 92004) EMLR 21 (ECHR). This was followed in England by *McKerrit v Ash* [2005] EWHC 3003 (QB) which repeated the words of the ECHR, in favour of the plaintiff.

information, one expert in the field has listed the factors which might import liability as:[65]

(1) The use of illegal means, such as breaking into a house to steal the DNA. The person who had so acted would be subject to test of good faith and conscience were the sequences of that DNA to be acquired or published.

(2) Improper or reprehensible methods, such as trickery or deception, not in themselves illegal. The blameworthiness would be enhanced if the owner took pains to safeguard the information. This is more or less the Douglas scenario – presumably they had security guards present. One can imagine this point to be apposite where the subject matter in question resides in a document which can locked away, but we have repeatedly noted in this pages that safeguarding one's DNA is virtually impossible.

(3) Notions based on property per se. (One must here hark back to Chapter 2.1 and note that there is no clarity about the property status of DNA, especially 'abandoned ' DNA.) The issue here would simply be theft.

(4) The possible importation of a tort of harassment. This is only tentatively advanced – the individual would have to ask himself if he feels threatened or made fearful by the purloining and/or publication of his genetic details. One supposes that it would all depend on the circumstances, but enough has been mentioned above to allow the conclusion that DNA privacy would stand a great chance of protection.

These are entirely speculative, as the author admits. Three further points: firstly, one might note that in both USA and UK the antiterrorist legislation following the 9/11 attacks is tending to nullify any progress towards greater privacy for their citizens. If Bush's minions can tap telephone conversations in defiance of the rule of law (a matter of some controversy as well as indignation), they certainly will not hesitate to collect DNA samples. These would aid in the identification of suspected terrorists who might have changed their appearance (and maybe even fingerprints) with surgery, say. They could also trace correspondence through saliva traces on mailed envelopes. The DNA of Osama bin Laden will be profiled, if and when he is captured, to check his true his identity; if the authorities do not at present have his DNA,

---

65 Wei, G. *An Introduction to Genetic Engineering, Life Sciences and the Law* (Singapore University Press, 2002) p 88. The writer comes to no firm conclusions as to the applicability of his scenarios.

they will most certainly have obtained samples openly or surreptitiously from his relatives. Recurring scandalous exposures in the UK (the suspected aid the government or possibly MI6 afforded to ' rendition,' for example) makes one suppose that the same suspicions apply there.

Secondly, DNA information is different from all the others in one crucial respect. All other evidentiary matter relates to the past – DNA readily looks to the future. Hitherto, throughout the centuries, politicians (to take a prominent section of the populace) have stood or fallen on what they did or did not do in the past. Very often resignation came upon the discovery of some past weakness. Now, with gene hunting, future weaknesses will be predictable. Suppose a public figure's base sequence reveals him to have a mutation in the apolipoprotein E gene, which happens to indicate an extremely high risk of developing Alzheimer's dementia, or even to have a gene predisposing to cancer, could he then look forward to a prolonged career? DNA, health and future prospects are all highly intertwined. Privacy in respect of one's past is one thing, in respect of one's fate, something different. As been written: 'All genetic information projects into the future. It has implications for the assessment not only of one persons' health but for the health of all that person's relatives, descendants, or potential descendants.'[66]

Thirdly, there is a recent international instrument, the 'Oviedo Convention' (Convention for the Protection of Human Rights and Dignity of the Human Being with Regard to the Application of Biology and Medicine) which in part goes to genetic privacy.[67] The Convention came into force on December 1999 and at the time of writing neither the USA nor UK has either ratified or even signed it. It was promoted by the Council of Europe whose Convention on Human Rights and Biomedicine it echoes, and the parties are all European states, except Turkey. It is a direct descendant of several other international conventions such the Universal Declaration of Human Rights. In Article 10 it states that: "Everyone has the right to respect for

---

66   Hubbard, R and Wald, E *Exploding the Gene Myth*. (Beacon Press, 1993) p 152; Laurie, G *Genetic Privacy* (Cambridge University Press, 2002).
67   Austin, MA, Crouch, J et al 'International organizations addressing databank issues' [2005] *Jurimetrics* vol 45, at p 115. These authorities cite the World Medical Association, Council of Europe, UNESCO, and the Human Genome Organisation as being concerned with informed consent, withdrawal of consent, legal incompetence, multiple use of data, privacy/confidentiality, anonymisation, and archiving. A consensus is that informed consent will be a sine qua non for future/unspecified research using DNA databanks. Among commentators agreeing that DNA testing is covered by the regulations is Nauwelaerts, W 'Whose DNA is it anyway? Testing genetics under the auspices of EU data privacy law' [2004/2005] *Bioscience Law Review* vol 3, at p 118.

private life in relation to information about his or her health, " which must of course include genomic information. It is interesting to speculate whether this would apply to personal STR sequences, which have no known relation to health at the moment. One would have to look back at the general privacy issues discussed above, in that STRs are an aspect of personal identity.

Summary of 3.3

- Privacy is difficult to define in any legal sense but socially it implies defence of one's autonomy against, for example, compilers of DNA databases.

- Various statutory provisions appear to safeguard genetic privacy in the US.

- Common law systems vary in their recognition of a tort of invasion of privacy; case law, at least in England, tends to oscillate. However with the enactment of the Human Rights Act a right to privacy can be assumed but there is still no tort of invasion of privacy *per se*.

- Personal genetic information may well be considered under the law of confidential information and acquiring it by dishonest means might give rise to a head of action.

- The Data Protection Act appears to be relevant to genetic information.

- Information about DNA is different from all other modalities of confidential information in that it can look to the future as well as the past.

- Article 10 in the Oveido Convention originating from the Council of Europe can be interpreted as protecting genetic/DNA privacy.

3.4 DNA and Medical Law

The main issues in medical law with respect to molecular biology, genetics and DNA can be listed as:

- Negligence *per se*
- Loss of chance
- Confidentiality
- Consent

- The status of genetic testing kits

- Issues surrounding gene therapy.

Negligence

The general principles of medical negligence law must necessarily apply to genetic/DNA or protein testing as set out in the standard texts.[68] Negligence can of course be generated by either acts or omissions, an example of the latter being 'loss of chance', dealt with below. The liability of laboratories for mishandling or other defects, for losing specimens, for carelessness in interpreting results, all potentially leading to loss to a patient, are no doubt actionable under the normal rules. Liability for defective genetic testing kits will fall in U.K. under the provisions of the Consumer Protection Act 1987. It is authoritative opinion that at the moment in the US genetic testing kits are essentially unregulated.[69] Some other aspects of genetic testing are addressed below.

There is a further question related to this type of liability. Was the test introduced into ordinary practice having been validated (see Section 2.6) and accepted by a majority of the relevant practitioners? If not, and there is some loss of injury to a patient, there is the possibility of an action in negligence. The negligence need not have been due to a medical practitioner – the case of *Adams and Another v Rhymney Valley District Council* (1999)[70] in the Court of Appeal established that the *Bolam* test for determining breach of duty need not necessarily be applicable only to a professional person (although the *Bolam* test itself is discredited.)[71] Thus the managers of a company providing genetic testing kits might well be liable.

Turning to DNA again, it appears that negligent genetic testing can give rise to a 'wrongful life' action, that is the claim of damages by a child (not the parents) who would not have been born had the tests been carried out. In *Parkinson v St James and Seacroft University Hospital Trust* (2001) the extra costs of bringing up a baby with an inherited disability, in this instance

---

68 Jones M,. *Medical Negligence* (Sweet and Maxwell, 1996).
69 Ossorio P, Product liability for predictive genetic tests. [2000] *Jurimetrics* vol 41 at p 239.
70 *Adams v Rhymney Valley District Council* [1999] EWCA CV 1257.
71 The Bolam test, from *Bolam v Frien Barnet Hospital Management Committee* [1957] 1 WLR 582, which became controversial in the nineties, and was substantially superceded by the judgement in *Bolitho v City and Hackney Health Authority* [1997] 4 All ER 771 and perhaps *Rogers v Whitaker* [1992]109 ALR 625 is dealt with in great detail in all the medical law textbooks.

Down syndrome, undiscovered due to negligent testing, were held to be recoverable.[72] The full costs of the child's upbringing could not be claimed (therefore the judgement did not go fully as far as wrongful life *per se*). However the extra costs could be claimed for the child beyond the age of 18, a recognition that the disability was most likely to last a lifetime. There are several ongoing cases in the US but it appears that only a minority of states recognise wrongful life as a head of action.[73] A legal technicality is liable to cause difficulties in wrongful life actions, namely, that the alleged negligence has taken place when the plaintiff was a foetus and a foetus has never been recognised as a legal person in common law jurisdictions. Additionally, it might be noted that the possibility of such actions is predicated on the legality of abortion, which is either a recent phenomenon or non-existent, still, in some areas.

If a genetic test is done, the patient himself being informed that it shows a positive result, should relatives who might be at risk of developing the same condition be informed? They might want to be tested, or they might prefer to desist (the latter now being referred to as 'the right not to know') but in any case might it be it negligence for the doctor *not* disclose the risk? Prime facie if he so does he is in breach of his obligation of confidentiality. If the patient himself gives consent to disclosure that is not quite the end of the matter, for the doctor has to ascertain if the recipient of the information, the third party, is in a position to understand what is being conveyed. The most-cited guidance in this situation is the *Rogers v Whitaker* (1992) standard[74] which requires health professionals to ascertain what significance a reasonable person in the position of that third party would attach to a risk if informed of it. We await case law when risk due to inheritable conditions is the issue.[75]

---

72 *Parkinson and St James v Seacroft University Hospital Trust* [2001] 546 CA. A similar case was *Rand v East Dorset Health Authority* [2003] Lloyds Rep Med 181, also following a Down syndrome birth.

73 Burns, TA. ' When life is an injury;an economic approach to wrongful life lawsuits' [2002/2003] *Duke Law Journal* vol 52, at p 807. Jurists distinguish between wrongful conception (damages sought by parents when a healthy child would not have been conceived but for somebody's negligence), wrongful birth (failure of genetic counseling resulting in a disabled child) and wrongful life (an action by an impaired child claiming that but for negligence he would have been aborted).

74 *Rogers v Whitaker* [1992]109 ALR 625.

75 Risk assessment in medicine is a large and formidable topic An informative article is by Prins, H 'Taking chances: risk assessment and management in a risk obsessed society' [2005] *Medicine, Science and the Law* vol 45, at p 93. See also Calman, KC. 'Cancer: science and society and the communication of risk' [1996] *British Medical Journal* vol 313, at p 799. There is an analogy here to the precautionary principle in environmental law.

There is a leading case on negligence by way of omission from the US. In *Safer v Estate of Pack* (1996) the Superior Court of New Jersey held that doctors have a duty to warn a family member of a patient who is at risk of avoidable harm from a genetically transmissible condition. The daughter of a man who had died some years before from hereditary multiple polyposis sued the doctor (of the father) in negligence for not warning her of the danger of contracting the condition. The daughter had not been a patient of the doctor and so arguably he had no duty of care towards her (normally one of the main heads of action in negligence.) The defence argued that a genetic condition was distinguishable from an infectious disease (for which a warning should be given and which in most countries is notifiable to the authorities as statutory duty) but the appeal court thought otherwise.[76] One commentator concludes that: '... when the usual principles of negligence are applied to genetic harm, the duty to warn unknowing blood relatives of their risk of serious genetic disease should be found in the common law. This duty should exist where there is a high correlation between the gene change and disease.'[77] This is debatable. The duty of patient confidentiality can be breached only be certain limited exceptions and they do not include sentiments of beneficence to spouses or relatives.[78] Again we await any rerun or extension of *Safer* v *Pack* in a higher court or some other jurisdiction.

The tort of negligence is revisited in the context of genetically modified food in Section 2 of Chapter 5.

Loss of chance

The tortious action for 'loss of chance' refers to failure of a practitioner to perform some test which, were it to be informative, would lead to a

---

76   *Safer v Estate of Pack*, 291 N.J. Super 619 (N.J. 1996). The case has been extensively dissected. See: Falk, MJ, Dugan, BR. et al. 'Medical geneticists' duty to warn at risk relatives for genetic disease' [2003] *American Journal of Medical Genetics* vol 120A, at p 374; Andrews, LB. 'Torts and the double helix: malpractice for failure to warn of genetic risks' *Houston Law Review*, Spring 1992, sourced on <file:///A:/Andrews.htm>; Laurie G. 'Genetics and patients' rights: what are the limits? [2000] *Medical Law International* vol 5, at p 25.

77   Keeling, SL 'Duty to warn of genetic harm in breach of patient confidentiality' [2004] *Journal of Law and Medicine* vol 12, at p 235.

78   Briefly, they are usually cited as: (1), consent by the patient himself, (2), a court order, (3), notification of an infectious disease to the relevant health authority, (4), communication to third parties strictly in the interests of the patient, (5), public interest, (6), disclosure to other professionals strictly in the interests of the patient, (7), use of the information for teaching purposes and (8), communication to healthcare management authorities.

modulation of treatment such that the patient's prospects would be improved, and so again the issue largely goes to negligence due to an omission. The task here is to determine whether established law applies to the modern genetic technologies. Slightly bizarrely, when the issue arises, the judges still entertain the case of *Chaplin* v *Hicks* (1911) which concerned a beauty contest, and was in itself decided on the law of contract (indeed it is embedded in all the contract textbooks).[79] An aspirant to a beauty contest had won the preliminary round but had for some reason had not been emplaced on the finalists' list, so that she did not have the chance to win the prize. Of course, she may or may not have won it, nobody could predict the future. But the court held that the chance was worth something, and she had lost that. The only difficulty was in computing damages, by a jury in those days. However the leading modern case is *Gregg v Scott* (2005) which, though not directly devolving upon DNA technology, enables some analogies to be drawn.[80] Mr Gregg found a lump which turned out to be a non-Hodgkin's lymphoma, but it was definitively diagnosed only at a late stage. Bearing in mind that the medical profession takes a 'cure' to be the attainment of a 10-year survival after the initiation of treatment, Mr Gregg's chance of survival – without the earlier treatment which he should have enjoyed – on the basis of expert evidence was reduced from 42% to 25%, the former figure representing the computed chance after an accurate, early diagnosis. In the House of Lords there was bare majority against the claimant, three to two, which suggests that the law is uncertain. (All the Lords gave reasoned judgements instead of the usual: 'I have read a draft of the speech of my noble and learned friend Lord......and agree with him.') This is not the place for a full analysis or a discussion of the Lords' unease about the venerable 'floodgates' spectre. Suffice it to note that Lord Hoffman pointed out that the previous successful actions for loss of chance were economic in nature (lottery tickets and the like) but that in the extant case the causal connection between the tort and the consequential loss could not be proved on a balance of probabilities, that

---

79 *Chaplin v Hicks* [1911] 2 KB 786. Another venerable case is *McGhee v National Coal Board* [1973] 1 WLR. 1 wherein the House of Lords decided that breach of duty by an employer 'probably' contributed to a dermatitis and therefore he was liable.

80 [2005] WLR 268. *Gregg v Scott* has been much discussed. See: Samuels, A 'Misdiagnosis leading to the loss or diminution of the chance of recovery or survival' [2005] *Medico-legal Journal* vol 73, at p 15; Lockart, KB 'Loss of chance in medical negligence: Gregg v Scott ' [2005] *Scots Law Times* vol 17 at p 93; Foster, C 'Last chance for lost chances' *New Law Journal* 18 Feb 2005, p 248. Some interesting Australian cases on loss of chance are discussed by Freckelton, I 'The evolution of loss of chance' [1999] *Journal of Law and Medicine* vol 7, at p 5. A recent case in the English High Court provides an addendum in holding that there is no objection in principle to damages for loss of chance in an action for deceit. *4 Eng Ltd v Harper and another* [2008] EWHC 915 (Ch).

is, over 50%. However any mandatory tipping of the probability over 50% was dismissed by Lord Nicholls, dissenting, who maintained that it could not be right to adopt a procedure which had the effect that, in law, a patient's prospects of recovery are treated as non-existent if they fall short of that level. For the three in the majority, though, all the claimant could prove was that he had lost the chance of a more favourable outcome. For the future, it was pointed out, everything is uncertain. Any one outcome could not be proved, on a balance of probabilities, to be more likely than not. It was also mentioned in respect of any appeal to the European Court of Human Rights that: "National tort law usually involves the social distribution of risk and usually does not impinge upon human rights principles."

Tardiness in carrying out a genetic test is likely to be distinguishable from the *Gregg* case in respect of some diseases or conditions, but not in others. Many inherited conditions are essentially untreatable, at least at present when gene therapy is in its infancy. An examples would be Down syndrome wherein late diagnosis would not then affect the eventual outcome. Many inherited conditions however are treatable if diagnosed early enough, for example phenylketonuria. If the screening for this is negligent, or missed, an affected baby might proceed to a diet high in protein, containing phenylalanine, and could suffer brain damage.[81] He might then have lost the chance of a normal life. It cannot be right that no redress would be forthcoming. According to *Gregg,* as a claimant he would have to prove on a balance of probabilities that extra care and resources needed for his disability would in fact not have been needed had the screening been properly conducted. This might not be easy – it would rest on expert evidence, of course. More, there is a category of genetic disease which goes to lifestyle and not survival as such. The prime example is the inherited condition called Huntington's disease (formerly Huntington's chorea), which when diagnosed in youth predicts a demise in mid life with absolute certainty.[82] A youthful potential sufferer, negligently not tested, might in his ignorance elect to become a surgeon (full qualification roughly age thirty) rather than a football player or pop star (in which professions one can flourish and gain fame and fortune in the late teens). How would an action for the loss of the chance of an appropriate

81   Phenylketonuria occurs in about one in 10,000 births. It occurs due to a defect in the gene for the enzyme phenylalanine hydroxylase, such that the normal metabolic pathway is blocked and a toxic ketone accumulates. It is treated by giving a diet low in phenylalanine. Since this amino acid is required for growth, the diet must be carefully formulated.

82   Huntington's disease, affecting about one in 20,000 people, is characterized by dementia, akinesia (inability to move in a coordinated manner) and rigidity, the onset being about 30 to 50 years of age.

148

career be decided? Would it make any difference if it could be shown that success in these fields was unlikely? In the cases wherein a solicitor has failed to act on instructions (and the result is loss of chance for a litigant) it has been held to be irrelevant that he might not have succeeded in court.[83] There are many interesting ramifications – for example, according to Lady Hale in *Gregg*, the claimant had adopted the wrong head of action. He might well have succeeded had this been based upon the extra pain and suffering he had experienced due to the late diagnosis. This might well be kept in mind for future claims.

Confidentiality

The medical aspect of the law of confidential information derives conceptually from the ' engineering' cases *Coco* v *A.N. Clark* (1968) and *Saltman Engineering* v *Campbell Engineering* (1963).[84] Its breach, unauthorised disclosure, was discussed above in connection with negligence and before that in respect of privacy (Chapter 3.3.) All bodies lending themselves to medical ethics and law, for example the delegates at the Oviedo Convention, have addressed confidentiality.[85] From the legal point of view it is important to note that most of these are merely declaratory, with no binding force. The appropriate binding language is to be found in the various domestic professional codes. Breach of these is usually followed by censure by the profession's governing body, and possibly deregistration as a practitioner, and of course if disclosure occurs negligently it generates a possible cause of action under that head.

More novel aspects of confidentiality relate to the creation of DNA databases. As has been written: 'Creation of biobanks (to obtain DNA) can give rise to a range of problems, which are not generally covered by regulations on research and experimentation in humans or by data protection legislation. The specimen is a medium carrying personal information… and should be granted at least the same protection in law as information relating to a patient's health.'[86]

---

83 *Spring v Guardian Assurance plc* [1995] 2 AC 296. Loss of chance has been addressed in a statistical manner by Evans, E. 'Lies, damn lies and the loss of chance' [2006] *Professional Negligence* vol 22, at p 99.
84 *Saltman Engineering v Campbell Engineering* [1963] 65 RPC 203 CA.
85 For a list of international declarations see Macklin, R ' Yet another guideline? The UNESCO draft declaration' [2005] *Jurimetrics* vol 5, at p 238.
86 Casabona, CMR. 'Genetics, tissue, and databases' [2004] *European Journal of Health Law* vol 11, at p 71.

Thus in respect of confidentiality nobody is prepared to put DNA sequences out with the mainstream of general medical information. The nascent UK Biobank with a proposed 500,000 donors of DNA will constitute an enormous bolus of genetic information, and equally, of controversy. (This database is not to be confused with the one held by the Home Office/Police, currently enrolling over three million 'members'.) Its whole existence will depend on how efficiently it practices anonymisation. This has its technical aspects. The personal identification information must be separated out from the data themselves and not in itself used. It must then be destroyed (this according to the Information Commissioner overseeing the Data Protection Act).[87] Moreover it can be operated at various levels. Some authorities advocate removal of name, address and full postcode; others suggest removal of the day or birth from the date, leaving only the month and year. Of course age has to be known for any medical conclusions from the research to be meaningful.

There is a further point on confidentiality, almost a footnote but very significant in the development of medical law, and that is the question of Gillick competence in respect of genetic tests.[88] The concept that a child of 16 can be given medical information if a doctor perceives he or she can understand its significance, without the knowledge of parents or guardians, presumably extends to the outcome of a DNA test, whether it relates both to genetic identity or genetic disease.

Consent

In medical law consent *simpliciter* usually refers to medical treatment and/ or investigation. If treatment or intervention is applied with no consent at all, this may well constitute the criminal offence of battery. The principle is enshrined in a much-venerated, much-cited statement by Judge Cardozo in a 1914 US case: 'Every human being of adult years and sound mind has a right to determine what shall be done with his own body; and a surgeon who performs an operation without his patient's consent commits an assault for which he is a liable in damages.'[89]

---

87 Goodman, C and Moore, G 'Personal genetic information, data protection and consent [2001/2002] *Bioscience Law Review* vol 3, at p 31.
88 *Gillick v West Norfolk and Wisbech Area Health Authority* [1985] 3 All ER 42 (HL).
89 *Schloendorf v Society of New York Hospital* 105 N.E. 92 (1914). This quotation hardly needs citation, since it appears in every book or article on medical ethics – incidentally the judge here used the word 'assault' interchangeably with 'battery', although the latter is more technically correct. Also he is here referring to the civil remedy of damages, not a criminal sanction.

However the extension of the legal concept of personal liberty to choose or refuse as applied to medical ethics does not appear to have become prominent until after the Nuremberg trials at the end of World War II, which revealed the horrendous experiments perpetrated on unwilling or unknowing subjects by Nazi doctors and the notorious Japanese Unit 371. As defendants the Nazis mounted the *tu quoque* (you also) defence (the Japanese were never held to account), that is they maintained that their experiments were no different in substance to many of those carried out routinely in the USA and Europe. This of course was an unacceptable argument, and as a result the Nuremberg Code was formulated by American physicians. It did not specifically use the phrase 'informed consent' which apparently appeared first in a judgement in the USA as late as 1957. The evolutionary process driving its incorporation into medical ethics culminated in the World Medical Association's Declaration of Helsinki of 1964, art 22 when it was realised that medical research had been neglected.[90]

> In any research on human beings, each potential subject must be adequately informed of its aims, methods, sources of funding, any possible conflicts of interest, institutional affiliations of the researcher, the anticipated benefits and potential risks of the study and the discomfort it may entail. The subject should be informed of the right to abstain from participation in the study or to withdraw consent to participate at any time without reprisal. After ensuring that the subject has understood the information, the physician should then obtain the subject's freely given informed consent, preferably in writing.

Onwards from this all-embracing provision, in itself without legal force, there have been efforts in most countries to educate organisers of clinical trials in so-called 'Good Clinical Practice' to the extent that trials will not be approved by ethical bodies unless the investigators have attended relevant courses which explore the nature of consent.

> It can be argued that well-informed donors have an absolute right to determine whether they will give tissue to benefit a recipient and that society (be it government, the courts, or professional bodies) has no right to obstruct an altruistic decision. If so, guidelines need only ensure that the donor receives all the information required to make a *well-informed decision* [my italics].. the donor must freely and willingly consent to the procedure having been given sufficient knowledge to make an informed decision.[91]

90   The Helsinki agreement, updated, is found on site <www.wma.net/e/policy/b3.htm>.
91   Neuberger, J and Price, D. 'Role of liver donation in the United Kingdom' [2003]

This alternative nomenclature, the 'well-informed decision' begs the question as to whether it is really possible to make participants in trials 'well informed' on the complexities of DNA and genetics, especially when the issues may relate to diseases which may or may not become manifest in the distant future and/or aimed at some vaguely-expressed beneficence to humankind in general. The values may not be easy to explain. The nature of consent of course is deemed to be especially important when the research is being conducted in developing countries, and the U.K. Nuffield Council on Bioethics among other bodies has turned its attention to this aspect.[92] It notes that inducements usually consist of money and/or healthcare for the families, but the point at which inducements become inappropriate is not always transparent. The greater the inducement, the more likely it is to be inappropriate, because it may cause an individual to devalue his or her concerns about the risks involved in a research project. And if a participant is ill and is promised medical treatment, the possibility of exploitation is all the greater. In addition, it seems inappropriate to test a new drug in a country wherein the study group will be too poor to afford it, should it be successful and come on the market. The report states that *inter alia* the concepts of harmfulness, proportionality and vulnerability should be addressed. This ethical body seeks to extend the concept of consent to a point not yet generally recognised. "The source of the investigational product may be culturally unacceptable." This can refer to anything from sponsorship by the widely detested tobacco companies, to the use of pork gelatine for capsules (anathema to Moslems), or the seeming exploitation of women.

Apart from that, many members of groups regard their genetic identity as belonging to that group (and the concept seems to be cherished equally by the Fraser clan in Scotland as the Wampanoag Nation in Massachusetts). If DNA sequences are to be divulged, consent is deemed to be the prerogative of the whole group, rather than of any individual within it. Problems of this nature were encountered by Human Gene Diversity Project (HGDP) (revisited in Chapter 6.4). It seemed a good idea to record the genomes of ethnic groups which were disappearing due to assimilation or destitution, by analogy with the efforts of linguistic anthropologists. But many of the tribes did not accept that viewpoint. It was reported that some of them: '... do not want their DNA used (even without their names attached) for research on race and intelligence, race and crime, or sex and mathematical ability,' because they think that the findings of the research might compromise, stigmatise,

---

British Medical Journal vol 327, at p 676; Mazur, DJ ' Influence of the law on risk and informed consent' [2003] *British Medical Journal* vol 327, at p 731.
92   <http://www.nuffieldbioethics.org>.

or stereotype the group.[93] It was not long before pressure groups such as the Indigenous Peoples Council on Biocolonialism made their appearance.

Any sanctions against exploitation of human biological material proceeds via domestic law at the moment, usually under the aegis of the commercial authorities – in some countries it is almost impossible to export any biological material at all. (Animal material is of course governed by CITES, see Chapter 6.1.) Obtaining permits in such countries as India and Sarawak are formidably difficult to obtain. Human DNA is yet another aspect of biodiversity and the possibility of patents based on it muddies the waters even further. In the 1990s the National Institutes of Health received a patent on cells from a male Hagahai (a man which contained a human T-lymphotrophic virus. The Hagahai were to have benefited from any spin-off from the patent, but it was forcibly pointed out that the nature of their consent to such a novel entity as to a patent was difficult to assess, assuming even that some form of consent had been offered.[94]

A few years ago nobody gave a thought to consent for the use of biological material, DNA included, considered to have been abandoned. Consider the 'blood test', for example. For analysis, normally 10 ml of blood is taken. This yields about 6 ml of serum and 4 ml of cells. The cells are normally not used for the routine testing of liver enzymes, glucose and the like. Why throw them away? They are a valuable resource, and associated with each specimen is information about the patient's age, sex, ethnic group (which can be inferred very often from the name) as well as provisional and/or final diagnosis. DNA can be prepared from the cells and used for research. The trouble is, that in each case the patient gave implied consent for the test but not for any subsequent research. However no scientist ever gave this potentially troubling glitch a moment's thought. It was all changed, in UK at least, by the Bristol and Alder Hey Hospital affairs. Pathologists therein were retaining rather large numbers of organs from deceased babies without the knowledge of the parents, who seem to have given consent for autopsy only, to determine the cause of death (and thus impliedly to advance medical knowledge). The reports on Bristol and Alder Hey protestations,[95] respectively the Kennedy and Redfern Reports, led to the Human Tissue Act

93   The HGDP website is <shg.Stanford.edu/hgdp>. See also Andrews, L and Neilkin D,. Whose body is it anyway? [1998] *Lancet* vol 351, at p 53.
94   The Rural Advancement Foundation International (US) on its website < www.cptech. org/ip/rafi.html> succinctly relates the history of this episode but it is of course written from a partisan point of view.
95   The Alder Hey Report Report can be found on <www.ricinquiry.org.uk> There is a good summary in <en.wikipedia.org.wiki/Alder_Hey_Children's_Hospital>.

(2004). This addresses 'appropriate' consent *ab initio*, in ss 2 and 3, and proceeds on to DNA in s 45. The aggrieved parents – and every thinking person respected their sense of outrage and loss – were seemingly howling for the blood of the pathologist who retained their infants' organs; the Crown Prosecution Service examined the possible issues of misconduct in a public office and dishonesty, but decided that there was not enough evidence for a successful prosecution. The equivalent furore in the US devolves upon the *John Moore* case, which was discussed in Chapter 2 (p 40) in connection with DNA as property.

The Human Tissue Act is especially concerned with consent as related to children. Of course parents can consent to medical intervention for their children, but what of the situation where there is no disease and the activities surrounding the sequencing of their DNA are merely speculative? It was announced in 2005 that 25,000 DNAs from newborns will be sampled at Bristol Children's Hospital by a researcher who says that their genomes can be examined to assess risk of diseases like heart attack or type II diabetes and that (presumably) avoidance measures can be adopted.[96] Presumably consent is sought for such projects, but can parents and guardians really allow it for the sequencing of their well children's genomes, the records of these to be kept in perpetuity for purposes which the later, grown, adults may not agree with? It has been pointed out that the babies cannot give their consent, and that as adults they may feel that their privacy has been violated.

The ancestry of consent constituted a legal framework, in the various Anatomy Acts, for example, which were the result of the body snatching activities of such luminaries as Burke and Hare.[97] There was a trend from law into medical ethics, as in the Nuremberg and Helsinki Declarations, but lately the law has largely again interposed. The Human Tissue Act is an eye-opener in that direction. Worldwide, the trend has been towards ever greater consultation of donors, DNA donors among them – in other words, ever greater restrictions on the researchers. In the eyes of many, the authorities in

---

96   This is fascinating 'sociomedicogenetic' territory. One would have to be very, very sure of one's ability to link DNA sequences to multifactorial diseases, possibly occurring half a century in the future, to advocate avoidance lifestyles for all those years. The argument deveolves on quality of life versus longevity.

97   Burke and Hare, of course, were the pair who disinterred the deceased in 18th century Edinburgh for sale to the anatomists; they could not be charged with stealing the dead bodies, for there was (and still is) no property in a dead body as such. The scandal lead to the Anatomy Act of 1832 and its successors, all to be repealed by the Human Tissue Act (2004).

UK have overreacted in the wake of the public outrage over the Alder Hey affair, but in any event it is clear that we have entered a new era.

Genetic testing kits

Testing for genetic disease, that is conditions both existing and predictable (as risk), has become big business in the sense that it is a vehicle for private enterprise rather than a component of coherent health services. Patenting aspects are considered in Chapter 4. The question here is whether private testing should be left unregulated. If regulated, should this operate by licence or by an outright ban? The former would represent yet one more extension of administrative law. The medical profession is in favour of the latter, assuming that it comes within the realm of the possible. This is not merely due to self interest, rather it springs from the conviction that the interpretation of any sort of medical test (even a serum cholesterol) is not safe without professional, interpretive, input.[98] The sentiment will become more acute when genuine self-testing, rather than the transmission of a sample to a commercial laboratory, becomes available (the so called 'home brew' scenario). Suffice to note that at the time of writing private genetic testing remains unregulated in most if not all countries.

Issues pending in respect of gene therapy

There is no doubt that gene therapy will one day be a successful technique for the cure of such conditions as diabetes, cardiac failure and a host of others. However for many years it will be expensive, outside the means of most sufferers, who will be dependent on either a prudent insurance policy or the national health services for the allocation of funds for the treatment. It is this last aspect which has the legal implications, and goes to the concept of 'distributive justice'. A well known argument between Rawls and Nozick revolved around this, but it is dealt with in detail in all jurisprudence texts. If a patient were to bring an action in judicial review following the failure of a health service to fund gene therapy the courts would have a number of precedents to draw on. Traditionally, however, it is clear that they have been reluctant to adjudicate on the allocation of scarce resources. This point has arisen recently in the context of the refusal of a health authority to pay for the drug herceptin, licenced by the European Medicines Agency for late breast cancer but not for early breast cancer. However it is habitually prescribed for

---

98   Hubbard, R and Lewontin, RC 'Pitfalls of genetic testing' [1996] *New England Journal of Medicine* vol 334, at p 1192; Burke, W 'Genetic Testing' [2002] *New England Journal of Medicine* vol 347, at p 1867.

the latter, since lack of a licence does not imply a prohibition. The relevant Trust declined to do so in Mrs Rogers' case and after judicial review the Court of Appeal in considering the matter came down in her favour, not because they were involving themselves in the allocation of resources, but because the Trust had been irrational in treating one patient rather than another. So it seems that the principle still holds.[99]

Summary of 3.4

- The normal rules of the tort of negligence apply to the examination of DNA for the diagnosis of inherited diseases.

- Negligent chromosomal and presumably then DNA testing can give rise to 'wrongful life' actions.

- The beneficence or otherwise of disclosure of the genetic information of an individual to relatives who might be put on alert presents an unresolved ethical and legal problem.

- The success of loss of chance with respect to genetic defects will depend upon the severity of the condition and its treatability.

- Confidentiality with respect to DNA banks is creating a problem, for in contrast to biobanks complied for criminal investigation, research based banks will have to practice anonymisation in conjunction with a written consent form.

- The meaning of consent is nebulous, especially in respect of DNA harvesting from groups who are not sophisticated, and see their genetic heritage as belonging to the whole group.

- In UK the issue of consent has been legislated by the Human Tissue Act is (2004).

- Genetic testing kits in their private aspect are unregulated.

- The justiciability of scarce resources may reenter the arena when gene therapy becomes general.

---

99   *R on the application of Ann Marie Rogers v Swindon NHS Primary Care Trust* [2006] EWCA Civ 392. For a commentary see Foster, C 'Buying Life: the herceptin case in the Court of Appeal' [2006] *Solicitors' Journal* vol 150, at p 558. For an earlier statement of the principle see *R v Cambridge Health Authority ex p B* [1995] 1 WLR 898.

3.5 Genetics, Insurance, and Employment

What insurers and employers have in common is taking a risk; in the context of occult genetic defects, for the former it is the risk of having to make a premature pay-out, and for the latter, it is that a carefully nurtured employee will turn out to have a greatly diminished period of utility to the corporation. The employment scenario is often discussed as an aspect of privacy, and in respect of both the bugbear of discrimination is readily applied. Any taint of discrimination is sharpened by the fact that certain debilitating diseases are clustered in specific ethnic groups, sickle cell anaemia in blacks for example. However one should not cast blanket aspersions on employers doing DNA testing without considering that it might be to a potential or existing employee's advantage – for example it might reveal a candidate's susceptibility to carcinogenic or allergenic chemicals used in the plant. In no quarters except their own, however, do DNA-fixated insurers attract a good press.

Insurance aspects

Presumably insurance companies wish to do genetic testing, not to detect the uninsurable, but to justify the imposition of high premiums. So, one of the many intrusions of DNA into the modern world has been its role in the actuarial assessment of future disease and/or (premature) death. Insurers like to argue that genetic data are no different from other information routinely requested when someone applies for cover and used to assess risk.[100] They point out that generally a life insurance policy is taken out voluntarily, and essentially is like any other contract, you can take it or leave it if you do not like the conditions attached to it. This sentiment however only relates to individually life purchased insurance. Especially in the US, employment group insurance schemes are usually compulsory. And there is another view of insurance, that it is a component of social justice, in which case everybody should have the right to obtain cover. In this, the 'solidarity' model, all the insured share costs across the range of risk, with the exception of certain modifiers, like smokers and the obese.

> Essentially it is argued that the essence of insurance is to spread risks of certain illnesses and diseases throughout society and not to burden those who bear the exclusive risk with its full costs. This social policy should seem to prevent precisely that type of rate setting data [genome analysis] from being used. This type of law is quite distinguishable from the legally permissible policy of raising rates for

---

100   Pokorski, RJ 'A test for the insurance industry' [1995] *Nature* vol 391 at p 135.

those who engage in voluntary pleasurable activities that increase the risk of illness, such as smoking.[101]

The tension is between those in the insurance industry who would like to perform genetic tests on all applicants and adjust premiums individually, and the consumers who see this as outright discriminatory. Countries with legislation limiting access to genetic information by insurers include Norway, Slovakia, Switzerland, Belgium, Austria, France, Denmark, Estonia, Georgia, Israel and Luxemburg (the US is not in the table) so it seems that in many European countries insurance is seen as a basic socioeconomic right, not a privilege.[102] And at the international level this view is taken in the Oviedo Convention. It would appear that art 12 (predictive genetic tests) applies to insurance (and employment) in stating that such tests may be performed 'only for health purposes.'

In UK there is little concern with group health insurance, more with mortgage-linked schemes, for it does not seem right to many that somebody would be rendered unable to buy a house due to a genetic defect. As elsewhere, too, there is a feeling that individuals who might benefit from predictive genetic test would refrain from undergoing them if they were necessarily disclose to insurers under the *uberimae fides* provisions of the contract, that is the obligation to disclose any fact which might possibly be relevant to the risk. At present however there is a moratorium on genetic testing as the result of an agreement between the government and the Association of British Insurers. Originally it was to expire on Oct 2006, but has been extended for another five years. There are exceptions for very large cover, in that the industry is concerned that individuals who have had genetic tests predicting early death or illness will not reveal these while at the same time taking out very large policies (called 'adverse selection'). Since 2000 there has also been an exception for individuals with the defect for Huntington's disease, but only if cover of more than £300,000 is sought. The Association is said to be anxious to make an exception also for individuals with mutations in the BRCA1 gene. About 5% of breast cancers are a result of such mutations, and 70% of the women who develop breast cancer as a result will die prematurely. That is 30% will not, and medical opinion is that we should be directing our energies to discovering what protects the 30%.[103] Exceptions are only granted after discussion with the Genetics and Insurance

---

101   Broyde, M 'Insurance risks' [1992] *Nature* vol 364, at p 665.
102   Knoppers, BM Godard, B et al 'A comparative international overview' *Genetics and Life Insurance*. (MIT Press, 2004).
103   Wall, W. *Genetics and DNA Technology: Legal Aspects* (Cavendish Publishing, 2001) p 121.

Committee (GAIC), a governmental body set up in 1999 to monitor events in this area.[104] Interestingly, it has recently been realised that negative results of genetic tests can be taken into account. Thus if an applicant for insurance whose family has a history of breast cancer turns out to have the normal BRCA1 gene, then she may be offered some sort of discount in premiums.

Many but not all states in the US have enacted provisions to prevent insurers discriminating against genetic defects. In the US, with no universal health service, health insurance is as important as life insurance. The (federal) Health Insurance Portability and Accountability Act (1997) provides that when a worker leaves a job in which he was participating in a group health plan, he could not be denied the same protection in a new job because of some genetic defect.[105]

There are however ominous signs pointing to the future – a German company has a patent pending for an opioid receptor which it is claimed will allow the detection of predisposition to addictive disease, especially to cocaine – how could that affect both insurance and job prospects? The University of California already has a US patent on a dopamine receptor, which may be material in detecting susceptibility to alcohol dependency. The insurance companies presumably retain officers to track these developments with close attention, and those of us with some inherent or inherited weakness must beware (that is, most of us). Will there be any bulwarks against the inequalities of private health insurance systems, which raise the spectre of a 'genetic superclass' of the well and insurable, and an underclass of the unwell and uninsurable, when the moratoria expire?[106] As has been pointed out, the decision will be a politico-social one: 'If on the other hand the costs of insuring those with genetic defects is proposed to be passed to the 'normal' population, it is a matter for Parliament to decide; ultimately,

---

104 The GAIC website is < File:///A:/The%Genetics%20and%20Insurance%20 Committee.htm> See also Jackson, E *Medical Law: Text, Cases and Material* (Oxford UP, 2005) p 359.

105 Hunter, JR 'A consumer approach', in: Rothenstein, MA *Genetics and Life Insurance* (MIT Press, 2004) p 212. An informative consumer pressure group's website is < http://geneticalliance.org> See generally the site of the American Academy of Actuaries at <www.actuary.org.pdf.health/geneticmono.pdf> The document states that any ban on genetic testing before insurance is issued would have greater impact as the accuracy of the test improves. The word 'accuracy' is not helpful. Presumably what is meant is predictive value, that is the ratio (true positives) / (true positives + false positives).

106 Aldhous, P 'Victims of genetic discrimination speak up' *New Scientist* 5th Nov 2005, p 7.

we cannot escape from the fact that insurance, like most social contracts, is a cultural phenomenon.'[107]

One other DNA-linked scenario which may turn up more frequently in the future is the insurance fraud. In 1987 in Singapore one Morganarubin faked his brother Gandarudin's death and claimed insurance. His sister in law went back to Ceylon, met up with Gandarudin, 'remarried' him and had a child. In 1996 the child's DNA along with the date on his birth certificate proved that Gandarudin had not died at the time claimed.

Employment aspects

An article some years ago in the science magazine *Nature* puts the perspective rather well:

Imagine four potential cases of genetic disablement. (1) When a haemophiliac wants to become a butcher it makes sense to discourage him. (2) When a colour- blind man wants to become a truck driver, he fails at a colour test: his DNA does not need to be tested. (3) When a healthy young man asks for employment and his employer wants to know whether his genotype indicates that he may die in his forties from Huntington's disease, this is unfair. (4) When a healthy black person seeks employment and is tested for the sickle cell anaemia gene, then is refused employment because there may be a risk under certain conditions, this is unfair.[108]

It has to be asked, then: is there a legislative framework to balance an employer's economic interests with the autonomy of the employee ?[109] In UK unfair dismissal due to some genetic weakness might be remedied by the Employment Rights Act (1996) s 98. To be covered of course one has to be in employment already – any such provision is void for job applicants. If the genetic defect happens to be ethnically segregated (like sickle cell anaemia) or sex chromosome-linked then presumably the Race Relations Act (1976) and the Sex Discrimination Act (1975) respectively might apply. The latter, by s 1 states: 'A person discriminates against a woman if...... he applies to her a requirement which applies .... equally to a man but .... which is to her detriment because she cannot comply with it.' Clearly this will apply to an advertisement which states that: 'The position is open to all regardless of

107   Mason, JK, McCall-Smith, A et al *Medical Law* (Butterworths, 2003) p 220.

108   Muller-Hill, B 'The shadow of genetic injustice' [1993] *Nature* vol 362, at p 491.

109   These are the words of Gannon, P and Villiers, C 'Genetic testing and employee protection' [1999] *Medical Law International* vol 4, at p 39. They provide a very thorough discussion of the topic as applied to UK.

age or sex, but the person selected must have a toothbrush moustache.' It is less easy to envisage genetic scenarios. If the advertisement were to read: ' The position is open to any person who can demonstrate the absence of a mutation in the BRCA1 gene' it would not discriminate against most women, only a substantial portion thereof, but one would suppose that the courts would take a dim view of it, and invoke proportionality principles.

The Disability Discrimination Act (1995) s 1 may be more relevant in that it refers to a disability as 'a physical or mental impairment which has a substantial or long term adverse effect on his ability to carry out day to day activities.' Presumably this would apply to inherited conditions such as sickle cell anaemia with its recurrent crises but not to occult genetic defects which have a delayed effect on the phenotype, like a mutation in the BRCA1 gene. In the absence of imminent legislation to address this point, the Nuffield Council on Bioethics[110] and the House of Commons Science and Technology Committee[111] both recommend that a genetic test should only be taken into account when there is clear evidence of a link between the working environment and the diseases or condition that the test seeks to investigate. In other words, the thrust must be to health of the employee. This is once again the sentiment of art 12 of the Oviedo Convention.

In US the Civil Rights Act (1964) is said to cover discrimination in general but the Americans with Disabilities Act (1995) is presumably more proximate in that while it formerly only protected against employment discrimination on the basis of traditional disability, it was extended to protect those with genetic impairment.[112]There is one keynote case which may relate to it. In *Bragdon* v *Abbott* the Supreme Court held that a man with asymptomatic HIV infection is covered as disabled under the Act.[113] The supposition is that genetic defects not yet leading to a set of symptoms would be sheltered under the same umbrella.

---

110   *Genetic Screening Ethical Issues*. Nuffield Council on Bioethics (1993) p 90.
111   *Human Genetics: the Science and its Consequences*. House of Commons Science and Technology Committee, Session 1994 – 95, vol 1, para 225.
112   Miller, P ' Analyzing genetic discrimination in the workplace' *Human Genome News* vol 12, February, 2003 (this from the Commissioner of the Equal Employment Opportunity Commission). See also Silvers, A and Ashley, MA ' Human rights and genetic discrimination: protecting genomic's promise for public health ' [2003] *Journal of Law, Medicine and Ethics* vol 31, at p 337. This article discusses the case of Terri Sergeant, who had α 1-antitrypsin deficiency (an inherited condition). She was dismissed from her job on this account, although she was asymptomatic. She was awarded compensation by the Equal Employment Opportunity Commission.
113   *Bragdon v Abott* [1998] 524 US 624.

Thus, in respect to the matters at hand, the legal situation is fluid. Older statutes can be interpreted to safeguard workers with inherited diseases, but there is still little or no case law as a guide.

Summary of 3.5

- Use of information on genetic defects by insurers and employers goes to discrimination law generally.

- Occult genetic defects are perceived as adding to their risks and as the science progresses, there will be proportionately more pressure to take them into account.

- Opinion is very much against an insurer using genetic information to adjust premiums – statutorily in the US and by means of a moratorium in UK.

- But exceptions are pressing, and Huntington's disease is already exempted in UK.

- Probing of employees' DNA is seen in all quarters as an invasion of privacy unless it goes to health and safety on the job.

Chapter 4

Intellectual Property

4.1 Intellectual Property and DNA

The main component of intellectual property law as related to molecular biology is, of course, the patent, usually described as a type of intangible personal property. All the elements of a successful patent, namely the familiar triad of novelty, inventive step (its antonym being 'obviousness') and industrial application, have been considered by the courts in relation to molecular biology. (See Box 4-1). Equally important has been the role of the 'hypothetical skilled artisan', who is no horny-handed artificer, rather a notional PhD from one of the major universities, and who has the honour of joining the corpus of fictional legal persons, like the officious bystander, the person of ordinary fortitude and, the paragon of them all, the man on the Clapham omnibus. Of the previous triad, the last has possibly been the least contentious - almost any genuine advance in DNA and protein technology is potentially useful. Most of the keynote cases derive from the US, whose scientists developed modern molecular biology techniques and which in any case retains the largest quantum of activity in the field, possibly contributed to by the fact that the US patent Office (USPTO) appears to be preternaturally generous to applicants. Patenting is largely (if not entirely) related to commercialisation, and worldwide there has been a creeping commercialisation in universities, unknown in the heyday of Crick and Watson, which has impelled them to ever more assiduous protection of the fruits of their research. For commercial companies of course patenting has always been of the essence. Overall, then, this has lead to a burgeoning of cases in which counsel must have some familiarity with nucleic acids and proteins. In a sense molecular biology has 'come home' to intellectual property law, experts on which have consistently noted, within it, judicial admiration for the entrepreneur and respect for the watertight contract. At any rate, as we shall see, it is the view of many that genetic information is over-protected by legal systems, entirely to the advantage of the commercial sector.

In addition to patenting, some aspects of confidential information are relevant to molecular biology. It has been considered under the general heading of privacy in Chapter 3. Obviously, confidential information has always been a tradable commodity, throughout the ages - hence the value of spies, variously military, industrial, and matrimonial. New ways are constantly found to protect it. In the US in 2001 a grand jury indicted a Japanese national under counts variously of conspiracy to violate the Economic Espionage Act,

---

Box 4-1 Conceptual Matrix for Assessing Molecular Biology Patents

Enabling	*Challenging*
Novelty	Already in the public domain (except for some scientific exposure)
Inventive step	Obvious to the scientific community (persons 'skilled in the art')
Precise claims	Overbroad claims
Utility	No defined application (or merely idea or discovery)

1996, stealing trade secrets and interstate transportation of stolen property. The suspect, while a supervisor in the Cleveland Clinic Foundation, Ohio, was said to have purloined DNA useful in the investigation of Alzheimer's dementia, in order at some later date to transfer it to a Japanese laboratory which would benefit commercially from it. One Hiroaki Serizawa was later sentenced to probation, community service and a small fine for lying to the FBI, but the economic espionage charges were dropped. He was the first person to be charged under the Act, designed to penalise the selling of trade secrets to foreign governments, but it is salutary that this novelty involved DNA.

In the ordinary way, information as a commodifiable entity must carry with it a degree of exclusivity - if everybody knows it, it loses its value. Patenting restores the value - it is in a sense complementary to confidential information since it demolishes any worries about spies and other leakage of sensitive information.

A further point harks back to criminal law – if I am arrested and the police take my DNA for sequencing, and put the sequence in their database, is it protected as their confidential information? Although the DNA is mine, it would seem so. Logically, I have not possessed the sequence information in the first place. (In any case, the law of confidential information - common law – has been largely superseded by statute in its criminal aspects, see Chapter 2.) Criminal matters aside, if I happen to know the sequence of my genome, wholly or partially, and keep that information under circumstances which imports confidentiality, then it is no doubt protected under the law.

Passing off is at most marginally relevant. It might find an application in the area of plagiarism and its elder brother, publishing fraud, but these are not areas peculiar to molecular biology.

The other important arm of intellectual property law, of course, is copyright. The essential principle of copyright is that it protects expression in a material form. Long printed sequence of bases can be copied as easily as anything else. If such sequences from a scientific paper are copied such as to constitute 'substantial taking', along the lines laid down (at least in English law) in *Hubbard* v *Vosper* (1972),[1] obviously this constitutes a breach of copyright (unless the copying falls under the "course of instruction" exception – Section 32, Copyright, Designs and Patents Act, 1988). It is equally obvious that one cannot copyright one's genome *per se*. Plainly, having a sequence of bases in the DNA in my cells in no way constitutes a mode of expression. The same precept would seem to apply to segments of DNA, whether haplotypes or VNTRs/STRs.[2] (With the advent of home-based sequencing kits, which will inevitably appear at some stage, the operator will be able to capture his own genome either as a print-out or a screen display, or both, would presumably attract copyright. (Section 3 of the 1988 UK Copyright, Designs and Patents Act and the equivalent in other jurisdictions cover the screen display and storage in the computer.)

Bizarrely, some parties have been trying to use copyright to overcome difficulties in patent protection. It seems that gene sequences, whether man-made or natural, can be encoded as 'music' in MP3 files and then copyrighted!

---

1   *Hubbard v Vosper* [1972] QB 84. As a further complication, a DNA database may be an amalgam of other databases, namely a compilation. Such are generally protected by copyright after *Ladbroke (Football) Ltd v Wm Hill (Football) Ltd* (1964) WLB 273, wherein Lord Devlin said that 'There is copyright in every original literary work which by definition includes compilations. The product must originate from the author in the sense that it is the result of a substantial degree of skill, industry or experience.' Compliers of DNA databases will no doubt strongly claim these attributes. In US the keynote case is *Feist Publications Inc. v Rural Telephone Service Co Inc.* [1991] 111 USC 1282.

2   Copyright in relation to DNA is discussed in great detail by Harris, RK and Rosenfield, SS 'Copyright protection for genetic databases' [2005] *Jurimetrics* vol 45, at p 225; also Madhavan, M. 'Copyright versus database right of protection in U.K: the bioinformatics bone of contention' [2006] *Journal of World Intellectual Property* [2006] vol 9, at p 61; Cate, FH ' The commodification of information and the control of expression' [2002] *Amicus Curiae* vol 43, at p 3.

4.2 Patenting Genes

Patent law devolves on the same principles of precedence and analogy as other branches of law, but has presented its own difficulties.

Although patent law operates at the frontiers of technology, like all fields of law it resolves new controversies by looking to how similar issues have been resolved in the past. In theory, this approach should make the applicable legal rules stable and predictable. In practice, however, it can yield surprising outcomes that contradict the intuitions of researchers who work in rapidly changing fields.[3]

In other words, common law principles run up against novel problems. The intuition of researchers -"pure" researchers, moreover, is often to decry the importation of patent law in the first place. Drs Bruce Alberts and Aaron Klug, then respectively Presidents of the US National Academy of Sciences and of the Royal Society of London, wrote an article to *Nature* in which they stated that: 'The intention of some university and commercial interests to patent the DNA sequences themselves, thereby staking claim to large numbers of human genes without necessarily having a full understanding of their functioning, strikes us as contrary to the essence of patent law.'[4]
Such views are not popular within biotechnology corporations and university technology transfer offices, nor with entrepreneurial scientists and (most of all) patent attorneys. All of these regard the arguments for patenting genes sequences, and indeed fragments of gene sequences, as unassailable.

Gene patents in the US

Some exceptions having been met, it appears that in the words of the Supreme Court in the oft-quoted case of *Diamond v Chakrabarty* (1980) '… anything under the sun made by man….' is patentable.[5] Thus the system in the US can be said to be particularly enabling, at least traditionally, in contrast to

---

3   Eisenberg, RS. 'Structure and function in gene patenting' [1997] *Nature Genetics* vol 15, at p 125.
4   Alberts, B. and Klug, A 'The human genome itself must be feely available to all human kind' [2000] *Nature* vol 404, at p 325.
5   *Diamond v Chakrabarty* [1980] 447 SC 303. This patent is cited so frequently in any discussion of biotechnology patents that it is ironic that the invention, the modified bacterium for disposing of oil slicks, did not in the end work. An up to date and extended discussion of the US enablements is to be found in Safrin,S 'Hyperownership in a time of biotechnological promise: the international conflict to control the building blocks of life' [2004] *American Journal of International Law* vol 98, at p 641.

the position in Europe, in which the patent offices and the courts have had to contend with ethical issues:

> Although similar [ethical] arguments have been raised in the US in the absence of an applicable statutory exclusion from patent protection, the burden of inertia has rested on those who oppose such patents rather than on those who seek them. The US courts have accordingly confronted certain doctrinal questions regarding such matters as the patenting of DNA sequences before their counterparts in other countries.[6]

The enabling language in the USA is usually quoted as 35 United States Code (USC) 101 (Patent Act 1970) which states: 'Whoever invents or discovers any new and useful process, machine, manufacture, or composition of matter, or any new and useful improvement thereof, may obtain a patent therefore subject to the conditions and requirements of this title.'

In respect of DNA this has been amplified by the Director, Biotechnology Examination, Technology Center of the USPTO, whose language is distinctly uncompromising:

> Without the incentive of patents, there would be less investment in DNA research, and scientists might not disclose their new DNA products to the public. Issuance of patents to such products not only results in the dissemination of technological information to the scientific community for use as a basis for future research, but also stimulates investment in research, development, and the commercialisation of new biologics. It is only with the patenting of DNA technology that some companies, particularly small ones, can raise sufficient venture capital to bring beneficial products to the marketplace or fund further research. A strong US patent system is critical for the continued development and dissemination to the public of information on DNA sequence elements.[7]

(One can here recognise the argument repeatedly used by the pharmaceutical companies ['Big Pharma'] to protect their innovations in medication – if they cannot patent drugs they do not have funds to develop new ones.) It is noteworthy that the Director uses the word 'products' several times, that is, he does not for one moment entertain the idea that DNA sequences, as elucidated, might be in essence products of nature. Turning again to Dr Chakrabarty, this microbiologist was originally refused a patent in that the

---

6   See note 3 above.
7   Doll, JJ 'The patenting of DNA' [1998] *Science* vol 280, at p 689.

relevant bacterium was a product of nature, such remaining unpatentable in the US as well as in most other jurisdictions at that time. But when the case went to the Supreme Court it was pointed out that *Pseudomonas cepacia,* with the capacity to digest oil slicks (technically, 'dissimulating environmentally persistent chemical compounds'), was extensively modified by man and thus an article of manufacture, within the act. Thus it is clear that even in the USA, in its natural form as an informational array of bases, the gene remains unpatentable. But the cynicism engendered the persistent efforts of the biotechnology companies has provoked more than one wry comment, viz: 'Human gene sequences, in their natural state, cannot be patented: this is true in all patent systems. However, in real terms, this statement has not been regarded as a fundamental barrier derived from the justifications for the patent grant, but rather as an inconvenience to be overcome.'[8]

This thought can be kept in mind during the evaluation of cases involving genetic material and proteins. It is clear though, that if the barriers have been overcome, they have been overcome most successfully in the US. That is not to say that there was no opposition there, but it was stoutly resisted by the USPTO on strictly statutory grounds. The present attitude of the USPTO (which can be read in conjunction with the remarks of the Director above) is summarized as: 'An excised gene is eligible for a patent as a composition of matter or as an article of manufacture because that DNA molecule does not occur in that isolated form in nature' and 'Synthetic DNA preparations are eligible for patents because their purified state is different from the naturally occurring compound.'[9]

But the USPTO rejected a 1997 patent application by Dr Newman of New York Medical College for a human-animal chimera. His real intention was either to obtain the grant and then not use it (and of course others would have been so prevented in the absence of a licence from him), or to have such an entity declared non-patentable. The USPTO invoked the 13th (anti-slavery) constitutional amendment.[10] The question remains: when is something 'too human' to be patented?

One topic of note in relation to biotechnology patents in the US is the 'doctrine of equivalents.' described as an equitable doctrine designed to

---

8   Foster, C 'Current issues in the law of genetics' [2003] *New Law Journal* vol 29, at p 76.
9   'Utility Examination Guidelines' [2001] *Federal Register* vol 66, at p 1092; the difference between the US and European enablement policy is discussed by Roberts, T 'Examples of disputed patent claims' [2005/2006] *Bioscience Law Review* vol 5 at p 75.
10   Anon. [2005] *Biotechnology Law Reports* vol 24, at p 290.

prevent somebody copying a patented invention while at the same time avoiding the literal meaning of the claims in the patent copied. The court will look at the way the potentially infringing claim is worded and try to discern whether it is in fact equivalent to the one granted, despite its language. The test is applied to each individual claim, not to the invention as a whole; this was established by the Supreme Court in *Warner Jenkinson* v *Hulton Davis Chemical Company* (1997). Some have discerned a UK version as enunciated in *Clark v Adie* (1873) - a patent would be infringed were it to be copied by taking its 'pith and marrow' without violating its language.[11]

A much-discussed decision in the context of the doctrine of equivalents is *Festo Corp v Shoketsu Kinzoku Kogyo Kabushiki Co* (2000) (an engineering case) on remand from the Supreme Court to the Court of Appeals of the Federal Circuit (CAFC), a specialist court hearing patent cases on appeal. It involved a staggering 27 amicus curiae briefs, indicating its importance, and it restricted the scope of the doctrine of equivalents.[12] Thus, where an application has a claim rejected, and then makes an amendment to render it more suitable, the amended item in the claim is not entitled to enter into the doctrine of equivalence. Thereupon the principle of 'prosecution history estoppel' applies. ('Prosecution' in this sense is the shepherding of an application through the patent office; 'prosecution history' is the file of the correspondence between the applicant and the office.) *Festo* was estopped from amending the application purely to meet the provisions of the Patent Act. In the US courts there is also the concept of 'file wrapper estoppel'. (The files of published patents are referred to a 'file wrappers'.) In effect, the patentee cannot tell the USPTO one thing then tell the court, during infringement proceedings, something else.

Festo was followed by the *Enzo* (2002) case[13] which was firmly biotechnological in nature. It was a claim for a probe to detect the gonorrhoea bacterium *Neisseria gonorrhoeae*. Previous probes had tended to hybridise to other bacterial species, that is, produce false positives during the diagnostic process. The patent had been challenged by as many as six biotechnology companies for failure to meet the statutory written description

11 The citation of the old *Clark v Adie* case is [1873] LR 10. Ch 667 but it is mentioned in all the intellectual property texts.
12 234 F.3d 56 (Fed.Cir.2000); cert granted [2001] 533 U.S. 915 Among the many commentaries see Anon. 'Patent Litigation: Massachusetts court examines Amgen-Transkaryotic dispute in light of most recent Festo decision' [2004] *Biotechnology Law Report* vol 23, at p 59. There were three Festo cases in all. The prodromal case is *Warne-Jenkinson Co v Hilton Davis Chemical Co* [1997] 520 US 17, 40.
13 For example *Biogen v Madera*, discussed below.

requirement under s 112, 35 USC (1975). The application did not include the sequences of the DNA probes, but three DNA segments were deposited with the American Type Culture Collection (ATCC), a public depository for biological specimens. (This is one of many deposit authorities which will hold stocks to validate patent claims – ATCC is particularly comprehensive however in holding algae, animal viruses, animal cell cultures, pathogenic/ non-pathogenic bacteria, bacteriophages, embryos, eukaryotic DNA, pathogenic/non-pathogenic fungi, human cell cultures, hybridomas, moulds, mycoplasmas, oncogenes, plant cell cultures, plant viruses, RNA, seeds, and yeasts. In UK there is a the European Collection of Cell Cultures, and in Japan the International Patent Organism Depository.) In its initial decision the CAFC affirmed the invalidity of the patent, in that as genetic material, the claimed substances required description of structure, formulae, chemical name, or physical properties. Ability to bind somewhere, a functional description, was not a chemical property and so inadequate. On petition for a rehearing however, the court reversed its opinion, and instructed the District Court to determine whether a person of skill in the art would be able, on the basis of both the written description and the DNA sample deposits, to 'demonstrate possession of the generic scope of the claims.' In other words, the matter had to go back to the court of first instance on a determination of fact. Thus '*Enzo II*' held that making a biological deposit of the invention may be used to demonstrate possession but the accession number of the deposit must be recited in the specification. There has been bitter criticism of this decision in that it may create a special law for biotechnology, rather than regarding patent law as unitarily applying to all technology.

Gene patents in Europe

In Europe, on the other hand, the student of patent law has to contend not only with the 1973 European Patent Convention (EPC) and the European Patent Office (EPO), plus national patent offices, and the European Union (EU) itself. Of course the EPO is merely a facilitating organisation offering a centralising procedure for the granting of patents in contracting members, but having no role in enforcement. A party, though, can still seek protection through national patent systems. It is also possible to oppose a patent grant in the EPO, (within nine months of the application) but once granted, revocation can only be accomplished in a national court. It is possible for a patent to be pending in the EPO while undergoing revocation proceedings in the UK, for example. Moreover, national decisions are not subject to reversal or scrutiny at any international level. Thus, a decision of the House of Lords is final for the UK.[14]

It is art 23 (d) of the EPC which is relevant to molecular biology, since it sets out that which is not patentable - namely processes for cloning human beings, for changing the genetic identity of human beings, using embryos as a tradable commodity, and changing animal genomes in such a manner as to cause undue suffering.

The EU issued a directive 98/44/EC on the protection of biotechnological inventions in 1998. It derived from the European Commission, which is the executive arm of the EU. National courts in Europe considering a national genomic patent are bound by the Biotechnology Directive as community law. To begin with art 3 (1), this states:

1. For the purposes of this directive, inventions which are new, which involve an inventive step, and which are susceptible to industrial application shall be patentable even if they concern a product consisting of or containing biological material or a process by means of which biological material is produced, processed, or used.

2. Biological material which is isolated from the natural environment or produced by means of a technical process may be the subject of an invention even if it previously occurred in nature.

This merely holds that biological material (which is defined as any material containing genetic information and is capable of reproducing itself) shall be subject to the same rules as other materials for which patent protection is sought. Generally-held opinion is that the stance does not differ materially from that of the USPTO.

Art 5(1) restates the anti-slavery point in that the human body and its elements, including genes, cannot be patented. But 5(2) reduces the scope of 5(1) in stating: 'An element isolated from the human body or otherwise produced by means of a technical process, including the sequence or partial sequence of a gene, may constitute an invention, even if the structure of that element is identical to that of a natural element.'

---

14 *Enzo Biochem Inc v Gen-Probe Inc* [2002] 296 F. 3d 1316; 63 U.S.P.Q. 2nd 1609 (Fed. Cir.). There is a verbatim report in *Biotechnology Law Review* vol 21, at p 277 (2002). See also Gibson, H 'In the wake of Enzo: the impact of the Federal Circuit's Decision on the US life science industry.' [2004] *San Diego Law Review* vol 41, at p 903; Lathrop, BK and,Bent, SA 'Enzo and "hybridisation" claims: will the Federal Circuit meet Watson and Crick half way? ' [2002] *Biotechnology Law Report* vol 21, at p 333.

Provisions contained in art 6 of the EU Biotechnology Directive illuminate perhaps the most significant difference between European practice and US practice (although it must be stated at this point that many commentators feel that the difference between Europe and the USA is becoming smaller).[15] This article states:

1. Inventions shall be considered unpatentable where their commercial exploitation would be contrary to ordre publique [this is an echo of art 53 (a) of the EPC] or morality; however exploitation shall not be deemed to be so contrary merely because it is prohibited by law or regulation.

2. On the basis of paragraph 1, the following, in particular, shall be considered unpatentable:

- processes for cloning human beings

- processes for modifying the germ line genetic identity of human beings;

- uses of human embryos for industrial and commercial purposes;

- processes for modifying the genetic identity of animals which are likely to cause them suffering without any substantial medical benefit to man or animal, and also animals resulting from such processes.

The EU directive was adopted by the EPO in 1999. The latter's art 23c states: 'Biological material isolated from their environment, even if known in nature (is patentable). This particularly applies to genes that are isolated from their natural environment by means of technical processes and made available for industrial production.' Informed opinion is that this clarifies the sense of EPC art 53(b) which states: 'European patents shall not be granted for plant or animal varieties or essentially biological processes for the production of plants or animals; this provision does not apply to microbiological processes or the products thereof.'

---

15   Herdegen, M. 'Patenting human genes and other parts of the human body under EU biotechnology directive' [2001] *Bioscience Law Review* vol 3, at p 102; Dunleavey, K and Vinnola, M 'A comparative review of the patenting of biotechnological inventions in the United States and Europe'. [2001] *Journal of World Intellectual Property* vol 3, at p 65. Aerts, R.J. 'The industrial applicability and utility requirements for the patenting of genomic inventions: a comparison between European and US law' [2004] *European Intellectual Property Review* vol 8 at p 349.

The EU released its second report on the implementation of the directive recently (2005) and notes that the provisions have been transposed into national law in 21 member states. The Directive was a compromise and not all states are happy with it, to the extent that non-implementation has led to proceedings being initiated against them in the European Court. France for one has banned the patenting of human gene sequences across the board. In the new Protocol to the directive, published in 2000, art 69 states: 'For the purpose of determining the extent of protection conferred by a European patent, due account shall be taken of any element which is an equivalent to an element specified in the claims. '

This seems entirely analagous to the US doctrine of equivalents and was considered by the House of Lords in *Amgen v Transkaryotic Therapies* (below). Greece being the 15th state to ratify the Protocol, the latest date on which it had to come into force was 15th Dec, 2007. Sixteen contracting states (as at March 2006), including France and Germany, had not ratified it, but are bound to do so before that date. In the UK the Patents Act of 2004 was framed to bring UK law into line with the Protocol.

International treaties

Worldwide, however, all of this is potentially upstaged by the Trade Related Aspects of Intellectual Property Protection (TRIPs) (1994) as an arm of the of the World Trade Organisation (WTO). Nonetheless, this by no means lays down a multinational patents system. Patents must still be granted in each country, in which protection is sought, in an individual application for each. (The 1970 Patent Cooperation Treaty [PCT] also in no way supersedes domestic law but facilitates a streamlined procedure whereby patents in many countries may be acquired by filing a single application in a number of designated patent offices.)

TRIPS under its art 27 attempts, as explicitly as possible, to foster the Chakrabarty-type 'everything manmade underneath the sun' philosophy. The enablements it pertains to were hotly debated, in that many countries hitherto recognised little or no protection for computer programmes, integrated circuits, plant varieties, pharmaceuticals and life forms, and foresaw the payment of heavy licence fees as all these became progressively and perhaps exclusively patented by the more technologically advanced nations. Indeed some of these latter wished to see no restrictions whatsoever. Naturally, some sort of compromise was eventually reached. Art 27 states:

Subject to the provisions of paragraphs 2 and 3, patents shall be available for any inventions, whether products or processes, in *all fields of technology*, provided they are new, involve an inventive step, and are capable of industrial application. Subject to paragraph 4 of Art 65 [delays in implementation are allowable for developing countries], paragraph 8 of art 70 [there need not be retroactive implementation] and paragraph 3 of this article [below] patents shall be enjoyable without discrimination as to the place of invention, the field of technology, and whether the products are imported or locally produced.

Members may exclude from patentability inventions, the prevention within their territory of commercial exploitation of which it is necessary to protect ordre publique or morality, including to protect human, animal, or plant life or health or to avoid serious prejudice to the environment, provided that such exclusion is not made merely because the exploitation is prohibited by their domestic law.

Members *may* also exclude from patentability:

1. Diagnostic, therapeutic and surgical methods for the treatment of humans or animals.

2. Plants and animals other than microorganisms, and essentially biological processes for the production of plants or animals other than non-biological and microbiological processes. However members shall provide for the protection of plant varieties either by patents or by an effective *sui generis* system, or by any combination thereof.

Proponents of the widest application of patenting tend to emphasise 'all fields of technology', italicised above. However the word 'may', is also italicised because it is crucial. Traditionally there was absolute abhorrence, in most minds, of the patenting of therapeutic methods as such. (In 1862 the inventor of ether anaesthesia, Morton, was refused a US patent on it.) One can also note the European influence implied in the term 'ordre publique'. But consider, in the context of 2(a) the US Patent 5563132 granted in 1996.

A two-step cancer treatment method consisting of the initial administration of a cancer-localising peroxide-reactive metal-ion containing compound, and then administering a peroxide compound to the patient after allowing sufficient time for the localisation to the cancer of the metal-ion containing compound to occur. The product of the chemical reaction between the cancer-localising metal-ion containing compound and the peroxide compound is an oxidant species which acts to destroy the cancer.

Not only is what is proposed here purely a therapy, the chemicals themselves remaining unnamed because they are ordinary compounds which have been known for half a century or more, but the whole thing is merely an idea anyway. There is no evidence that it actually works. The USPTO has ignored the 'may' in 2(a) above in this instance, as in many others. (The UK Patents Act of 1977 specifically excludes methods of diagnosis and treatment from patentability and this was reaffirmed by the 2004 Act.) In some jurisdictions, the law has been changed to accommodate TRIPs, in others there is a time lag. Still, any member of TRIPs, must eventually adhere to these provisions and bring domestic law into line with it. This means of course that if they are fortunate enough to have burgeoning biotechnology industries, these will be able to acquire extensive protection for their inventions as they appear.

Other views on gene patents

In addition to the justifications in these bodies of international law, more homely legal rationales for the patenting of genes have been adduced. Genes have been likened to *ferae naturae*, that is wild animals, which in common law systems, once captured, become the property of the captor. It has been pointed out that in an early US case in 1805, *Pierson v Post*, the plaintiff Pierson had interfered with Post when the latter was pursuing a wild fox, after which he killed it and carried off. (The case presumably went against Pierson at first instance, so he was the plaintiff on appeal.) The fox was available and unexploited, it was argued, like genes in our body, till its status was changed by actual possession by somebody:

> Ownership ....is reasonable. The alternative would be too uncertain. A claim by one person to one gene as it exists on his chromosome is likely to be contested by another who believes it exists on his chromosome. At the very least, siblings will share some of the same genes and thus would be forced to settle among themselves as to who is the rightful owner. Moreover, even if siblings had a common goal and were willing to settle on joint ownership, the controversy would not end there. Shared genes of course extend in all directions, familial, geographical, and temporal. As they exist on chromosomes, genes cannot be considered personal property. If gene ownership were decided by who in the population had a chromosome having a particular allele in the gene pool, who would get paid? Only those who have it? Or all contributors to the gene pool as conservators

of the genetic material? Can you buy the right to a gene in future offspring?[16]

It seems that this writer could have gone further and adduced the analogy of *res nullius*, the term in international law for property without an owner. The analogy is with *terra nullius*, land which belongs to nobody because it is unoccupied or unclaimed. (and in Chapter 2 there is indeed drawn the analogy between the information in DNA and real property, that is, land). Ownership of a territory could be obtained, formerly, by conquest, by cession, by settlement, and by occupation if it was owned by nobody, or at least inhabited by 'backward peoples'. At the end of the First World War so-called mandates were issued by the League of Nations for occupation of this last category, although it quickly became apparent that occupation meant ownership. Why not regard genes in the same light? The only *terra nullius* now is Antarctica and the deep sea bed, often described as the 'common heritage of mankind'. Article 137 (2) of the Law of the Sea (notably, *binding* international law) states that this is not now subject to alienation. Extremely similar language is used by the opponents of the patenting of human genes.

Moreover the argument in the quotation above seems to confuse the physical ownership of an entity with the information it contains (a physical book and the copyrighted information in it, say). Certainly I can sell a cell containing my choice allele, as I can sell my hair. All over the world however I cannot however sell my kidney or any other organ under the various tissue transplantation laws. Also, the rejoinder to the above came swiftly from others. Genes are not free ranging, it was reiterated, but parts of genomes, and are components of the bodies of persons who in free societies retain rights in them by virtue of the rules and conventions of informed consent: 'Samples and sequences unaccompanied by documentation of genuinely informed consent belong in the same category as other goods of dubious ownership: presumed to have been obtained extralegally and barred from commerce. Antiquities markets provide more relevant precedence than *Pierson v Post*.'[17]

The writer is here maintaining that extraction of DNA sequences without the consent of their bodily owner is more akin to the purloining of say, carvings from Angkor Wat than it is to the capture of some free ranging entity. This echoes the still substantial body of opinion worldwide that the information in DNA should not be the exclusive property of a patentee, in other words, that genes (human ones at least) should not be patented. There are various

---

16   Lebovitz, I 'Ownership of human genes [1996] *Nature* vol 382, at p 17 See also Chapter 2 herein for some background to the concepts of the ownership.
17   Eckhart, RB ' Foxy logic on gene pursuit' [1996] *Nature* vol 382, at p 750.

strands to the arguments, delivered both in the courts and in academic debate (in addition to the privacy considerations which are mentioned at the end of Section 4.2 herein).

First of all, it is held, genes should not be subject to the property of individuals, even for the limited period of a patent, as they are the common heritage of mankind - as part of the 'commons.' (This is not quite the same as maintaining that they are *terrae nulliae*, but somewhat analogous thereto.) Famously, the concept of the commons was introduced by a an article in the journal *Science* by Dr Garret Hardin some thirty years ago. He put it this way:

> The tragedy of the commons develops this way. Picture a pasture open to all. It is to be expected that each herdsman will try to keep as many cattle as possible on the commons. Such an arrangement may work reasonably satisfactorily for centuries because tribal wars, poaching, and disease keep the numbers of both man and beast well below the carrying capacity of the land. Finally however comes the day of reckoning that is, the day when the long –desired goal of social stability becomes a reality. At this point, the inherent logic of the commons remorselessly generates tragedy. As a rational being, each herdsman seeks to maximise his gain. Explicitly or implicitly He asks 'What is the utility to me of adding one more animal to my herd? ' This utility has one negative and one positive component.
>
> 1. The positive component is a function of the increment of one animal. Since the herdsman receives all the proceeds from the sale of the additional animal, the positive utility is nearly + 1.
>
> 2. The negative component is a function of the additional overgrazing created by one more animal. Since, however, the effects of overgrazing are shared by all the herdsmen, the negative utility for any particular decision-making herdsman is only a fraction of -1.
>
> Adding together the component partial utilities, the rational herdsman concludes that the only sensible course for him to pursue is to add another animal to the herd. And another ... But this is the conclusion reached by each and every rational herdsman sharing a commons. Therein is the tragedy. Each man is locked into a system that compels him to increase his herd without limit – in a world that is limited. Ruin

is the destination towards which all men rush, each pursuing his own best in a society that believes in the freedom of the commons....[18]

Is the idiom of the commons, or 'global public goods' in any way apt? Or, more appositely in the present context, does it have legal application? The genome, in a sense, must be a limited resource – there are a finite number of genes in the body, estimates varying, but perhaps as many as 100,000. The genome cannot be 'overgrazed' like the pasture, but perhaps, by analogy, it can be over-investigated, with wastage of mainly public money. No doubt patenting saves both private and public money because it avoids repeat investigations of genes already discovered (and cloned), which might otherwise be retained by the investigators as confidential information. Of course money must be spent to gain a licence to operate the patent, so there may well be a trade-off. And further, arguments have been put forward that the commons are better cared for when they are enclosed, that is managed privately. The idea of the commons was taken up once again in 1998 and indeed represents a very succinct way of looking at the whole issue. 'Since Hardin's article appeared, biomedical research has been moving from a *commons* model towards *privatisation* model'.[19] That observation is very obviously correct in general, but it may not apply to the third world, wherein for example, it is still not possible to patent traditional medicines.

This however does not exist the list of analogies. Further, there is the idea of trusteeship. In equity (and non-common law jurisdictions have equivalent provisions) ownership of an asset can be vested in another party (the trustee) who holds the property for the benefit of somebody else (the beneficiary). It might be argued that knowledge of gene sequences is to be held in trust for the benefit of individuals providing it, or even for humanity as whole. This

---

18   Hardin, G 'The tragedy of the commons' [1986] *Science* vol 162, at p 1243. The idea of the commons is of course quintessentially applied to the environment, *vide* the nature reserves and national parks set up in most countries. The universality of the idea has been cogently expressed by Maienchien, J, Collins, JP et al ' Biology and law: challenges of adjudicating competing claims in a democracy' [1998] *Jurimetrics* vol 38, at p 151 thus: 'Underlying such actions is the sense of a transcendent aesthetic or moral principle of such high value that it overrides individual economic interests.' There is also a fine discussion of the commons in Gibson, H note 13 above. See also an up to date discussion in Chadwick, R and Wilson, S 'Genomic databases as global public goods' [2004] *Res Publica* vol 10, at p 123.
19   Heller, MA and Eisenberg, R S. 'Can patents deter innovation? The anticommons in biomedical research' [1998] *Science* vol 280, at p 698. The juxtaposition of genes and the commons may be thought strained, but the UN *Universal Declaration on the Human Genome and Human Rights* states that ' The human genome is the heritage of humanity' albeit that the phrase '… in its natural state' was added somewhat later.

would certainly be very apposite to the DNA sequences derived from the genes of primitive and indigenous peoples, a topic which is again addressed in Chapter 6.

Yet one more argument against biotechnology patents is that historically, natural products other than DNA, when isolated by human ingenuity, have not attracted patents. Rifkin, the founder of the NGO known as the Council for Economic Trends, has consistently argued the case against gene patenting, and points out that pure helium, for example, is in a different form when taken from nature and used in industrial processes; a patent on helium *per se* was never contemplated.[20] Moving on again, a further objection by those opposed to patenting genes relates to unbridled power. A gene may have been isolated and used to make some protein, but it is still in my body (as well as in the bodies of others). It would appear that I cannot use my own gene for that purpose if I later isolate it from my own body. That would infringe the pre-existing patent. This does seem a bizarre situation. Again, is a gene not really a discovery, rather than an invention? The wording of 35 U.S.C. 105, quoted above, seems to allow discoveries to be patented, if they are useful, but most other countries have provisions contrary to this, albeit that they may gradually be expunged in the face of pressures from the commercial interests.

Another objection is that the effort involved in isolating any gene and making it useful necessarily depends on a vast body of fundamental research which was largely funded (in the universities) by public money (and, one might add, by ill-paid and toilworn scientists.) Particular umbrage was taken by the research community when in 1994 Myriad Genetics, a biotechnology company based in Utah, proposed to charge $2,500 for a patented (in the EPO) test of breast cancer susceptibility using mutations in the BRCA1 gene. (The cost subsequently dropped somewhat. However it has been pointed out that if a test is developed by a public authority the bill is invariably very much lower – the test for Tay Sachs disease offered by the US Department of Health and Social Security currently costs about $100.) Strenuous objections came especially from French scientists, who pointed out that the gene had been identified after intensive investigation by workers in many countries. The test as developed in France was priced at about $700. Subsequently, in 1995, a team of mainly British researchers attempted a pre-emptive strike at the patenting business by publishing the sequence of the BRCA2

---

20   Rifkind's website is <www.foey.org> (The Foundation for Economic Trends). See Rifkin, J and Tarcher, JP *The Biotech Century: Harnessing the Gene and Remodelling the World.* (Putnam, 1999).

gene in *Nature* magazine, that is putting it into the public domain and so beyond patenting by another party. Unfortunately, a patent had been filed in the US a day before the publication of the *Nature* article, subsequent to the EPO's rejection of its essentials in January 1995. It does not appear to have been noted among all the verbiage generated by the case that Myriad claimed only that the company *believed* the mutation increased the *risk* of cancer, a double hedging of bets if ever there was one. Since the predictively important mutation on the BRCA1 gene is largely confined to Ashkenazi Jewish women (the Eastern branch of the Jewish diaspora), there has been particular outrage in Israel, where the patent is widely held to import a racist slur. In so far as the invention claims to be a diagnostic method, it should summarily be refused in Europe under the provisions of Article 52(4) of the EPC. Indeed the patent was narrowed to exclude the diagnostic aspect by the EPC in Jan 2005. Other objections are that any new test should be subject to evaluation and endorsement by an expert, preferably statutory, body before introduction into practice; this should be combined with licensing, compulsory if necessary, and directions as to reasonable costs to be borne by the consumer. Thus, on the basis of Myriad Genetic's technology, unvalidated by any public authority, many women have been persuaded that they are at high risk of cancer and have undergone bilateral mastectomy.[21] At the time of writing the EPO application is before the Technical Board of Appeal (The Opposition Division, the lower tier, revoked it in May 2004). The legal tussle over the BRCA2 gene is similarly ongoing. At some point a conclusion will be reached and a timeline can be constructed to indicate the lessons for all concerned, specifically, when and where can a commercial entity seek ownership of a gene in a particular ethnic group?

Perhaps the most comprehensive (if highly technical) set of objections to gene patenting are contained in the 2001 USPTO Consultation Document. Twenty two comments/objections were made following the agency's

---

21   Matthijs, G and Halley, D 'European-wide opposition against the breast cancer gene patents' [2002] *European Journal of Human Genetics* vol 10, at p 783; Anon, 'Myriad Genetics BRCA2 patent under fire' [2005] *Biotechnology Law Reports* vol 24, at p 444; Bostyn, SJR. 'A critical analysis of the (non)-patentability of diagnostic methods and consequences for BRCA1 gene type patents in Europe' *Bio-science Law Review* 27th March, 1993. The matter also has also some resonance with employment law, see Chapter 3.5 (In the US the ADA Act 1990 offered some protection and the EEOC expanded the definition of 'disabled' to include deleterious genes. – but the issue does not appear to have been tested in the courts at the time of writing.) The risk for breast cancer of Ashkenazi women with the mutation in BRCA1 is 50-89% as opposed to 12% in the population worldwide.

invitation, which are somewhat paraphrased and somewhat simplified as below:[22] They echo many of the considerations expressed above.

(1) Genes are discoveries rather than inventions, therefore not patentable.

(2) A gene is a product of nature, therefore not patentable.

(3) There is no legislative basis for patenting genes.

(4) The DNA sequences are the core of what it is to be human and no person should control something so basic.

(5) Patents for genes will confer a broad protection for unproven uses and applications.

(6) Gene patenting will, *inter alia*, undermine research on indigenous peoples, as well as violating the 13th (anti-slavery) amendment to the constitution.

(7) Patents on genes delay medical research.

(8) A DNA sequence in itself has little utility.

(9) DNA sequences should patentable even if there is no indication of utility (like some of the others, this is an enabling item rather than an objection, relevant to expressed sequence tags, as discussed below).

(10) Patents should only be granted for utilities, rather than DNA sequences per se.

(11) Speculative uses for a DNA sequence, over and above those disclosed in the application, should be disallowed.

(12) DNA should be freely available for research.

(13) DNA sequencing is so routine it cannot be considered inventive under the act.

(14) Short DNA sequences should not be patented (even if of demonstrated utility) only whole genes.

(15) The patent application should disclose 'why' an invention, i.e. the process generated from the DNA sequence, works.

---

22   Note 9 above.

(16) Patented matter should be freely available to others to make improvements.

(17) The USPTO should be stricter in its utility guidelines.

(18) The patent examiners need more training.

(19) Computer based assignation of homologies to predict protein function are too uncertain to predict utility.

(20) The examiner should state whether there was acceptance of an asserted utility or a well-established utility.

(21) The examiner should not have to prove that a person with skill in the art is not aware of a well established utility (in other words here is the venerable difficulty of proving a negative).

(22) The nature of the required "nexus' between a showing supporting a well-established utility and the application as filed was unclear.

Many of these came from a single person or organisation (for example number six above) but those of a more technical or legal nature are identifiable as deriving from attorneys and academics. Nonetheless the USPTO had no difficulty in rejecting them (the actual language used being the more diplomatic "not accepted"), except for items 21 and 22 which were "taken aboard" in part. It is essential to note that the guidelines issued by patent offices in no sense have the force of law; it is the decisions of the courts based on precedence and statute which remain decisive. However, the tendency to consult the public before crystallising the patent examiners' stance is a modern phenomena and of course to be welcomed. In a word, nonetheless, the objectors to gene patenting do not appear to be prevailing. Finally, it has been established in patent law that the final arbiter is the courts, not the patent office.

Summary of 4.2

- There is a lingering conflict between some 'pure' scientists and patentees in respect of the patenting of biotechnological inventions, particularly genes.

- In the US the breakthrough in patenting biotechnological inventions came with *Diamond v Chakrabarty* (1980).

- The USPTO regards an excised gene as eminently patentable.

- Alleged infringements of biotechnological patents will be assessed in the US in the light of the doctrine of equivalents following the *Festo* and *Enzo* decisions.

- Patents are still territorial (conferred by the individual nation state).

- The European systems at least formally import the ordre publique (morality) doctrine.

- In Europe, diagnostic methods, including those based on biotechnology, remain unpatentable.

- Arguments against gene patenting based on ethics, *res nullius*, morality, or the 'commons' have generally not been successful, whatever the jurisdiction.

- The TRIPs agreement, while mandating the patentability of all forms of technology, yet has a derogation facility.

4.3 Expressed Sequence Tags and Single Nucleotide Polymorphisms

Expressed sequence tags (ESTs) are segments of DNA, usually containing 300-500 nucleotides known to code proteins; however the protein end products and their functions, by definition, are unknown. (What is now addressed is the sixth question posed in Box 2-1). They are generated by isolating messenger RNA from a cell or tissue, purifying it, and synthesising a copy (complementary DNA or cDNA) from it. This cDNA necessarily represents the coding for protein because the mRNA is produced in the cell as an expression product of the gene for that protein. The cDNA, now part of a 'library', is ligated into a phage vector used to infect a bacterium, which then synthesises large quantities of the cDNA library for sequencing. The amino acid sequences in the corresponding proteins, therefore, can be worked out from the base sequences. However, what is the role of such a protein - is it a functional molecule, and if so, how it is folded, and does it have prosthetic groups (attachments of non-protein molecules such as lipids, carbohydrates or metals)? The first patent for an EST, nonetheless, USPTO number 5,817,479, appears to have been granted to Incyte Pharmaceuticals in 1997. This patent, and its successors, proved to be controversial from the start:

> It is well known that the patent laws provide the patent owner with rights to preclude the use of the patented subject matter. Once a genomic invention is patented, the owner of the patent has the right to exclude others from making, using, importing, offering for sale or selling the patented invention. It is this right to exclude, if exercised, that provides exclusivity to the patented invention. If the USPTO or other patent offices granted patents for genomic technologies [for example, the generation of ESTs] based on their unknown future

potentials, it would have a destructive impact on the incentives for the industry to research and develop new drugs and therapies based on genomic technology. Companies could invest years of work and hundreds of millions of dollars to identify a unique gene that expresses a crucially important protein that is unique to a specific disease, for which there is no known treatment, only to find that research is blocked by a purely putative patent.[23]

The Human Genome Organisation has stated that patenting ESTs would 'reward those who make routine discoveries, but penalise those who determine biological function or application' (a discovery as such, of course, being non-patentable). There were similar deprecatory statements by the various societies of human genetics (the professional organisations) throughout the world. In the face of all this, USPTO made a final ruling in 1999 that fragments like ESTs can only be allotted a patent if they can be shown to have specific, substantial and credible utility.[24] These three adjectives need interpretation, of course. Specific utility means a utility specific to the claim *per se*. The bare claim that a polynucleotide sequence is a probe is not specific enough, because all polynucleotide sequences are potentially probes. (This means that if a cDNA sequence is synthesised from an EST it may bind to a segment of a chromosome which may identify that segment as either a specific known gene or a candidate gene). The Association Internationale pour la Protection de la Propriété Intellectuale (AIPPI), which appears to be a pressure group of patent attorneys pushing primarily for the protection of business methods, believes that even this mild derogation must be challenged - it maintains that the claim 'as a probe' in itself is quite good enough. 'Substantial utility' relates to utility in the real world, as it were. Thus a claim that a sequence is a specific probe (the first hurdle) will not be acceptable for an as yet unknown disease. Finally, credibility attaches to realistic and sensible utility. The Harvard oncomouse could be used as a snake food in herpetaria - there is no doubt about that - but using such a valuable commodity for such a trivial

---

23 Elliston, K. and Tribble, JL. ' Access to genomic inventions'. [1996] *Expert Opinion on Therapeutic Patents* vol 6, at p 543.

24 The 2001 guidelines on ESTs issued jointly by the USPTO, the EPO and the Japanese Patent Office can be accessed on < http://www.european-patent-office.org/tws/sr-3.htm> See also Crespi, S 'Patenting for the research scientist' [2004] *Trends in Biotechnology* [2004] vol 22, at p 638. In accordance with the organ in which it is published, a highly technical discussion is provided by Flattman, G J and Kaplan, J M 'Patenting expressed sequence tags and single nucleotide polymorphisms' *Nature Biotechnology* [2001] vol 19, at p 777. See also Aerts, RJ. 'The industrial applicability and utility requirements for the patenting of genomic inventions: a comparison between European and US law' [2004] *European Intellectual Property Journal* vol 26, at p 349.

purpose is manifestly not within the bounds of the credibility criterion. Even then, apart from AIPPI, not everybody agrees that the utility of ESTs has been correctly challenged. A succinct list of their proposed usefulness is:

(1) The provision of a cheap and effective short cut for identifying the majority of an organism's genes.

(2) Surveys of ESTs can provide a global view of the gene expression patterns that distinguish different tissues of cell types.

(3) The large collection of human ESTs will soon permit the majority of genes to be placed on the chromosomal map.

But whether these fulfill the criterion of specificity is a matter of opinion. The present situation has been further explained by Dr Francis Collins, the head of the National Human Genome research Institute in the USA.[25] He writes that some years ago the USPTO tended to look upon any DNA sequence as useful because potentially it could be used as a probe (This was a 'generation one' patent.) Now these are rejected. 'Generation two' versions are patent applications where a sequence and homology to other sequences suggests a function (meaning that the sequence might correspond, in part, for example, to a receptor which would enable the design of a drug to block the receptor). These may or may not be granted, depending on their specific claims. But 'generation three' which have 'biochemical, cell biological, or genetic data describing a function' do comply with the criterion of usefulness. To it another way, there must be the ability to correlate the structure of the claimed base sequence with the function. To quote the Human Genome Project:

> The patenting of gene fragments is controversial. Some say that patenting such discoveries is inappropriate because the effort to find any given EST is small compared with the work of isolating and characterizing a gene and as gene product, finding out what it does, and developing a commercial product. They feel that allowing holders of such "gatekeeper" patents to exercise undue control over the commercial fruits of genome research would be unfair. Similarly, allowing multiple patents on different parts of the same genome sequence – say on a gene fragment, the gene, and the protein – adds undue costs to the researcher who wants to examine the sequence. Not only does the researcher have to pay each patent holder via licensing for the opportunity to study the sequence, he also has to pay his

---

25   Collins, F. 'In the crossfire: Collins on genomes, patents and "rivalry"' [2000] *Science* vol 287, at p 2396.

own staff to research the different patents and determine which are applicable to the area of the genome he wants to study.[26]

As the other major authority in the world of patenting, the EPC has adopted the statement in the EU directive 94/44/EC of 1998, art 5 (3) which reads: 'the industrial application of a sequence or partial sequence of a gene must be disclosed in the patent application.' The matter appears to be settled and unless some new scientific breakthrough occurs it is reasonably predictable that patent examiners outside the US and Europe will find these policies generally acceptable for their own practice.

In any case, as the totality of the human and other genomes are elucidated and the base sequences identified as functional genes there will be a natural limit to the generation of ESTs, the human genome being finite. (For practical purposes the genomes of the millions of animal and plant species are infinite.) This is not the case, however, for single nucleotide polymorphisms (SNPs), the patenting of which induced a controversy parallel to that of ESTs. SNPs are substitutions of single bases in the coding triplets for the amino acids. Since these can occur at any point in the genome, and vary from individual to individual they are, if not infinite, potentially extremely numerous. The single base substitution can prevent an amino acid being synthesised altogether, or a different amino acid can be synthesised. In humans there is said to be about one SNP per every thousand base pairs, or three million per genome. Although few of them are likely in themselves to cause a disease (since many of them occur in the non-coding segments of DNA, the so-called introns), they can act as markers for regions which are associated with a disease. (They are in due course likely to have forensic importance, and have been mentioned in Chapter 2.)

SNPs are said also to be useful in determining the genetic identity of an individual and apparently that specific application was patented some time ago by the Australian company Genetic Technologies, under the aegis of a Swiss parent company GeneType. The technique for 'high throughput' SNP analysis is available as a non-exclusive licence for about half a million dollars. The situation has given rise to yet more statements that biotechnology patents are too easy to obtain and that this portfolio must be challenged in the courts. In a no-loss situation however, Genetic Technologies is said to have insured itself against challenge to its patents. However the more ethical (as they would see it) arm of the biotechnology industry was moved to step in, for in 1999 ten large pharmaceutical companies together with the Wellcome

---

26   < http://www.ornl.gov/TechResources/Human_Genome>. See also Caskey, C et al. 'HUGO statement on patenting of DNA sequences' [2001] *Science* vol 291, at p 1304.

Trust in UK decided to set up a non-profit foundation to map some 300,000 common SNPs and to put this into the public domain. The SNPs are to be patented first, but with the sole purpose of preventing interlopers like Genetic Technologies from doing likewise. All one can say is that the dogged attitude of the biotechnology companies in placing DNA sequences – any sequences – under intellectual property protection inexorably reminds one of First World War generals – determined to attack on a broad front in pursuit of some vaguely expressed goal, gaining only yards of muddy and shell-pocked ground every day, confident nonetheless in themselves and their methods no matter what the cost in men and materiél, and imbued with moral imperatives valued only by themselves.

Summary of 4.3

- ESTs, if described as 'probes' but having no demonstrable utility, initially were successfully patented.

- However there was a rapid reaction to this, and utility must now be established.

- SNPs can be useful in the determination of identity and such applications have been patented. However public bodies have taken the ethical stance of putting them in the public domain free.

4.4 Some Keynote Cases

As usual issues crop up in more than one context, often several, and it has been more convenient to treat with the US *Verlander* case in Chapter 1 and the Canadian *Schmeiser* case in Chapter 5. The keynote cases are derived primarily from the courts in the USA, whose scientists are the acknowledged pioneers of both genomic technology and its protection by the laws of intellectual property. However some important cases have originated from Europe, and we await intellectual property law decisions the rest of the world as its biotechnology industry gets underway. Of course the cases in USA and Europe will be persuasive elsewhere in the world, as long as they do not militate against fundamental principles, for example the banning of patents for traditional medicines. Increasingly also, the TRIPs provisions will be decisive everywhere. In looking at the cases, what one is trying to do, as is usual in legal studies, is extract dicta which are likely to define the law, rather than relate the judgements themselves. In any case, it is often difficult to know what is the final judgement – most of these cases go on for years, even decades, as one appeal after another is mounted. (The *Biogen v Madeva* case, in England, dragged on for almost two decades. When it reached the House of Lords, Lord Hoffman stated that: 'Difficulties.... have been exacerbated by the fact that in the relevant field, genetic engineering, the state of the art has been developing with great rapidity throughout the relevant period. As will be appreciated, on the judge's findings, what was not obvious in 1978 had become obvious by November 1979' – and Lord Hoffman's speech was in 1996! This case illustrates another point very relevant to the fast moving biotechnology - that a patent should construed as of its application date, that is, the obviousness to a skilled person should be assessed at that point and not at some arbitrary date in the future.

Since the drafters of complex biotechnology patents try to put in as many claims as possible (some of which, regrettably, duplicate each other by the clever use of language), when these are challenged or infringed, in the ensuing litigation a portion only of the various claims may be sustained, or modified. These modifications as well as the residual claims can be subject to appeal by both sides, and if the infringing matter is a rival patent claim, then cross appeals can be entered by both parties too. Add the fact that some claims might be upheld by an appeal court while others are remitted to a lower court for redetermination and one can understand why it takes many hours of study to extract the principles at issue. Merely printing out the relevant documents is daunting in terms of costs and paper. The point may be illustrated by the *Invitrogen* case, the litigation over which stretched from 1988 to 2003: '... the Court of Appeals for the Federal Circuit vacated the judgment of invalidity and the district court's partial summary judgment ... affirmed the partial summary judgments that the claims-in-suit are enabled and satisfy the written description requirement, and affirmed the partial summary judgment of infringement of the '608 patent. The case was remanded for further proceedings....'[27] (This case involved a genetically modified reverse transcriptase, that is, an enzyme capable of constructing multiple copies of cDNA from RNA and being free from RNase H. That is, the mRNA would not be broken up an rendered useless by the RNase.)

The following then are in no strict order; they merely represent the bundle of issues which have been brought to the fore. The jumpstart to biotechnology was the series of so-called Cohen-Boyer patents in the late 1970s, held by the Universities of Stanford and of California, and which covered basic gene splicing technology, that is the introduction of genes into plasmids, which then infected bacteria which in turn produced, in bulk, the proteins coded for by the spliced-in genes. The licencing system is universally acknowledged

27 *Invitrogen Corporation (formerly known as Life Technologies Inc.) v Clontech Laboratories* [2005] No 04-1040 (Nov 15) For a commentary: Anon. 'Who conceived RNase H minus RT and when? ' [2006] *Biotechnology Law Report* vol 15, at p 71.

to have been liberal from the start and perhaps for that reason the patents do not appear on the contested list. These early patents expired in late 1997; the important patent for recombinant human insulin owned by Eli Lilly has also now expired. However contests there have been in plenty, in the interests of extracting, from the various legal systems, as much commercial advantage as possible.

An early English case is known as *Genentech Inc's Patent* (1989).[28] It involved the production of tissue plasminogen activator (TPA) a protein naturally occurring in the blood, with the property of dissolving clots, and therefore useful as a therapeutic agent for coronary episodes. The claimed invention was for construction of a cDNA to be inserted into a plasmid vector which in turn would express the TPA in a cell line. The techniques were convoluted and involved *inter alia* the isolation of the correct mRNA and the construction of a double stranded DNA for insertion into the plasmid. The challenges to the patent were that each of the steps was well established and the Genentech team had merely persistently applied them, albeit it in a highly skilled and competitive manner, in order to achieve their end. The Court of Appeal held that choosing to pursue such a course was like putting a bet on a race - if the backer were to win the race, it would be wrong to maintain that he had invented or discovered some way to pick winners. Other points which arose out of this case are that, however marvellous the technology might seem to the man in the street, it is the degree of obviousness to the qualified molecular biologist (the 'skilled artisan' in this context) which is important; also, as commented by Lord Hoffman in the *Biogen* case also, due to rapid advances in the relevant technologies, non-obviousness can emerge in the twinkling of an eye. One other factor which has been said to influence the decision, adversely for the applicant, was the role of management and the employment of large teams in what might be seen as more of a business venture than an inventive foray. Also, the issues here have some affinity with 'mosaicism' that is, putting pieces of established inventions together to produce what is claimed to be a novel, composite invention. Mosaicism however has not been an important issue in the courts, it merely lurks there awaiting an airing.[29]

In *Amgen Inc v Chagai* Pharmaceutical Co in the US in 1991, the claimed invention was a purified and isolated DNA sequence encoding the protein

---

28   *Genetech's Inc Patent* [1989] CA RPC 147.
29   Cornish, WR *Intellectual Property* (Sweet and Maxwell. 3rd edn, 1996) p 174 Cornish comments that the problem here has been solved in respect of the pharmaceutical industry, but is more difficult in the case of biotechnology claims.

erythropoietin, which promotes erythrocyte production in the bone marrow.[30] The original patent was claimed in 1983 but abandoned and revived in a series from 1987 onwards. It was opposed on the grounds of prior art. A Dr Fritsch had previously developed a probing strategy for the gene, but had not isolated it. The court affirmed that: "A gene is a chemical compound, albeit a complex one, and it is well established in our law that conception of a chemical compound requires that the inventor be able to define it so as to distinguish it from other materials, and describe how to obtain it." In other words the gene must be chemically isolated, not merely probed or detected. In this case although the DNA was indeed isolated the claim was a broad generic one covering all DNA sequences encoding any polypeptide with an amino acid sequence similar enough to erythropoietin to have the ability to increase the production of erythrocytes. The claim on the DNA itself was valid enough, but otherwise the details revealed an unacceptable breadth. This illustrates the consistently unacceptable face of many biotechnology applications – they seek to wipe out any future competition by putting claims on whole families of molecules, on techniques wide enough to exclude other related areas of development, and in the case of animals, they sometimes claim whole families if not phyla. This *Amgen* case was followed, again in the US, by *Fiers, v Revel* in 1993, in which it was affirmed the gene for interferon-beta was 'a simple chemical compound'.

The *Howard Florey/Relaxin* case came about because in its 1994 EPO Patent was opposed by the Green Party in Germany. The application sought to protect the invention of a gene coding for human relaxin, a protein hormone which relaxes the pelvic ligaments during parturition. The opponents submitted that the patent was not novel, since the gene coding for relaxin had always been present in the female body, that it was intrinsically abhorrent to take tissue from a pregnant female (this would be necessary for a licencee of the invention to repeat it), and that here was an offence against human dignity in the sense of making use of a particular female condition (pregnancy) for profit. Further, that the patenting of such human genes amounted to slavery since it involved the dismembering of women and their piecemeal sale to commercial enterprises throughout the world; moreover, that the whole process infringed the human right to self-determination; lastly, that the patenting of human genes is in any case inherently immoral. It will be appreciated that many of the objections were contiguous with Articles 27

---

30 *Amgen Inc v Chugai* is cited as 927 F.2D 1200 (Fed Cir), *Fiers v Revel* as 884 F.2d 1164 (Fed Cir 993). Both are discussed by Doll, citation 9 above. See also Crespi, S. 'Patenting and ethics: a dubious connection' [2000/2001] *Bioscience Law Review* vol 3, at p 71.

(2) of TRIPs, Article 6 of the EU Biotechnology Directive, and 53(a) of EPC, cited above. This being a case before the EPO, it was the last which was most relevant. The Opposition Division had no difficulty in faulting most of the objections. With regard to novelty, it established that the claim was for a cDNA, which cannot be found in nature. In any case, should the claim have been for the genomic DNA, this was patentable as long as it had been isolated from the body and shown to be useful. On the supposed exploitation of the pregnant female for profit, it was established that the lady in question had parted with the tissue on the basis of full consent, and so this objection too was not relevant. The board pointed out that DNA as a chemical could not be equated with life, and so the slavery point was invalidated in its turn. In general terms the board refused to place itself in the position of an arbiter of ethics, Article 53(a) being apposite only to inventions which were by any criteria completely outrageous and indefensible. So here again the biotechnology industry was not to be gainsaid.[31]

In *In re Deuel,* a US case in 1995, a claim for a series of DNA fragments coding for human and bovine heparin binding growth factor (a mitogen, promoting division for endothelial cells and therefore potentially useful, *inter alia,* for skin regeneration) was opposed on the grounds that the amino acid sequence had been known previously, and so the DNA sequence could have been predicted. In other words, the challenge went to obviousness. In an appeal to the Federal Circuit, it was decided that the patent was valid because the genetic code is degenerate. This means that each amino acid can be coded for by a number of trinucleotides (codons) and so, by working backwards as it were, nobody could have predicted which sequence in the DNA was responsible for that particular amino acid sequence. This was regarded as a victory for the biotechnology industry.[32] An attorney for Human Genome Sciences Corporation (the patent owner) immediately announced his hopes for the patenting of another 70 gene sequences generated by his company. The decision has been heavily criticised as a piece of casuistry, and as having little legal justification.

In 1996 the long running case of *Biogen v Madeva*, mentioned in passing above, at last reached the House of Lords; it is said to be the first purely biotechnology case considered by the highest civil court in UK.[33] The first

31 *Howard Florey /Relaxin* is cited as [1995] European Patent Office Reports, 541. See also Vossius, V 'Patenting inventions in the field of biology and chemistry: case law' [1997] *Bioscience Law Review* vol 1, at p 7.

32 Ducour, P 'In re Deuel: biotechnology industry v patent law' [1996] *European Intellectual Property Review* vol 35 at p 9.

33 The citation is [1997] RPC 1, 97; among the many commentaries are McInerney, A

instance applications were made in the UK in 1978, then to the EPO in 1979. At that time a vaccine against hepatitis B was badly needed, since the causative virus had been shown to be linked to liver cancer. The virus particle was well known to be composed of a double stranded circular DNA plus a core protein and a surface protein. The surface protein was potentially a vaccine, meaning that if injected as an antigen into a subject, that subject would produce antibodies to it and thereby would be able to neutralise the virus itself should he come into contact with it. The surface protein could have been isolated chemically from the blood of patients with hepatitis B, but only in small quantities and with the danger of carrying along impurities which might be toxic. (This baleful scenario was indeed enacted some years later when growth hormone preparations from cadaver pituitaries caused the sometimes fatal Jacob-Creutzfeldt disease.) It was decided by the founders of Biogen to try to prepare the protein by recombinant DNA methods. In the late seventies it was not clear whether or not viral DNA contains introns, the non-coding segments of DNA. (In fact now we know they do not.) Any artificially prepared segment of DNA containing introns would not express the desired protein. So the scientists cut the viral DNA into large segments with restriction endonucleases, prepared cDNAs from these, and inserted the cDNAs into a bacterium. Some of the cDNA containing bacteria expressed proteins, some did not, but one strain yielded the desired surface (protein) antigen. The view was subsequently expressed in court that the scientists were 'working in the dark' and merely 'got lucky.'

The claim was essentially for: 'A recombinant DNA molecule.... coding for a polypeptide or a fragment thereof displaying HBV antigen specificity .... in a suitable host cell molecule ..... [without contamination by other proteins].' That is, it was a product claim, the process being kept notably vague, as in a 'suitable host.'

In 1992 UK infringement proceedings against Madeva were instituted, accompanied by a counterclaim from that company. Madeva sought revocation of the Biogen patent on the grounds of: (a) obviousness (b) the patent did not describe an invention as defined in Section 1 of the 1977 Act

---

'Biotechnology: Biogen v Madeva in the House of Lords' [1988] *European Intellectual Property Review* vol 20, at p 14; Karet, I and Britton, I 'The U.K. courts tackle biotechnology and the EPO: the decision in the House of Lords in Biogen v Madeva ' [1997] *Bioscience Law Review* vol 1, at p 25. (This paper gives a timeline for the applications, infringement proceedings, appeals, cross appeals, etc in both UK and the EPO.) The US Supreme Court case *Reilly v Morse* 56 U.S. (15 How.) 62 [1854] was quoted in the context of similar broad claims; Samuel Morse had invented electronic communication, but claimed every conceivable future development of it, not merely the morse code itself.

and (c) insufficiency of description. There was also an issue surrounding the priority date. Biogen relied on the 1978 (UK) application date for the description and specifications incorporated into its 1979 EPO application. However it was common ground that the techniques employed had become obvious between the time of the UK application and the EPO application. Naturally Biogen wished to rely on the state of the art in 1978. In the House of Lords, Lord Hoffman was content to assume that what the inventor had done was non-obvious in 1978, the technological knowledge at the time being what it was - to consider a later level of knowledge had no merit. According to Lord Hoffman the inventiveness alleged in this case was said to lie in attempting something that a 'man less skilled in the art might have regarded as obvious but the expert would have thought so beset by obstacles as not to be worth trying'.

Assuming that the 1978 application was patentable, was the enabling disclosure sufficient to cover all the ways in which the protein might be produced? Was the invention described sufficiently to establish a monopoly of any recombinant method of making antigens? It was held that it did not. The same results could be obtained by means not described but which if described adequately could overcome a s 72 (a)(c) revocation on the grounds of insufficient disclosure. Thus, broadness of claim was fatal. Biogen's application was insufficient for 'a claim to a monopoly for any recombinant method of making the antigens'. It was too broad in the sense that the same results could be obtained by different means not described by Biogen. S 14 (5) (c) (claims to be supported by the description) has ipso facto been interpreted as a ground for revocation. 'The substantive effect of section 14 (5) (c) that the description should, with the rest of the specification, constitute an enabling disclosure, is given effect by 72 (1) (c) ' (that is the specification must be clear and complete). This is said by commentators to be a new approach, overturning decisions of the lower courts, as in *Genentech* for example. Previously there was more lattitude. The decision is believed to be a victory, in a sense, for the consumer; in plain language, from now on scientists who achieve a result will not be able to prevent others from marketing the same end-product manufactured by different means.

In their decision the Lords also dismissed the analogy of betting on the race, as cited in *Genentech* (above), as unhelpful. The question was not odds but the existence of an inventive step conceived in an effort to overcome a problem.

Historically then, the High Court held for Biogen, the Court of Appeal for Madeva, with the House of Lords agreeing with the latter. Notably, contemporaneously with the hearing in that House, the EPO was making the decision to allow the Biogen patent – but recall again that the territoriality of patent law means that the Lords decision is the decisive one in UK. Incidentally Lord Hoffman stated that the decisions of the EPO are of considerable persuasive authority in the House of Lords. At the same time, others hold the view that the EPO favours the economic health of the European biotechnology industry rather than the letter of the EU directive.

In 1997 Amgen was back in court again initiating actions for infringement in both US and Britain against Transkaryotic Therapies Inc.[34] The molecule in question was again erythropoietin, but the issue was now the method of its production. Amgen had taken out several patents in the eighties for the production of erythropoietin, as mentioned above. Their process involved splicing the erythropoietin gene into a bacterium via a plasmid, which then produced it in large quantities. Transkaryotic Therapies manufactured erythropoietin by stimulating its synthesis in a mammalian cell through the insertion of a promoter upstream (nearer the beginning of the reading frame) from the gene itself. A major technical challenge was to persuade the bacterium to glycosylate the protein, that is, effect a combination with carbohydrate molecules, as is the case in the human kidney. One interesting feature of the case is that Amgen had initially managed to take out five patents describing what essentially were different aspects of the same invention. It seems that patent attorneys advise that the protection of a valuable product should be sought not in a single patent containing broad claims, but should be part of a portfolio that permits back-up positions should the stand-alone patent fail. (In turn this seems to suggest that success may depend not so much on the originality and inventiveness of the scientists, as that of the patent attorneys.) In England the Court of Appeal and the House of Lords found that there had been no infringement by Transkaryotic Therapies. There were three key claims, among no less than 68 (ultimately) presented by Amgen:

34   The House of Lords citation is *Kirin Amgen Inc & Ors v Hoechst Marion Roussel Ltd & Ors* [2004] UKHL 46. Note that 'Transkaryotic' seems to have disappeared as a party - due to takeovers and mergers - the names of the big biotechnology companies change faster than their technology. See also: Crespi, S. 'Erythropoietin in the UK courts - further thoughts' *Chartered Institute of Patent Agents Journal* Feb, 2005, at p 98; Jones, N and Marsh, D 'Biotech patents: the U.K. and the U.S. disagree on the equivalents test '.[2003] *Bioscience Law Review* vol 6, at p 223; Moore, G and Gilbert, P 'Amgen v TKT: bye bye Biogen?' [2001/2002] *Bioscience Law Review* vol 4, at p 122; Godar, G, and Batteson, A 'Tread carefully: expert evidence after Kirin Amgen' *Patent World*, April 2005, p 171. Anon 'Patent Litigation: Transkaryotic Therapies succeeds in House of Lords' [2005] *Biotechnology Law Report* vol 24, at p 39.

Claim 1 described a DNA sequence which will cause a prokaryotic or eukaryotic host cell to produce a polypeptide that stimulates the formation of erythrocytes by the bone marrow.

Claim 19 (was for) '...a recombinant polypeptide [erythropoietin].... being the product of eukaryotic expression of an exogenous DNA sequence and which has a higher molecular weight .... than erythropoietin isolated from urinary sources.'

Claim 26 (was for) a polypeptide product of the expression in a eukaryotic host cell of a DNA sequence according to [inter alia] ... Claim 1.

The trial judge found that the word 'exogenous' as applied to the DNA claimed by Amgen precluded infringement by the 'endogenous' DNA of Transkaryotic. Thus it was a 'product-by-process' claim. The Court of Appeal decision was similar in that the patent was held to be valid but not infringed. In the Lords, Lord Hoffman identified the key question as: "Would a person skilled in the art have understood the patentee to have used the language of the claim to mean?" He stated that the *Catnic* tests[35] (broadly, that the purpose of the invention should be looked at rather than its language when considering infringement) are consistent with the Protocol on the interpretation of the Article 69 of the EPC but are only guidelines. Nonetheless, in line with the diplomatic conferences of the EPC (via the 2000 Protocol) a doctrine of equivalents is to be introduced and will automatically be incorporated into UK law by Section 125 (3) of the 1977 Patents Act.

Lord Hoffman agreed with the trial judge and the Court of Appeal that the man skilled in the art would not understand the claim to be sufficiently general as to include [endogenous] gene activation. So Claim 19 failed for insufficiency. As to the protein produced by the gene, Claim 26 for it was invalid on the grounds of anticipation; it had already been purified from urine, and the recombinant and urinary versions were indistinguishable. (In passing, it was stated that its amino acid sequencing was a discovery, not an invention.) In respect of Claim 26, the EPO policy was adhered to even though it was a change in UK law. Now, in UK, a claim written in terms of "product obtained by a process" cannot be novel if the product itself is not

---

35 *Catnic v Hill and Smith* [1982] RPC 183. Catnic was analysed by Hoffman J in *Improver v Remington* [1990] FSR 181; in turn it was stated by Laddie J in *Merck and Co v Generics* (UK) Ltd [2003] EWHC 2842 (Pat) that the Improver format should not be interpreted too literally. The real authority was the Protocol on the Interpretation of art 69 of the EPC, incorporated into the EPC by art 164 and the UK Patents Act 1977, by s 125 (3).

novel. A process *per se* should be claimed according to Section 60 (1) (c) of the 1977 Act, essentially the same as Article 64(2) of the EPC (where the invention is a process, use of a product produced by that process constitutes an infringement).

It was stated that the US doctrine of equivalents had no place in UK law then. (Here it is correct to cite 'UK law' rather than 'English law' since the Patent Acts apply to the whole of the United Kingdom.); also 'file wrapper estoppel', according (again) to Lord Hoffman, has no place in UK law (nor has it found a place in the EPO, apparently - it is the responsibility of the office to make sure that the applicant is consistent in his prosecution of the patent.)

It had been long standing policy in the EPO that a claim to a product when made by a new process is not allowed unless the product is in some way different from the previously known substance. Amgen relied on the fact that their product was extensively glycosylated in distinction to the urinary version. So, a slightly amended form of Claim 19 was allowed in the EPO. Thus the House of Lords and the EPO differed not on law but on fact - the identity or not of the two erythropoietins.

In the US the CAFC sitting in 2003-2004 found that some of Transkaryotic's claims infringed the Amgen patent and some did not, but in addition some aspects were remitted back to a lower court. [36] The gene claims had been abandoned in the US and Amgen being the first to clone erythropoietin sought protection for it as a protein even though its function was well known at the time of the application. The litigation stretched from 1988 to 2003 when the patent for 'an isolated non-naturally occurring erythropoietin glycoprotein, amino acid sequence described, with glycosylation distinct from human urinary erythropoietin.' One might note here how illustrative is this case of the competition - which can be conservatively described as cutthroat - between major biotechnology companies at the present day. Inspection of the transcripts of the case reveals that sitting in the Massachusetts District Court - the lowest in the pecking order - were no fewer than 30 counsel for Amgen and 27 for Transkaryotic. The costs must have been enormous, a financial

---

36   The citation is *Amgen Inc v Hoechst Marion Roussel Inc* 314 F 3rd 1313 [2003]. Some articles are: Lawson, C 'Amgen, TKT and the erythropoietin patents - patent privileges in preference to competition' [2005] *American Intellectual Property Journal* vol 16, at p 129; Chahine, K. 'Amgen preserves erythropoietin monopoly for now' [2003] *Nature Biotechnology* vol 19, at p 199; Anon 'Patent Litigation: Massachusetts court examines Amgen-Transkaryotic dispute in light of most recent Festo decision' [2004] *Biotechnology Law Report* vol 23, at p 59.

paradise for patent attorneys, and indicate the how high the stakes are, even leaving aside possible future sales. It is also a curious fact that the Amgen patent was about to expire at this time - no doubt it was testing the law.) During prosecution in 1995 Amgen cancelled 60 original claims, added eight new ones, of which several were later cancelled, to be succeeded by six fresh ones. In the event *Festo* was followed but the CAFC stated that a narrowing amendment to satisfy the Patent Act could give rise to an estoppel, and that the doctrine of equivalents is not available for an amended claim limitation when prosecution history estoppel applies. Amgen succeeded however in rebutting this doctrine. The claims in the US and UK were not exactly identical but commentators regard the final result in the two jurisdictions as divergent. It has been considered by many to be a win for old technology against Johnny-Come-Latelys. Thus in the US the main issue was Amgen's amendment of the original patent and the eventual outcome was that TKT were held to infringe Amgen's patent under the doctrine of equivalents, the CAFC in essentials supporting the trial court.

In UK law, such prolonged intermeddling with claims has not been allowed. In *Lubrizol v Esso* (1998) the judge, quoting precedent, held that a patentee had to put forward any proposed amendments prior to the trial so that all issues could be dealt with once and for all. Otherwise what would ensue would be effectively a re-trial, costing the courts time and resources.[37] In addition Article 123 (c) of the EPC precludes amendment of a European patent application in such a way as to contain matter that extends beyond the context of the application as filed. The factual aspects of such are a matter for the addressee skilled in the art.

In *Plant Genetic Systems* in 1995, in a European case, the inventors put in a claim for plants and seeds resistant to a particular class of herbicides, namely glutamine synthetase inhibitors.[38] There was opposition by the NGO Greenpeace, which opposes genetic manipulation *ab initio*, citing Article 53(a) of EPC, the 'morality clause'. This was a botanical, not a medical case of course (and plants have nothing resembling human rights) but certain principles were formulated in the course of the grant of the patent by the Appeals Board of the EPO. These included a statement that: ' Inventions the exploitation of which is not in conformity with the conventionally

---

37   [1988] RPC 727. This is discussed by Cordery, B and Nettleton, E 'Review of patent cases in the English courts in 2005' *Chartered Institute of Patent Attorneys' Journal*, April 2006, at p 255.

38   Llewelyn, M 'Article 53 revisited: *Greenpeace v Plant Genetic Systems NV*' [1995] *European Intellectual Property Review* vol 10, at p 506 See also *European Patent Office Reports* T356/93 [1995].

accepted standards of conduct pertaining to the *culture inherent* [my italics] in European society and civilisation are to be excluded from patentability as being contrary to morality,' or, in other words, that morality *does* play a part in the granting of a patent, even if the principle was not apposite to the patent in suit. (The Opposition Division of the EPO in the Oncomouse case took another view, see below.) An oft-expressed view is that patents are morally neutral, despite the provisions of art 53(a) of the EPC. However the Board held that the moral standards are not to be assessed by surveys (" Survey and opinion poll evidence are not decisive in this connection.") this following the citation by Greenpeace of a 1988 questionnaire given to farmers in Sweden and Switzerland, most of whom felt it was wrong to allow the granting of such patents as the one described to them. In respect of the former point, one might ask what is meant by 'culture inherent', in that large sections of the European population, one might adduce for example football supporters, have no discernable culture worth that name. For the latter, a survey of the views of the population at large, even if conducted correctly, can by long standing practice have no place in legal proceedings. But on the other hand, why not? How else could an appointed body like the patents panel assess morality, now that it has to be taken into account, otherwise than by survey of public opinion? The opposition panel's view is presumably that the peoples of Europe would have difficulty, when asked, of distinguishing genes from trousers made of blue cloth. This might well be true. But here at least here there was is an attempt to formulate a policy, however vague, rather than the "anything under the sun made by man" approach in the USA. There was also a challenge to the patent under art 53 (b) (the bar on essentially biological processes), but here there was a precedent in that an earlier case, *Lubrizol / Hybrid plants*, in 1988, before the EPO Technical Board of Appeal, wherein it had been stated that the exclusion of essentially biological processes stood as an exception to the general principle that processes are patentable subject matter. 'Exceptions to broad statutory principles were to be narrowly construed,' it was held. Therefore, although essentially biological process are not patentable, the amount of human intervention determines whether a process is biological or not.[39] (This was a plant invention, of course, but the reasoning is obviously entirely apposite to human biotechnology.)

Presumably Greenpeace, the complainant in the above, is now no longer looked upon as a collection of cranks, or it would not be given standing in court, but there are other pressure groups not so highly regarded. In this connection a prominent patent attorney comments:

---

39 'Lubrizol /Hybrid Plants' [1988] *European Patent Office Reports* T320/87.

Furthermore, if the patent debate is to be properly engaged, it ought to be tackled comprehensively and not selectively to suit the agenda of the Greens, animal rights campaigners, and their supporters. For example, the question of patenting abortifacient drugs has not so far figured in the anti-patent case although for many people this technology raises far more important moral questions than those of animal welfare.[40]

The view here, on which one must come to one's own conclusions, seems to be that the debate should be shifted from those with a moderate point of view to those who are extremists, and might be easier to dismiss. Consistently the patent attorneys wish the morality question to disappear, and just as consistently the general public, on whom the NGOs depend for their support, will not allow it to do so. But as the cases above show, in the keynote cases, the disputes between the biotechnology companies, the arguments are all about novelty, prior art, breadth of claim - indeed the technicalities. Morality, despite some statements to the contrary, is a very minor consideration indeed.

Anybody with even marginal knowledge of biotechnology will have heard of the saga of the 'Oncomouse' (incidentally a trademark owned by E.I. du Pont Nemours Inc). This started with a series of patents sought by the President and Fellows of Harvard University, in many countries, for a mouse which has been engineered to carry an oncogene, that is, a genetic element making it prone to cancer and therefore making this, a 'higher organism' eminently suitable for research on that condition. It is not strictly a molecular patent, but a patent on a living animal, and therefore somewhat outwith the present theme, but is so pervasive in modern intellectual property law that it cannot be passed over since it is quintessentially illustrative of a major issue that biotechnology has thrown in the face of the patent system. This is the challenge to the traditional dichotomy between a mere discovery and an invention, by the alteration, in some way, of an organism already present in nature.

The original patent which covered both the process and the product, was of course initially sought in 1985 in the US and granted in 1988 without challenge. Notably, both the process and product were claimed for all non-human animals. An application was also made that year to the EPO and refused on the basis that the EPC excludes the patenting of higher forms of life as such. On challenge there, since art 53 (b) of the EPC mentions

---

40   Crespi, S 'Biotechnology patenting: the wicked animal must defend itself' [1995] *European Intellectual Property Review* vol 9, at p 431.

only 'animal varieties' rather than something like 'living animals, ' the patent was granted in 1992. Opposition was then mounted on the basis of the ordre publique provision, art 53 (a). Subsequent to this the patent was maintained in an amended form, the claims reduced to 'transgenic rodents' (the claims had been overbroad, extending the techniques employed to all animals). This was in turn appealed to the EPO Board of Appeal which remitted to the original tribunal, the Opposition Division of the EPO, in 2004 with directions to maintain the patent in its amended form. The latter came out with number of cogent points, including the statement that in terms of an EPC Article 53(a) objection, '….no single definition of morality based on, for example, economic or religious principles represents and accepted standard in European culture.' Nor was it prepared to accept the results of opinion polls as evidence.[41] Compare the notes on the *Greenpeace* case above.

In Canada the process claims were initially allowed by the Examiner, but not the product. The various appeals reached the Supreme Court of Canada, wherein the nine judges and 12 objectors ('interveners') argued the matter out once more. By a majority, the Court held that a higher life form is not a 'manufacture' under Section 2 of the Canadian Patent Act (the wording dating back to 1869), thus refusing both process and product. Comparison with other countries was held to be of limited value: 'While a fertilised egg injected with an oncogene may be a mixture of various ingredients, the body of a mouse does not consist of ingredients or substances that have been combined or mixed together by a person.' However as many as four judges dissented, stated that: 'The extraordinary scientific achievement of altering every single cell in the body of an animal which does not exist in this altered form in nature …….. is an inventive 'composition of matter' within the meaning ….. of the Act.'[42] The divergent fate of the patent in two neighbouring and superficially similar countries once again demonstrates the territorial nature of patent law in general.

On a more technical stumbling block, the case of the *University of California v Eli Lilly* (1997), again in the CAFC, concerned human recombinant insulin, useful – indeed vital – for glucose control in diabetics. The 1987 patent awarded to the university scientists described a method for cloning the insulin gene starting from mRNA but failed to describe the

---

41   'Grant of European Patent No 0 169 762 (Oncomouse/Harvard)' *Official Journal of the EPO* 588 (1992). Schertenlieb, D ' The patentability and protection of living organisms in the European Union' [2004] *European Intellectual Property Journal* 203. For the official documents see < http:legal.european-patent-office.org/dg3/biblio/t03031ex1.htm>.
42   *Harvard College v Canada (Commissioner of Patents)* [2002] SCC 76, or see website <File:/// A:Supreme%20Court%20of%/20Canada%20-%20Decisions%> .

complete nucleotide sequence in the cDNA derived from it. On challenge by Lilly the relevant claim was held to be invalid for insufficiency, and dragged the other claims down with it. The case therefore defined the scope of the written description of claims in biotechnology applications, and was much cited in the *Enzo* litigation (above). It is said to have established a new form of written description requirement apposite to biotechnology – more stringent than enablement simpliciter and an impediment to biotechnology patenting. Previously the manner in which the written description was provided was not critical as long as the skilled addressee could match it to the claims as originally presented. The insulin battle had wider repercussions since the alleged infringer Lilly fought out a battle over suspected 'inequitable conduct' by the UC scientists.[43]

One might note here that some nations, concerned to protect their indigenous species and varieties, and still rather dependent upon traditional medicine and agriculture, may well be much more restrictive in their patenting than are North America and Europe.[44] For example s 9 of the Thai Patent Act excludes any substance extracted from animals or plants from patentability. It is uncertain though whether this applies to genes, or even to steroids and enzymes. There is no specific exclusion for biological processes (as opposed to animal or plant varieties in themselves). On the face of it, were a transgenic mosquito to be invented, protection would apply to the process of producing the mosquito, but not to the mosquito itself, nor the gene in itself, used to produce the mosquito variant. Any decisions might devolve merely on the way the application is framed. In any case, under s 36(2) the law confers monopoly rights on the holder of a process patent to exploit not only the process, but also the products obtained from that process. This is seen as a threat to Thailand because of the domination of Western bioengineering companies, who are of course quite free to apply for patents within that jurisdiction. We will perhaps see a deepening fissure between countries which have traditional flora and fauna to protect, like India and China, and those which have become heavily urbanised and industrialised, like Singapore and Taiwan.

---

43   *University of California v Eli Lilly* USCAFC 96-1175 [1997] For the transcript see <file:///C:data/Hokker/fed96opinions/96-1175.html>. Discussions available are: Runkle, D and Granger, E 'A bitter battle over the insulin gene' [1997] *Science* vol 277, at p 1028; (1997); Crespi, RS. 'Patenting for research scientists.' [2004] *Trends in Biotechnology* vol 22, at p 638.
44   Thamisetty, S 'Patents and human genome research in developing countries' *Journal of World Intellectual Property* [2002] vol 5, at p 685; Kuanpoth, J Major issues in the Thai legal system: <http://members.tripod.com/asialaw/articles.jakpat1.html>.

Summary of 4.4

- Parties to patent disputes often persist in their efforts for decades, even after the patent in suit has expired, primarily to test the law (*Invitrogen*).

- Non - obviousness at the point of application might well be obviousness 20 years later (*Genentec*).

- To be successfully patented, a gene must be isolated, (*Amgen v Chugai*-US) when it becomes a simple chemical compound (*Fiers*-UK).

- Generally, objections to gene patenting on the basis of morality fail to impress patent examiners and appeal tribunals (*Howard Florey* as well as *Plant Genetic Systems*).

- It might be possible to argue that a protein, although previously well characterised, is not predictive of a DNA sequence due to the redundancy of the genetic code, rendering the DNA sequence novel. *(Deuel*- US).

- An end-product produced by its inventors by a process different from that embodied in an existing patent generally infringes the latter. *(Biogen*-UK).

- Broadness of claims in applications for biotechnology patents can be fatal and can be interpreted as protection for the consumer. (*Biogen*-UK*).

- A product obtained by a process is not novel if the product itself is not novel. (*Amgen v TKT*).

- In UK the doctrine of equivalents is paralleled by the EPC's Article 69.

- In the US an older biotechnology invention may well be infringed by a newer method even if the product is identical (*Amgen v TKT* –US).

- The Oncomouse patent suffered different fates in various jurisdictions, being successful in US and partly so in Europe (after overbroad claims were modified) but foundered in Canada, largely over repugnance at patenting life forms.

Box 4-2 DNA in Steganography

Steganography is the transmission of concealed messages, invisible ink being the means we all hear about at an early age. (It is contrasted with cryptography, the transmission of a message whose existence is apparent but whose meaning is concealed.)

Thus it is rumoured that cartoonists incorporate their DNA into the inks to prove the authenticity of their work. It is not clear however how this is accomplished - possibly they use hair roots. One company markets a 'DNA Print-kit' which encourages customers to place thumbprint on a precious object then write a security number or message on it.[1] The DNA would appear to have a fluorescent label for quick identification by a UV lamp. The SigNature ™ programme uses parts of a plant genome; these are unique for each customer, in that the DNA fragments are re-assembled for reading. [2] The product, be it a pill, a leather handbag, or a manuscript, can be traced through a commercial process. An initial success is claimed to be the authentication of high grade US cotton as the basis of finished textile products. An obvious and urgent application is the tracing of authentic pharmaceuticals so that the flood of fakes can be eliminated before they can wreak their damage. Thus DNA steganography embodies elements of intellectual property law, international trade, medical law, forgery and theft.

1   http.www.dnaaware.co,uk

2   http://www.adnas.com/Signature/the_signature_program

Chapter 5

Food

5.1 Gene Manipulation in Plants and Animals

In the production of food, biotechnology, as opposed to genetic engineering, is age-old. The manufacture of cheese, bread and beer involving the use of microorganisms are only a few examples. The so-called 'ploughman's lunch' served in many hostelries, contains at least three products of traditional biotechnology. The novelty of genetic engineering in food science is to supercede the intact microorganisms used in the traditional processes and to manipulate the DNA of food crops and animals such as to alter protein, carbohydrate, fat, flavour and toxin production. (See Box 5-1.) In Chapter 1 some of the scientific background was outlined. It can be noted here that the technological principles apply as much to plants as to animals. The universal genetic code applies to green plants and, like mammals; they are eukaryotes (having chromosomes). Scientists are quite prepared to alter the germ line in a plant to produce a different type of self-replicating organism. This is illegal for humans in all countries whose legislatures have considered the matter. Permanent alteration of the germline is also performed with some reluctance in animals, if not fish.

Somewhat tediously, the nomenclature as well as the abbreviations must be addressed. Any genetically modified organism (GMO) may have had its DNA engineered permanently, that is from generation to generation, or somatically, only within its own lifetime. And genes may either be inserted or deleted, usually the former. Sometimes the term living modified organism (LMO) rather than GMO is used. A non-plant GMO/LMO might be a vertebrate like a fish or an invertebrate like a prawn; it might even be a fungus, like a mushroom, or a bacterium. A modified plant grown in a field for food is a genetically modified crop (GMC). A GMC may be sold in the shops as the intact organism, e.g. a tomato or a banana, or may be processed and packaged to appear in the shops in some other form, e.g. textured protein from genetically altered soya beans. products. The blanket term for all these is a genetically modified food (GMF).

Perhaps the most famous of such products is 'yellow rice'.[1] The yellow rice project was initiated in the context of some hundreds of thousands of

---

1   Sommer, A and West, KP *Vitamin A Deficiency: Health, Survival, Vision* (Oxford University Press, 1996).

children in Indonesia suffering from vitamin A deficiency. Much of the investigation was done by the American scientist Sommer, who brought the situation to the attention of the scientific community and pioneered the combating of measles and other infections by making the vitamin available to children. This is supplied in the diet in two ways, as precursor carotenoids, or preformed, as retinoids. The former are abundant in highly coloured fruit and vegetables, the latter in dairy products. Of course orange or red fruits such as papayas, mangoes and watermelons are abundant in Indonesia, as are green vegetables, so it might seem that vitamin A deficiency should be rare. However this is not the case, and children either do not have access to such foods or do not eat them if they are available. By all accounts in families where the parents are busy working the children are merely filling their stomachs with rice and tapioca, unsupplemented by ingredients with sufficient vitamins. In any case it appears that food is generally in short supply in Indonesia and dairy products, specifically, are even less available to the population in general. In January 2000, however, the Institute of Plant Sciences in the Swiss Federal Institute of technology at Zurich announced that it had produced a carotenoid-enriched rice. This of course is yellow, and if adopted by farmers in South East Asia will go a long way to eradicating the growth and eye problems associated with vitamin A deficiency. The achievement was unique, at the time, because the scientists inserted not a single gene, but the genes for a complete synthetic pathway, and one of them, surprisingly, was from the daffodil. Here we have an altruistic effort to produce a genetically modified organism (GMO).

When it was realised that that foreign genes might be introduced into plants and into soil bacteria symbiotic with plants (importantly, those bacteria capable of fixing nitrogen, for they would provide nitrogen for the host plant) a vast improvement in agricultural production (most of these of course being linked to marketability) seemed in the offing. And of course food animals were next on the list - salmon, for example, were soon genetically engineered to make them grow faster. However plants still form the main corpus of GMOs at this time, and achievements in their technology seem modest in comparison to what is envisaged, *inter alia* plants which express human insulin or viral proteins as vaccines in their sap. Whereas there has been much concern, indeed outrage, over the introduction of GMCs for food, their development for pharmaceutical production has been looked upon as transcending no ethical boundaries. There remain reservations, however, about the possibility of a GMO carrying the genes from a vaccine entering the food chain and exposing people to uncontrolled doses of the vaccine. In 2003 the US company Prodigene was fined $250,000 for contaminating a soya bean crop with corn engineered to produce an experimental pig vaccine.

Box 5-1   Genetic Modifications of Food Plants and Animals

Food content per se

Post-harvest preservation (slow ripening/sprouting)
Enhancement of protein or essential fatty acid content
Reduction of saturated fat or cholesterol content
Increased vitamin content
Reduction of allergens or toxins

Crop well-being and performance

Resistance to fungal/viral disease
Resistance to insects
Resistance to frost and drought
Faster growth
More abundant fruiting
Herbicide resistance

(Evidently some items apply to plants only)

GMOs and concerns about their safety emerged simultaneously. If used as food, human health is the issue; if transgenic crops and fish in the agricultural industry itself are considered, damage to the environment, and particularly biodiversity, is the concern. Both plant and animal cells can be infected with viruses. When the splicing of genes into viruses became possible, there was general concern that if this were done in respect of (specifically) tumour viruses their inter-species pathogenicity might be enhanced. There might also be altered patterns of disease and geographical spread. Thus it was that at an early date in the history of biotechnology, around 1973, there existed among scientists a moratorium on constructing recombinant cancer viruses, whether human or plant, lest there be harm if they escaped into the environment, and especially into that precious component of the environment, ourselves as human beings. Obviously were escape to occur, removal from the environment would be rather difficult, for experience has shown that even large animals like rabbits in Australia are impossible to eradicate if they reach threshold numbers. And viruses are notoriously resilient particles. Neither at the stage of initiating the moratorium, not for a long time afterwards, was public or legal opinion engaged. However one can see here the genesis of a regulatory framework for genetics and molecular biology, later to mature into administrative and (even later) criminal law.

The next step was a conference held at Asilomar, California in 1975. This saw eminent molecular biologists agreeing to restraint in cloning (i.e. making multiple copies of) DNA in those organisms which had not been specifically disabled in some way to restrict their growth outside the test tube. National Institutes of Health (NIH) guidelines were produced after the conference; they effectively forbade the use of recombinant DNA (rDNA) techniques in cancer viruses. They were not applicable to private industry, however. In any case they were revoked in 1979, for by then two safe plasmid vectors (rather than viruses) had been developed. Many scientists then came to view the concerns expressed in seventies as premature. Any GMO released into the environment, it was theorised, is likely to be less well adapted to stress than the wild types – being highly selected for survival under restricted conditions - and will tend to die out. Ordinary microorganisms in the free-living state have been known, for many years, to mutate spontaneously, travelling long distances and even exchange genetic material with other microorganisms. If GMOs do this too, it was said, there is unlikely to be any dire consequence. Moreover, by the early 1990s there had been many controlled releases of transgenic plants without apparent harm, and in 1992 for the first time the US Department of Agriculture (USDA) stated that it would no longer bother to monitor a new genetically engineered product. The first product exempted was a tomato produced by the Calgene Corporation, having a longer shelf life and better flavour than the traditional crop. Recently however fresh warnings have been articulated by scientists and these find strong resonance among the public and in the non-governmental organisations (NGOs). There is concern that transgenic plants might become competitive and weedlike. And there is certainly some evidence of genetic exchange between GMOs (as crops) and weeds.[2]

Transgenic livestock like sheep or goats are held to be of low risk to the environment but transgenic fish and live virus-based vaccines a priori pose some conceivable risk. The former might escape from farms and alter the

---

2   Poppy, GM 'Geneflow from genetically modified plants – towards a more quantitative risk assessment.' [2004] *Trends in Biotechnology* vol 22, at 436; Barton, J, Smith, P et al ' A model protocol to assess the risks of agricultural introductions: a risk-based approach to rationalising field trial regulation.' [1997] *Nature Biotechnology* vol 15, at p 845; Douma, WT and, Matthee, M. 'Towards new EC rules on the release of GMOs.' [1999] *RECEIL* vol 8, at p 152.

ecological balance in the wild; the latter might spontaneously mutate and become virulent for animals or plants. Moreover agricultural botanists in France have claimed that genes for herbicide resistance in oilseed rape can spread to wild radish and that potatoes engineered to resist aphids can also harm natural predators of the aphids, namely ladybirds.

The so-called marker genes have caused particular concern. These are genes inserted to check the validity of the gene insertion process. Thus, suppose a gene for enhanced protein synthesis is inserted into a plant cell. This gene is ligated to another gene conferring antibiotic resistance. The transformed cells can then be placed in a suitable antibiotic - if they survive, there has been successful insertion of the gene for the protein. But what if the plant containing the cells, on being ingested, transfers the gene for antibiotic resistance to the microflora in the human intestine? They would then become antibiotic resistant - not a hazard in itself certainly, but any antibiotic resistant microorganism is intrinsically undesirable. The danger has long been deemed to be negligible, but the test is whether genes ingested in plants can be found intact, or nearly so, in the large intestine, where the microflora reside. Recently researchers had the bright idea of feeding GMFs to colostomy patients, who of course pass foods down the small intestine but avid the colon with a colostomy bag. Sure enough, the colostomy contents appeared to contain plant genes.[3] In an alternative strategy Novartis Corporation has developed a new marker gene which codes for an enzyme converting the phosphate of the simple monosaccharide mannose to glucose. Plants with this marker gene thrive when fed mannose, for they can convert it to glucose, and so the success of the bioengineering is confirmed. In any case the EU has now banned any GMFs containing marker genes via the enablement to make fast decisions in Article 21 of Directive 90/220.

The yellow rice venture notwithstanding concerns about the safety of GMFs have led to them being banned in many countries, and described quite ludicrously as 'frankenfoods', an emotive term much used by the media and most unhelpful in the context of reasoned debate. In this connection one canard at least can be shot from the sky – there is no way that a GMF can affect the characteristics or health of a consumer merely by being a GMF. We consume the genes of plants and animals every day, and in large quantities, and they do not in any way affect us (apart from providing small molecules

3 For a discussion see <http:/www/rense.com/general27/intes.htm</A>. In another incident reported in *Nature* in 2005, stray Bt corn seeds were found to contain antibiotic resistance genes. ('Bt' represents Bacillus thuringiensis toxin – a powerfully insecticidal protein.) See also Burke, D, 'Novel foods: the changing response', in Belton PS and Belton T (eds). *Food, Science and Society* (Springer, 2003) p 135.

- purines, pyridines, pentoses and phosphate - for metabolism), certainly not our genomes. Sir Colin Berry has pointed out that we share 60% of our genes with the banana![4] Henry II of England was said to have died from a 'surfeit of lampreys,' but he had no resemblance whatsoever to a lamprey when he died.

Notwithstanding that irrefutable fact, GMOs, GMCs, GMFs and LMOs across the board attract concern from individuals, governments and NGOs interested in safety, ethics and regulation. In the medicine/ healthcare field, an alternative focus is on ethics, particularly, in connection with GMOs designed to produce vaccines or spare organs. In nutrition/ food science, concerns have been fuelled on the one hand by the growing desire of educated populations to know what they are putting down their throats, and on the other by a number of unfortunate scares, near-disasters, and actual disasters, relating to such diverse entities as cholesterol, salt, prions causing 'mad cow disease'.[5] There is a feeling in some circles that reassurances from governments, usually ministries of health and their attendant scientific advisors, cannot be trusted. Given that the safety of food (and the environment) is seen as a matter of vital importance, regulations, national and international, are clearly necessary, it is equally clear - at least to the objectors - that preexisting regulations are not sufficient – even those of a stringency required by the EU.

Summary of 5.1

- GMOs/LMOs have attracted a regulatory framework from their inception.

- Marker (antibiotic resistance) genes which may have posed a danger are being phased out by the agricultural industry and by regulation.

- Despite the fact that ingested genes cannot alter the characteristics of a human individual, GMFs are banned in many countries.

- NGOs have been particularly active in leading public opinion in the direction of perceived risk from all GM products.

4   Berry, C. Baseball, lobsters and our genetic relationship to the banana [1995] *Medicine, Science and the Law* vol 45, at p 277.
5   'Mad cow disease' is known more properly as bovine spongiform encephalopathy. The infective agent of this, the prion, when taken up by human tissues can cause the delayed onset, but very serious Jakob-Creutzfeldt disease.

5.2 Tortious Possibilities

Consider the sequence of events in Box 5-2 (p 222). Such a concatenation might seem unlikely, but all disasters happen due to the random occurrence of untoward but interlinked events, including, of course, human error. In mathematical terms, the separate odds against misfortune, when subjected to the multiplication rule, yield 'x' to one against, and 'x' may be massive, but the 'one' never disappears. The legal issues that might arise out of the scenario as presented are as follows:

Negligence

If actions in negligence lie in a duty of care, (conjoined with foreseeability, proximity, and what is fair and just under the circumstances) with the addition of breach of the duty and causation, they are relevant to many aspects of the events in Box 5-2.[6] The great advantage of negligence (to a plaintiff) is universally acknowledged to be its flexibility, since anybody can sue irrespective of territorial interests, and every sort of injury, even psychological, is now actionable. Here there are a clear variety of possible plaintiffs and defendants, these two categories being somewhat interchangeable. Aggrieved parties include the chicken, banana and fish farmers, with the Ministry, the EIA consultancy, and the biotech company as potential defendants. Environmental NGOs, if they are given standing in this country's courts, may well be enjoined as plaintiffs. The mothers with mastitis will certainly explore the possibilities.

The cases would largely hinge, presumably, on foreseeability and proximity. In some aspects perhaps even *res ipso loquitor* could be adduced,[7] perhaps for the fact of the GMO infesting the banana plantations. Of course, beyond observing that if rats die off it is foreseeable that other animals will proliferate, the cases would be argued on facts more detailed than those

---

6   The development of tort is related by Baker, JH *An Introduction to English Legal History* (Butterworths, 3rd edn, 1990) p 477. The heads of negligence now usually cited are originally as in Lord Bridge's speech in *Caparo Industries plc v Dickman* [1990] 2 AC 617 and reiterated in *White and Another v Jones and Another* [1993] 3 All ER 481. In *X and Others v Bedfordshire County Council* [1995] AER 353 Lord Browne Wilkinson in the House of Lords quoted Caparo once again, in that in deciding whether to develop novel categories of negligence, the court should proceed incrementally and by analogy with decided cases. *Rylands v Fletcher* as head of action has not been discussed in the text herein but cases involving GMCs might be expected to crop up in the context of non-natural user of land and escapes from that land.

7   The locus classicus for *res ipsa loquitur* is usually given as *Scott v London and St Katherine's Dock* [1865] 3 H & C 596.

presented in the box. The chain of events leads through three agents from BC to the mastitis in the mothers, and no doubt in court there could be much argument as to causation and proximity with respect to each. A modern case which presents dicta on causation is *Fairchild* v *Glenhaven Funeral Services Ltd* (2002)[8] in which the House of Lords considered three conjoined appeals. The instant case involved asbestos dust, which causes mesothelioma, a lung cancer, and the difficulty in ascribing to blame to any of a series of employers for whom the claimant worked, two of them in particular being identified for the action. It had previously been a tenet of the law that the claimant was required to discharge the burden of showing that the breach complained of was due to the negligence of a specific tortfeasor. In this case Lord Bingham reviewed the 'but for' (or *causa sine qua non*) test (i.e. but for the breach by the defendant the plaintiff would not have suffered injury or harm). This gives rise to the difficulty that there are cases, like *Fairchild*, wherein there are two or more acts or events each of which could possibly have caused the harm. The strict application of the test gives the result, at variance with common sense, that none of these is a cause. Lord Bingham observed that the claimant was not able, due to the current limits of human science, to prove, on the balance of probabilities, that his mesothelioma was the result of his inhaling asbestos dust during his employment by B or during his employment by both A and B. Thus, there was room to question the appropriateness of the established rule. In the event the HL reluctantly concluded that both respondents should be considered liable since they contributed to the risk of the mesothelioma. Lord Hoffman said that the agents (the supposed tortfeasors) had to be 'operating in substantially the same way'. *Fairchild* was succeeded by *Barker v Corus* (2006). This was also a mesothelioma case. Again, proof of causing an increase in risk was considered a material contribution to the injury (by two of the judges). Others, the majority, were of the opinion that the creation of the risk that the plaintiff might contract the disease, in itself, constituted the damage caused. If this is followed, each of

---

8 *Fairchild v Glenhaven Funeral Services Ltd* [2002] UKHL 22. An interesting feature of this case was that the judge at first instance held the defendant companies liable. The companies appealed but in the meantime paid out the damages without prejudice to later proceedings; in other words the law was to be tested, as it was – very thoroughly – in the HL. For a comprehensive discussion of the relationship of tort in relation to biotechnology including a discussion of Fairchild see Howarth, D 'Civil liability for GM farming: unanswered questions' [2004] *Environmental Liability* vol 4, at p 137. This article also contains an in depth discussion of the Biotechnology Commission. An official document is *GM Crops - Coexistence and Liability*. (Department of Trade and Industry, 2003). The *Barker v Corus* case is cited as [2006] UKHL 20.

the defendant parties in the scenario discussed herein would be liable, but not *in solidum*, rather in proportion to the risk that each generated.

The scenario as a whole has certain analogies to the so-called *toxic tort,* a term said to have been borrowed from the courts in US. These are reputed to be on the rise in most countries and to have added a fresh cause of action, namely injury to nature. The dispute usually arises when chemicals are released into the environment, causing illness or damage, sometimes many years later. In UK one can read the *Sellafield* (leukaemia) case, the *Cleveland* (asthma) case, the *Camelford* (aluminium toxicity) case, and the docklands (respiratory illness) case.[9] Many of the cases in the US devolve on contamination of housing by moulds, due to faulty plumbing or deficient damp courses; moulds of course being living cells offer at least an analogy to damage by GMOs. In the artificial scenario here, dispersion of the avocado toxin would certainly qualify under the heading of the toxic tort. Causation is said to be the one of the central problems of such cases (as indeed it is in tort generally) and certainly in the scenario in the box scientific evidence would have to be adduced on both sides in relation to the initial probabilities (see para 5.4 for further discussion). The causal linkage of the toxin to the mastitis might be especially difficult to justify. It could never be proved in the absolute sense. Science as a whole, and epidemiology in particular, does accommodate the concept of absolute proof - probabilities only can be deduced.[10] Although not explicitly stated in this manner, evidently the principle is legally endorsed in *Fairchild.*

9   Pugh, C and Day, M 'Toxic torts' *New Law Journal* 14th Nov 1989, at p 1549; Garrett, N 'Life is the risk we cannot refuse: a precautionary approach to toxic risks we run' [2004] *Georgetown Environmental Law Review*, vol 17, at p 67. It will be recalled that perhaps the most famous of cases on nuisance, *St Helen's Smelting Co v Tipping* [1865] 11 HL Cas 642, was in a sense a toxic tort, although there was no difficulty in establishing causation.
10   Eschewing certainties in favour of probabilities should be familiar from the contents of Chapters 2 and 3 herein. The criteria for probable causal connections in epidemiology were promulgated long ago by the famous statistician Bradford Hill. These are (A) strength of association, (B) consistency, (C) specificity, (D) temporal relationship, (E) biological gradient, (F) biological plausibility, (G) coherence - and, if possible, (H) experimental verification. See Hill, AB and Hill ID *Principles of Medical Statistics* (Edward Arnold, 12th edn, 1972). For a recent cogent discussion with a legal leaning see Danne, A. 'McTear v Imperial Tobacco: understanding the role and limitations of expert epidemiological evidence in scientific litigation' [2006] *Journal of Law and Medicine* vol 13, at p 471. The Bradford Hill criteria were adopted in, *inter alia*, in *Reay v British Nuclear Fuels plc* [1994] 5 MLR 1. It appears to be established that the standard of proof is the usual civil one of the balance of probabilities, as in *Bonnington Castings v Wardlaw* [1956] 1 All ER 615.

Nuisance

Nuisance is the common law crime of interfering with certain public rights is the more important head, namely public nuisance, herein. In the scenario in Box 5-2, there has certainly been public nuisance, namely release of both the GMO and its toxin into the environment. Historically the law of public nuisance focussed largely on the highway, but has travelled somewhat along it, in that notably in 1994 in England a surgeon who practised professionally, while being aware throughout that he was a carrier of the hepatitis B virus, was prosecuted and convicted of the offence of public nuisance.[11]

Private nuisance is still held to derive from property rights, reaffirmed in UK in the House of Lords case *Hunter* v *Canary Wharf* (1997).[12] The case gave the House of Lords the opportunity to discuss the categories of nuisance. It appears that the owner or occupier (with exclusive right of possession) can suffer:

(1) Encroachment on his land by a neighbour

(2) Direct physical injury to his land

(3) Interference with his quiet enjoyment of the land.

GMOs/GMCs would seem to be well within the compass of the first of these, and probably the second and perhaps the third might be relevant if the GMO happened to be obnoxious *per se*. In the context of food, examples might appear to be far-fetched, but what if the GMO/GMF happened to be a self pollinating bean which sent out clouds of asthma-engendering spores to a neighbour? In the scenario in Box 5-2, though, no doubt the banana growers would have a strong case against the farmers in nuisance under (2) above.

Breach of statutory duty

There are two venerable cases oft quoted in this area.[13] In *Gorris v Scott* (1874) a shipowner was bound by a statute imposing a variety of quarantine on the sheep he was transporting. Some sheep were washed overboard and their owner brought an action in damages for their loss. The court held that

---

11   Mulholland, M 'Public nuisance – a new use for an old tool' [1995] *Professional Negligence* vol 11, at p 70.
12   *Hunter v Canary Wharf Ltd (conjoined with Hunter and others v London Docklands Development)* [1997] 2 All ER 426.
13   Discussed by Hepple, BA and Mathews, MH. *Tort: Cases and Materials* (Butterworths, London, 1991), at p 540. The original citations are Gorris v Scott [1874] 9 LR Exch 125; *Read v Croydon* [1938] 4 All ER 631.

the statute did not cover loss for this reason, it implied liability only for the failure of sanitary precautions. Therefore the claim failed. In *Read v Croydon Corp* (1838) a baby contracted typhoid due to faulty maintenance of the municipal water supply. Damages were awarded, but not to the baby, rather the father as ratepayer. Before straying into later cases, one can extract the principles as follows: the relevant statute offers protection to a class of people, other than the public at large (ratepayers in the *Read* case); injury or damage was in fact caused; the breach caused the damage; and the reading of the statute corresponds to the damage caused. (The claim failed in the *Gorris* case on this point.) In *Y v UK* (2001)[14] the European Court of Human Rights (ECHR) declined to accept a House of Lords ruling (*X v Bedfordshire County Council,* 1995) limiting the extent to which the tort of breach of statutory duty could be applied to a case where the local authority apparently failed to make adequate care orders for neglected children. The ECHR decided that there had been breach of Articles 3 (illegality of cruel and unjust treatment) and 13 (mandatory nature of an effective remedy). Article 3 seems remote from any scenario involving GMOs but Article 13 might well crop up if a domestic court were to refuse restitution for harm done by GMOs which the ECHR thought unreasonable.

In these cases, a distinction between operational and policy decisions was again made (the concept not being novel), liability usually being attached to breaches of the former rather than the latter. In Box 5-2, the decision by the Ministry to adopt the EIA the GMO was undoubtedly operational, therefore potentially actionable. (The Ministry will of course sue the consulting company, who will complain that they were not given sufficient information from the biotechnology company; the recrimination runs back and forth as usual.) The farmers might have a cause of action, also, in the failure of the authorities to tackle the bird menace or the lack of compensation. The courts, moreover, will seldom ascribe blame to harm resulting from scarce resources or distribution of risks.

Trespass

Leaving Box 5-2, there is a UK case in trespass directly emanating from the introduction of GMOs. In *DPP v Bayer* (2003)[15] the defendant was charged with aggravated trespass under the Criminal Justice and Public Order Act 1994, s 68 because with others he entered private land which was being sown with GM maize as part of government sponsored project and effectively

---

14   *Y v U.K.* [2001] (ECHR) quoting *Barret v Enfield LBC* [1999] 3 All ER 193.
15   *DPP v Bayer* [2003] EWHC 2567 (Admin.)

halted the project. The district judge held that the defendant was an aggravated trespasser under the meaning of the act but dismissed the charge since at common law he had the defence that he genuinely believed that GM crops were dangerous and had genuine fears for the property surrounding the trial field. The Crown appealed by way of case stated, and the appeal was allowed by the Divisional Court since the common law defence related to the fear of unlawful or criminal acts. Here there was nothing unlawful about planting GM maize. The case was remitted to the lower court with a direction to convict. Section 68 of the Act was drafted to combat hunt saboteurs, but found an obvious application in the GM context. Once the prosecution has established that the activity disrupted is lawful, there is no defence available. Lord Melchett (see below) in his equivalent foray was charged with criminal damage – this was not available for the *Bayer* trial since he merely blocked the operation of the tractors.

The threat to non-GM farmers of contamination arises from consumer aversion to GMOs. They are apparently put into the same mental compartment as pesticides, which of course is what organic farmers claim to eschew. Thus if organic or non- GMO crops are thought to contain GM material then their value plummets, possibly in terms of the following elements. In terms of loss, the organic/non GMO farmers:

(1) Cannot obtain market premiums.

(2) Lose accreditation (from the organic farmers' organisations).

(3) See a fall in the value of their land.

(4) May have to spend money to ward off contamination.

Indeed the mere threat of contamination might be sufficient to generate these adverse circumstances. As has been articulated by one writer: 'As the political debate on GM farming rages on, with no obvious settlement yet in sight, lawyers continue to ask themselves a simple hypothetical question. If GM farming were eventually permitted, what liability would GM farmers have to organic farmers, or to conventional non-GM farmers, whose crops and land are contaminated by GM organisms?'

In UK the Biotechnology Commission (a cabinet-constituted advisory body in tandem with the Human Genetics Commission and the Food Standards Authority) has considered the question of liability and has produced a report which examines these issues. It proposes a code of practice, inspection and a compensation fund but does not rule out criminal proceedings. If there is environmental damage, GM farmers would have to pay for clean up if so ordered by the authorities. Otherwise of course there would have to be actions in negligence.[16]

As a final note here, under the Consumer Protection Act (1987) implementing EC Product Liability Directive 85/374, as amended by 99/34, it is irrelevant that the producer of defective goods (for example a GMO which has a toxin content too strong for its intended the purpose or is more vigorous in colonizing untoward environments than expected) does not know of the defect before the damage occurs. Moreover: '… product liability would be a chilling prospect if the courts were in future to link human illness or environmental change to GM foods. Companies no doubt will have learned from the travails of the tobacco industry that it is best not to hide those memos that discuss the discovery of deleterious side effects.'[17]

As has been stated above, although there is lingering suspicion that some of them may have altered allergenic properties, significant damage to the health of human beings by GMOs/GMFs seems unlikely, but when the hypothetical complainant claims to have contracted colon cancer from one of Monsanto's products, we will see.

Food forensics (detecting genetically modified products)

It has long been important to be able to detect, in food, ingredients which a specific consumer may not wish to ingest. The best known example, of course, is the abhorrence of any products derived from swine by practicing Moslems and Jews. Traditionally, and in the case of GMFs, any legal action in this context must rest upon science. Formerly the science was describable as immunochemistry, now it is DNA probing. It is essential, if for example GMFs are to be accurately labelled, or banned, that the authorities (ministries of the environment, local authorities, inspectorates of weights and measures, whosoever is applicable) be able to tell what is a GMO/.GMF or not, wholly or partly. This activity has been described as 'food forensics' (alternatively the work of the 'gene police').[18] Several points of science are relevant

16 This report is discussed in great detail by Howarth, D 'Civil liability for GM farming: unanswered questions' *Environmental Liability* [2004] vol 4, at p 137. The report itself is entitled: *GM Crops?-Coexistence and Liability*.

17 Ball, S and Bell, S *Environmental Law* (Blackstone Press, 3rd edn 1995) p 42. In addition, in some circumstances involving GMOs, judicial review might be sought. Recently this has arisen in the proposed application for judicial review by Friends of the Earth against the UK Food Standards Authority. It is alleged that it failed to prevent GM rice entering the food chain. See the *Guardian* 18th Sep 2006.

18 For exhaustive discussions of food forensics see Streinz, R and Fuchs, LO 'The legal

here, and would have to be understood by attorneys if such questions of identification became an issue. Firstly, if an organism, plant or animal, is engineered to produce more of a certain preexisting material, and that material, in itself, is harvested and incorporated into foods, there is no way that one can ascertain, by inspection of the processed food, that the material was derived from a GMO. Thus soy protein, for example, is incorporated into many processed foodstuffs and there is no doubt that frequently some of this comes from engineered soya beans in the US. It is usually, indistinguishably, the same protein as found in non-GM beans. The only way that consumers or buyers can become aware of such presence is by the process of traceability. Traceability then becomes an important facet of food forensics – it has a direct analogy to the 'chain of custody' concept in the handling of criminal evidence – the progress of the evidence from hand to hand must be carefully documented. (See Box 4-2 on 'steganography'.)

Secondly, if the organism is engineered to produce an altered soy protein, then that is detectable and traceable by isolating it and determining its amino sequence. However the industry has been accustomed to identify a food protein by listing the first five to 50 amino acids of the sequence at one end of the chain. Proteins can however be composed of chains of many hundreds of amino acids and those sequences remaining undisclosed could potentially be allergenic. A change of practice has been advocated.

Thirdly, it is difficult for the public (and presumably a jury) to understand the statistical basis of 'detectability'. Zero presence is one of the many things that science cannot prove. In asserting absence of a GMO or a GMO-derived protein, analysts can only state the probability (usually at a 95% standard) that a test material is not different from a graded series of standards of the same material, when the latter is extrapolated to zero on a graph.

For proteins in GMFs the techniques may still involve immunochemistry, that is the suspect protein is made to react with an antibody, thus revealing its presence; for cellular material, which inevitably contains DNA, PCR is used to amplify segments of that DNA, which can then be detected or

situation for genetically engineered food in Europe', in: *Genetically Engineered Food: Methods and Detection.* Heller, KJ (ed) (Wiley-VCH, Weinheim, 2003); Einspanier, R and Rief, S 'DNA –based methods for detection of genetic modifications' *ibid* at p 155. Wolfe, M and Primrose, S 'Food forensics: using DNA technology to combat misdescription and fraud' [2004] *Trends in Biotechnology* vol 22, at p 222; Henemann, JA, Sparrow, AD et al. ' Is confidence in the monitoring of genetically modified foods justified?' [2004] *Trends in Biotechnology* vol 22, at p 331; For specific examples see Rodriquez, MA, Garcia, T et al. 'PCR identification of beef,sheep goat and pork in raw and heat treated mixtures' [2004] *Journal of Food Proteins* vol 67, at p 172.

even quantitated. Remarkably, PCR techniques have been successful in distinguishing farmed from wild fish (the latter of course attracting a premium).[19]

Summary of 5.2

- Evidently GMOs like other products of technology, will in due course generate actions in

  - negligence

  - nuisance

  - breach of statutory duty

  - trespass

- At least in UK, juries, perhaps unduly influenced by media panic, seem reluctant to convict those who choose to interfere with GMCs.

- In UK, after *Fairchild*, a plaintiff might succeed in damages by proving only that GMOs/GMFs enhanced the risk of a harm suffered.

- Legal proceedings will increasingly depend upon food forensics - particularly the detection of specific DNA sequences amplified by PCR.

5.3 Genetically Modified Products in Administrative Law

Leaving aside disasters, opponents of genetic modification claim that it is unnatural, therefore impermissible, and should be banned by law. This has been described as a naturalistic fallacy - a plethora of entities encountered by humans are both natural and extremely harmful. 'Natural' does not mean 'good'. Nonetheless the fallacy is widely held and is the basis for attempts to introduce legislation to limit or even ban the dissemination of GMOs and GMCs. Democratically elected legislatures are compelled to respond to public pressure. To illustrate something of the panic engendered, consider the actions of the Marquess of Landsdowne, who wrote that after he had planted rapeseed he was informed by his supplier that it was 'contaminated' by 0.4%

---

19   Renshaw, MA, Saillant, E et al 'Application of hypervariable markers for forensic identification of 'wild' from hatchery-raised red drum, Sciaenops ocellatus' [2006] *Forensic Science International* vol 156, at p 9.

of genetically modified seed.[20] He killed off the entire crop with Gramoxone. Given that Gramoxone is a form of paraquat, which is not entirely harmless to the environment, and that neither rapeseed nor rape oil is eaten by humans, but used for animal feed and for modification to canola oil respectively, this reaction might be considered disproportionate.

United States regulation

In 1986, the Coordinated Framework for the Regulation of Biotechnology set up by the President's Office of Science and Technology empowered three agencies to consider new developments:

- US Department of Agriculture (USDA) for the development and field testing of GMCs. In turn this incorporates the Animal and Plant Inspection Service (APHIS).

- The Environmental Protection Agency (EPA) has responsibility for the safety of pesticides and pesticide producing plants, for example approving the use of *Bacillus thuringiensis (Bt)* toxin, which occurs naturally.

- The Food and Drug Administration (FDA) assesses food and nutritional aspects of new plant varieties and animals if used as food. In 1992 in this role it decided that genetically modified products must merely meet the same standards as other foods, not fresh standards.[21] The policy is to treat modifications to foodstuffs, including genetic modifications, as additives if they significantly alter the properties of the food, in other words, not sustaining 'substantial equivalence', of which more below. The FDA recently announced that it regarded foodstuffs deriving from cloned animals (*vide* Dolly the sheep) as substantially equivalent to established ones, that is, demanding no separate regulations.

If a GMO indeed contains a pesticide, then all three agencies may be involved in its approval. However it is notable that in the US there has been relatively little debate about GMCs/GMFs, and since the regulators did not

---

20   *The Times* 26th June, 2001.

21   See the FDA website < http://vm.cfsan.fda.gov/~lrd/biocon,html>. Also Pelletier D,. 'Science, law and politics in the Food and Drug Administration's genetically engineered foods policy: FDA's 1992 Policy Statement' [2005] *Nutrition Reviews* vol 63, at p 171. (This paper provides a very comprehensive timeline for anybody interested in biotechnology regulation in the US.) A useful list of US food laws is to be found in Omaye, ST *Food and Nutritional Toxicology* (CRC Press, 2004) at p 79.

see biotechnology as posing any special risks, so that existing laws were entirely applicable. Agribiotech companies may voluntarily ask the FDA for a consultation, however. Indeed all would have been well in the US were it not one of the world's major exporters of food. Its farmers planted millions of acres of GMCs only to find that in the last few years they have been branded as unacceptable in most other countries, notably in the EU. This has led to complaints to the WTO.

European regulation

As a reminder, in the EU the Commission, consisting of appointed officials, proposes legislation ('directives') which are approved by the Council of Ministers (usually the foreign minister of each member country) and can be vetoed by the European Parliament. Directives must be transposed into domestic law by the dates stated, and legislation should be 'effective, proportionate, and dissuasive.' Before a sort of panic ensued in 1997-98 any company which sought to introduce a GMC into the EU milieu approached a member state to act as rapporteur. The rapporteur decided if EU regulations were met, after which the application was sent to the Commission. A vote was taken and on a majority the product went on the market or not. Each member state was however free produce its own regulations. By Directive 258/97 a novel food was defined as one which did not have a significant history of consumption before May, 1997 and all such had to be subjected to premarket safety assessment.[22]

---

22   To explore the intricacies of the EU one can first enter website < europa.eu.int> which will allow navigation via the search facility to all directives. For faster access to food and biotechnology see <http://ec.europa.eu/food/food/biotechnology/index_eu.htm> For GMOs authorised for release before the 2003 revisions see <http://www.europa.eu.int/ comm/food/food/biotechnology/gmfood/gmo_authorisations_en_pdf.>
The website of Dr Jukes of Reading University is invaluable for a student in this area, but even he is careful to state that his coverage is 'probably not comprehensive'. See: <http//www.fst.rdg.ac.uk/foodlaw/main htm.> . Other useful sources are: Streinz, R and Fuchs, LO cited in note 18 above; (This volume contains a list of national authorities responsible for the implementation of European Parliament and Council Regulation No 258/97 concerning novel foods and novel food ingredients, e.g. in UK the Food Standards Agency with separate bodies for Scotland and Wales); Sampson, T 'Would you know your GMO? An assessment of regulations 1839/2003, 65/2004 and GMO unique modifiers' [2004/2005] *Bioscience Law Review* vol 3, at p 113; Gottweiss, H 'Regulating genomics in the 21st century; from logos to pathos' [2005] *Trends in Biotechnology* vol 23, at p 118, who advocates '..... more stringent agro-environmental norms, greater scrutiny of safety evidence, the acknowledgment of more complex causal pathways of potential harm and the introduction of new forms of transparency and accountability in the regulatory process.'

There was some change as the century due to a close. All new GM technology, beyond what was already in place or being tested as crops was effectively banned. At a meeting in Luxembourg in October 2001 EU Ministers of the Environment rejected a proposal to lift the ban and this gave rise to the ongoing dispute with the WTO. In 2003 the regulators relented somewhat, but the subsequent directives are of a byzantine complexity and realistically must be left to full-time specialists in the field.[23] (There is enough digestible material to support a specialist journal called *European Food Law*!) In general, though, the EU holds fast to the precautionary principle, in contradistinction to the authorities in the US.[24]

The EU in Directive 90/220/EC and subsequently 2001/18/EC defines a GMO as an organism as one in which the genetic material has been altered in such a way that does not occur naturally by mating or natural selection, and in addition, there are excluded organisms derived from polyploidy induction (increasing chromosome numbers) mutagenesis (chemical transformation) as well as cell fusion, on condition, in turn, that such procedures do not employ recombinant nucleic acid molecules. It incorporates the information required before authorisation of experimental release.

Directive 90/219 This is a system of risk management during any process involved in the development of a GMO. It is overwhelming concerned with administrative procedures. It is implemented in the UK by the Environmental Protection Act (1990) Sections 106 and 108. It is updated, by way of technicalities, by Directive 98/81.

Directive 2001/18 alludes to deliberate release of GMOs into the environment for research and development and also for sale. Environmental impact assessment (EIA) must be carried out before any releases; there

---

23   Among writings discussing the excruciating complexity of the rules are: Miller, H ' Unscientific regulation of agricultural biotechnology' [1995] *Trends in Biotechnology* vol 13, at p 123; Babinard, J and Josling, T 'The stakeholders and the struggle for public opinion, regulatory control and market development' In *Genetically Modified Organisms in Agriculture*, Nelson GC (ed) (Academic Press, 2001); Morgan, G 'Regulation of the use of genetically modified organisms in the EU' [2005/2006] *Bioscience Law Review* vol 15, at p 162.
24   Bridges, M 'Genetically modified organisms and the precautionary principle' [2004] *Temple Environmental Law and Technology Journal* vol XXII, at p 175; Levidon, L 'Precautionary uncertainty: regulating GM crops in Europe' [2001] *Social Studies of Science* vol 31 at p 842; Amman, K ' The role of science and discourse in the application of the precautionary approach' In: Fisher R and Schillberg S (eds) *Molecular Farming*, (Wiley, VCH, 2004) p 291. For another extensive discussion see Ball and Bell, note 17, at p 45.

must be consent of a local authority for this (and there is list of national authorities in the website); and an EU approval procedure for commercial release must be developed. Importantly, this stipulates that the Cartagena Protocol on Biosafety (dealt with substantively in Chapter 6) shall govern the interpretation of the rules. In train comes a four-way imbroglio which imports international legal facets:

> The tension between the WTO and ... the Convention on Biological Diversity (CBD) ... is an example. Many developing countries, as well as the EU, would prefer that the CBD take the lead though the recently agreed Biosafety Protocol [See Chapter 6] and that the WTO fall into line, allowing countries to choose whether to accept GMOs in their markets. But the United States (not a signatory to the CBD) along with other exporters, insists that the WTO must prevail in matters of trade policy and that the established requirements for customs procedures and market access be respected even in the case of GMOs. The role of CODEX in setting standards and labeling regulations is another question that divides countries and often ministries within national governments. [25]

Directive 1829/2003 is concerned with placing GMOs on the market as food. Where the GMO has been favourably reviewed by the EU Scientific Committee or the European Food Standards Authority (EFSA) the adventitious or technically unavoidable presence of the GM material below 0.5% is allowed. This however is a transitional measure and is to be reviewed in 2007. In the case of GMOs to be used as seeds for propagation, EIA must be performed by the relevant national authority.

The authorization procedure for emplacement of food on the shelves is detailed into four steps initiated by the manufacturer (termed the "GM event owner"). He approaches the EFSA which submits a opinion to the Commission for a final decision.

Directive 1946/2003 governing the transboundary release of GMOs adheres EU to the well known principles of advance informed consent (AIA) in terms of the Cartegena Protocol.

Hitherto the (intended) releases have been quite various - canola, soya beans, tobacco, corn, radish and carnations. (Thus not all transgenic organisms are designed for food) The NGOs Greenpeace, Genewatch and others however have influenced public and legislative opinion to the extent

---

25   See Babinard and Johnson, note 23. Also Editorial 'GM proposals breach WTO rules' EU [2002] *Food Law Monthly* vol 121 at p 5.

Box 5-2   GMOS in the GENESIS of a DISASTER

Biotech Co (BC) an international corporation with legal personality in a tropical island republic (TIR) is able to engineer plants according to local needs. TIR has an extensive free range chicken industry, exporting 95% of its high quality product, but 20-40% of the grain expensively imported to feed the chickens is consumed by rats. Could BC engineer a toxic plant made attractive to the rats and so eliminate them? The scientists ponder, and suggest using a recently-discovered toxin, called persin, in avocado plants. They will engineer the plants to greatly enhance the content of persin, which is a fatty acid at the same time possessing a flavour which has been found to be attractive to rodents. The toxin produces mastitis and agalactica (lack of milk) in lactating rats as well as extensive myocardial damage in all individuals. Humans seem to be unaffected. At the same time the scientists will engineer the avocados for disease resistance, rapid growth, enhanced fruiting, and nitrogen fixation. As a bonus a new cash crop might be generated after suitable safety tests in other non-human animals.

The technicalities are accomplished and a licence is sought from the Ministry for the release of this LMO into the environs of the chicken farms. The Ministry awards the licence after suitable EIA (conducted by a private consultancy on contract) and the farmers buy the avocado saplings for planting.

At first all goes well. The rats eat the avocados temptingly strewn round the farms and are largely eliminated because the offspring die for lack of milk and the adults of heart failure. Unfortunately the carcasses of the rats are eaten by avian raptors which experience huge increases in numbers. The rat carcasses being eaten up, the raptors turn on the chickens, which are all but eliminated in their turn. The poultry farmers become destitute and on being refused compensation by the Ministry take to the hills in armed gangs, which raid BC's premises and cause extensive damage.

Meanwhile the avocado becomes rampant in banana plantations and extra workers have to be hired to clear it. On top of all of this, environmental scientists claim that they have found persin in the fatty tissues of fish in the local fish ponds. It appears that persin may be subject to bioacummulation like many other fat-soluble compounds. Some months later an epidemiologist in the Ministry of Health claims that there is an increased incidence of mastitis in the post-partum women in the villages surrounding the ponds.

There have been many victims of the bioengineering initiative, but who is blameworthy, and what compensation might be available? Further, are criminal charges possible?

that some countries do not agree to follow the permissive aspects of the directives, being yet suspicious of any GMO whatsoever, and are in the course of being taken to the European Court by the Commission. Greenpeace especially has been willing to go so far as to risk prosecution for criminal damage. Lord Melchett, the CEO of Greenpeace UK, led a party of saboteurs on to private land in 1990, and destroyed a herbicide-tolerant maize. Against the judge's direction, the jury acquitted. [26] (This case incidentally revived controversy on the status of the jury trial, given that here it returned a perverse verdict by any standards, but was said to reveal the depth of feeling in the public, unease that was fuelled by the mad cow imbroglio.)

International interventions

It may be that this section would be more suitably emplaced in Chapter 6, but the two can be read conjointly. The concerns of WTO supporters have been mentioned above. They find themselves oddly in agreement with such organisations as the UN Environmental Program (UNEP), which has pointed out in numerous texts that malnutrition affects over 800 million people worldwide and affirms that GM technology will be instrumental in improving their lot. Modern varieties of millet, sorghum and cassava have to be developed. These are the foods of the poor, for at present GM technology is held by UNEP to cater mainly for the rich (tomatoes with a prolonged shelf life, for example - the poor eat their food immediately). The NGOs Greenpeace, Action Aid, Intermediate Technology Development, and Genetic Food Alert among many others agree neither with UNEP, nor the US farmers in that they seem to want to ban any transgenic entity across the board. On a worldwide basis there is no organization more pervasive than Greenpeace, which seems to have a spokesman in every country denouncing the slightest move, by any other organization, commercial or not, to test or market GMOs, GMCs, or GMFs. It has been quick to challenge the International Rice Research Institute in Manila, which has been handed the yellow rice technology for further development, by accusing it of 'using the misery of children to gain acceptance for GMCs.' Greenpeace has acquired respectability, and has been given *locus standi* in various courts of law - a recent jurisprudential departure in common law countries, wherein for previously a party to proceedings had to have a direct, usually property interest in a case. The Greenpeace view seems to be prevailing, except in the USA, China and Brazil. Elsewhere, in conjunction with local consumer

---

26   *Guardian* 22nd Sept 2000: 'Seed trial by jury'. For a contemporary discussion see Blom-Cooper L 'Judge and jury or judge alone' [2004] *Medicine, Science and the Law* vol 44 at p 6. The judge was equally sympathetic in the Bayer case, see note 15.

groups, it has effectively engineered the banning of both the cultivation of GMCs and the sale of GMFs.

One would expect FAO and WHO to offer an input into the area. Like UNEP, these bodies are basically in favour of further progress in the biotechnological production of food and its acceptance by the public.[27] The Organisation for Economic Cooperation and Development (OECD) has produced numerous papers on GMFs. In the context of the possible maturation of exhortations into domestic and/or international law, it is much preoccupied with the harmonization of regulatory oversight and the production of consensus documents.[28]

In a regional grouping, the Association of South East Asian Nations (ASEAN), whose members (with one exception) operate largely agricultural economies, there is as yet no directive on GMCs. However throughout the region there is deep suspicion. Early in 2001 the Thai government decided to stop all field trials of GMCs, even those already underway. The crops were cotton and maize, strains developed by Monsanto. In the Philippines Congress, a bill was introduced to mandate the labelling of any food containing a GMO. As in most environmental and food legislation, infractions are to be criminalised, up to 12 years in prison in this case. The government as well as its Department of Agriculture has stated that it wishes to protect the public against harm. However Monsanto succeeded in sowing and harvesting a *Bt* (that is pest resistant) corn near Manila in the teeth of local opposition. One report has it that Indonesia's Ministry of the Environment is now opposing the use of GMCs until they are established to be harmless both to humans and to the environment. However the Ministry of Agriculture is said to favour their introduction and specifically, a transgenic cotton named *Bt* DP 569B was licenced for planting in Sulawesi. If Indonesia became less dependent on imported cotton, and grew its own, this would fuel the country's textile industry and result in major savings. However existing strains of cotton do not grow well in any of the countries of ASEAN, including Thailand, Malaysia and the Philippines. A transgenic cotton like *Bt* DP569B, with superior qualities of yield and pest resistance might be the answer. The Environment Minister claims however to be applying the precautionary principle. In Singapore, at the time of writing, GMFs are banned. Its stance is interesting, as a non-agricultural economy heavily dependent on technology of all sorts. It has no fewer than three committees

27   Instructive sites are <http://www.fao.org/es/esn/biotech/tabconts.htm> and < www.dfao.org/newsroom/en/focus/2004/41655/index.html>.
28   <http://www.oecd.org/subject/biotech>.

sitting under the aegis of the Genetic Modification Advisory Committee to ponder the issues. Nonetheless concern about the safety of GMFs/GMCs in Singapore itself has not led to restraint on commercial development of them for application elsewhere. Thus Agrogen Pte Ltd is a Singapore-based consortium with Monsanto with a holding company in China to produce and commercialise insect resistant cotton there.

The only way to attempt to halt a technology totally in its tracks, if it is regarded on all sides to be an abomination, is for the whole world to agree that it is such, and to convene an international conference to try to ban or limit it. In this tradition we have the Convention on the Development, Production, and Stockpiling of Bacteriological, Biological and Toxin Weapons (which the most powerful country in the world refuses to ratify) and the Comprehensive Test Ban Treaty (which is now all but dead). Similar efforts, unsuccessful as these have been, are not likely to be made in respect of GMFs - it is too late in the day - and there is hope still that they will considerably help to feed the poor. There is perhaps a parallel to the GMF saga in the story of indigo, which was grown in the East Indies (modern Indonesia) for centuries and was used to give Javanese - and later good quality European cloth - its lustrous blue sheen. It was also an important cash crop in the Philippines for some time. It contributed greatly to the Dutch revenues till 1875 when the English chemist Perkin synthesized it. This destroyed it as a crop in the East. Both the practical and moral consequences were unpredictable and potentially catastrophic; the disaster was said to have underlined the helplessness of the individual in the face of science. But who worries about natural indigo now? The analogy to GMFs is that these also, in the long run, will be cheaper, more lasting, and just as attractive as the 'natural' products, which may not be phased out like farmed indigo, but which may become the purchases of specialised consumers only.

Summary of 5.3

- Administrators and legislators have to take into account the public's fear of GMOs/GMFs as being 'unnatural'.

- In the US the main regulators are the USDA and the FDA with the EPA involved in the case of pesticide incorporation.

- In the US the regulations may be described as minimalist.

- In the EU, however, numerous directives regulate the import and sale of GMFs as 'novel foods'.

- Other EU directives control the release of GMOs into the environment.

- In general the EU adheres to the advance informed consent and precautionary principles.

- There is a conceptual divide between the WTO and US on one side and the EU on the other.

- As a simplistic observation the FAO and, WHO and UNEP favour the WTO/USA stance.

- Governments in Third World/Asian countries are on the whole deeply suspicious of GMOs/GMFs.

- A global treaty to regulate dispersion of GMOs seems unlikely.

5.4 Environmental Risks

In general conversation the terms 'hazard' and 'risk' (like 'accuracy' and 'precision') tend to be used interchangeably. Environmental scientists among others must carefully distinguish them. A hazard (or danger) is a state or condition which may lead to an undesirable outcome; a risk is quantitative measure of the probability of the harm occurring. Thus it can be ascribed any value from zero to unity, like any other probability. The principal harm conceived for GMCs is contamination of other crops. This could possibly arise by rotting GMCs releasing DNA in the soil, this DNA to be taken up by bacteria and transferred to other plants (in practice deemed of very low probability).

By the middle of 2005 there had been eight incidents of GM contamination in the UK. There seems to be no record of a prosecution but there is one report of compensation paid to a farmer because his rape oilseed became unsaleable.[29] Writers on English environmental law are wont to state that pollution offences are generally regarded as morally neutral and that cooperation, not prosecution, is favoured by the authorities. Minor pollution incidents are evidently so frequent that presumably the authorities in very few jurisdictions would like to see the courts clogged up with them. Although it is convenient for legislators to criminalise delict of the environment, by general agreement the fines are derisory, at least when levied on large corporations. It seems however that it is convenient to criminalise every infringement rather than set up the breach of regulations courts which operate in some countries. The point has also been made that if heavier fines were to be introduced, this would overcome the uncertainty of claiming punitive damages in civil actions. What seems clear in any case is that large sections of the community

---

29   Brown, P 'Call for tighter GM controls' *Guardian* 1st June, 2005.

view the activities of the companies ('Big Agro') with extreme suspicion. Monsanto Corporation especially has been demonised, outside the US at any rate. Much of the animus against it derives from its precipitate introduction of terminator genes which render second generation seeds sterile, thus tying the farmer to the supplier every year.[30] However it is reported that Monsanto has agreed to stop producing such seeds. Its pernicious nature, in the eyes of some, has been demonstrated by the Canadian case of *Monsanto Canada Inc v Schmeiser* (2004).[31] This was an environmentally orientated case, but not involving damage to the environment as such. Schmeiser was a farmer in Saskatchewan who had been growing canola (an oil-yielding plant, called rape in UK) for many years. In the 1990s some of his neighbours decided to plant the Monsanto genetically modified (herbicide-resistant) canola. He was found in 1998 to be using the transgenic seeds although it is established that he never purchased them. Their source remains unclear but pollen may have blown in from the neighbours' fields, since Schmeiser maintained that he detected herbicide resistant plants in his own fields in 1997. Monsanto brought an action for patent infringement and was awarded injunctive relief as well as damages at first instance as well. The issue at this stage was not the source of the plants in 1997 but the fact that, whatever that might have been, Schmeiser was using the seeds without a licence in 1998. Moreover he 'knew, or ought to have known', that the seeds he planted were restricted to licencees. A principle item of the defence was that he had not used herbicide on the (Monsanto) plants, and so had not used the invention. This argument was rejected because the patent description did not in itself specify the employment of the herbicide. However the case proceeded through the appeal court, which held again for the company, and on to the Supreme Court of Canada. This last reiterated the point that although Schmeiser had not used the herbicide, he could have done so if necessary; the analogy was made with the pumps on a ship - if such are manufactured by the competitor of a patent holder without a licence, they infringe the patent even if they are not

---

30   Pendleton, CN 'The peculiar case of "terminator" technology: agricultural biotechnology and IP protection at the crossroads of the third green revolution' *Biotechnology Law Reports* [2003] vol 23, at p 1. Muscati. S. 'Terminator technology: protection of patents or a threat to the patent system'. [2005] *Idea: the Journal of Law and Technology* vol 45, at p 477). It has even been argued that the farmer's right to retain seeds for future planting is enshrined in common law.

31   [2004] 1 SCR 902;2004 SCC 34; Supreme Court of Canada. There is an excellent account in Wikipedia: <http://en.wikipedia.org/wiki/Monsanto_Canada_Inc.v.Schmeiser>; see also Cullet, P 'Monsanto v Schmeiser: a landmark decision concerning farmer liability and transgenic contamination' [2005] *Journal of Environmental Law* vol 17, at p 83; Schmeiser's personal website is <http://www.percyschmeiser.com/>.

actually used on the ship. However Schmeiser was victorious on one point – he did not have to pay damages since he had made no excess profit merely due to the presence of the GMC in his fields. More importantly perhaps, this judgement meant that Schmeiser did not have to pay Monsanto's enormous legal costs. One can readily conceive of the outrage generated by the apparent oppression of an ordinary farmer by a massive corporation. Interestingly, a judge in partial dissent followed the Canadian Supreme Court's 'oncomouse' judgement (Chapter 4. 4) in that he held that the canola plant being a higher life form could not in itself be patented. The patent was only good for the founder plant, as a product by process invention, but not for all its progeny. In *Schmeiser* there was no perceived general danger to the environment but two main heads of this have generally been articulated:

A GMCs acquiring weed-like characteristics. In other words a GMC might be so superior in terms of survival that it is able to choke out other vegetation, including other crops.

B GMOs not preexisting in the environment, but escaping. Thus GM algae, for example, might be grown in factory for a product, perhaps a protein they have been engineered to produce, but are released for some reason and swamp the waterways for miles around. This, as well as the previous item, obviously relates to biodiversity.

Summarising the writings on the subject, it seems that such risks can be put on a sequential basis - there must be at least four consecutive events:

(1) A pathogenic or dangerous GMO (plant, animal, bacterium or virus) must be constructed.

(2) It must escape from the contained environment (laboratory or field) or alternatively become involved in horizontal gene transfer,

(3) It must be viable in the larger environment

(4) It must compete successfully with other organisms.

The odds against final harm is the product of the odds of each of these separately. (Handling odds and probabilities is dealt with in both Chapters 2 and 3). Although nothing is absolutely certain, here, logically, we may take the probability of number one above as unity. Thus if there is only a one in a hundred chance of event 2, the escape, and a one in two chance of event 3, and a one in three chance of event four, the odds against harm are 1/100 x 1/3 x 1/3 or about a thousand to one against. Tighten up the laboratory security ten-fold and the odds against become a hundred to one. If any one risk can be considered zero, then the danger as a whole evaporates. However the dangers inherent in this sort of calculation are highlighted by the US *People* v *Collins* case (also referred to in Chapter 2, note 66) in that the odds on each sequential event (a) tend to be determined arbitrarily, and (b) they must be completely independent of each other for mathematical rigour. For example it might well be argued that items 3 and 4 above are in reality not independent of each other. The precautionary principle taken to its extreme, of course, would dictate that the construction of GMOs, first item above, must be cancelled.

Unlike the labelling question, which seems to be well on its way to a resolution, or at least becoming subject to regulations made uniform in Europe, the debate about risk is not likely to be resolved soon, if only because an exponentially growing output of a variety of GMOs will come from the laboratories. Another stumbling block is that the general public does not seem to accept the fact science is unable to prove that any activity is completely free from risk. It can only compute probabilities, as above, and even then cannot take account, at all, of human error (or stupidity!). Moreover the *perception* of risk, rather than the risk itself, can never be rationally addressed by the specialist, be he or she a scientist, statistician, engineer, or lawyer. We are assured that flying to New York is less risky than driving to work, but we feel safer driving our own cars to work than hurtling through the air in a metal box surrounded by tons of highly inflammable fuel, with freezing cold sea beneath us. And yet the public appears to think that it should be assured of zero risks, in whatever field of technology - this has generated the precautionary principle and has held up the development and marketing of GMOs. (Similar precepts have not been applied to surgery or aviation, to take other examples of rapidly advancing technologies.) The sentiment can be translated into legislation, as in the US via the 1958 Delaney Clause, which applied to food rather than the environment, but which illustrates the point. This was an amendment to the Federal Food, Drugs and Cosmetics Act (FDCA) (1938) whereby the FDA was enjoined not to approve any additive found to induce cancer in man or, after tests found to induce cancer in animals, at any dosage. The view among many who have studied risk analysis in relation to science it that this is a misguided approach. As has been reiterated many times above, science cannot prove with certainty that anything is safe. Absence of evidence is not evidence of absence.[32] (The Delaney clause in fact applied only to processed foods, and was abandoned by further legislation in 1996.)

32 Blanchfield, JR 'European Union Regulations with an emphasis on genetically modified foods' In:. Schmidt RH and Rodrick GE (eds) *Food Safety Handbook* (John Wiley and Sons 2003) p 59. Aikami, AS and Slovic, PA. 'Psychological study of the inverse

EU Directive 2001/18 has already been mentioned above. It is shot through with the precautionary principle, for example in the Preamble, item 8. 'The precautionary principle has been taken into account in drafting this Directive and must be taken into account when implementing it.' The directive was mandated to come into force in May 2003, but at that date 11 member states (UK not being among them) had not introduced compatible domestic legislation and were facing action by the Commission. This was reputed to be giving solace to the three countries – US, Argentina and Canada - who had complained to the WTO about the alleged restrictive action of EU in respect of GMOs/GMFs.

In England and Wales (Scotland has separate legislation) the Environment Act of 1995 welded all preexisting environmental bodies into yet another agency, the Environmental Agency. However it is part Part VI of the older act, the 1990 Environmental Protection Act which provides the legal framework for the regulation of release of GMOs. The technical details (in the associated statutory instruments) are largely derived from the EU directives (90/219/ EEC and 90/220/EEC) mentioned above, dating from 1992, but the breadth of control is essentially precautionary and non-technical in that Section 107 refers to organisms which are merely *capable* of causing harm, whether by themselves or through the activity of their descendants, 'harm' meaning harm to human health, to other living things, or to ecological systems. The Minister has an Advisory Committee on Releases to the Environment to which detailed proposals must be put by anybody planning to put GMOs into an environment outside a laboratory. This committee is designed to be independent of the Ministry and includes relevant experts from all related fields. Each applicant for a release must attach a risk assessment and full technical information, i.e. the nature of the gene spliced into the GMO. The applicant is also required to inform various bodies like local authorities and to advertise in the newspapers. Inspectors (the 'gene police') have the right of entry to all save domestic premises. In conformity with modern practice, breaches of the regulations are criminalised, but the Advisory Committee has taken the view that 'naming and shaming' is a better deterrent, at least for wealthy corporations. Thus recently a company called Plant Genetic Systems was chastised for failing to notify conservation officials about the controlled release of a herbicide resistant rape.

---

relationships between perceived risks and perceived benefits.' *Risk Analysis* [1994] vol 14, at p 1085; Finucane, JR 'Mad cows, mad corn and mad communities: the role of socio-cultural factors in the perceived risk of genetically modified food' [2002] *Proceedings of the Nutrition Society* vol 61, at p 31; also generally, Bennett P and Calman K (eds). *Risk Communication and Public Health* (Oxford University Press, 1999).

Summary of 5.4

- Contamination of fields by GMOs represents a potentially novel aspect of environmental law.

- Criminalisation of GMO contamination is a more attractive prospect than recourse to the civil courts.

- In the keynote Canadian *Schmeiser* case the defendant's fields were contaminated but he was prosecuted under patent law.

- Risks to the environment by GMOs as with all other risks can be assessed by the multiplication rule.

- Unfortunately (For GMC farmers) the perception of risk is more important than the risk itself.

- The perception of risk is reinforced the precautionary principle (vide the theme of EU Directive 2001/18).

5.5 Assessing Risk from GMFs

Foods not crops

Here risks posed by GMFs (in the shops) are hereafter distinguished from the risks of GMOs/GMCs in the larger environment, as above. The risk at issue is the risk to human health. Foods in general may be associated with

(1) microbial/parasitic contamination

(2) endogenous toxins

(3) the presence of allergenic proteins

(4) metabolic incompatibility

(5) gross imbalance

(6) adulteration

GM ingredients as 'adulterants' gives a suitably pejorative feel to the arguments of the objectors, but perhaps points (4) and (5) above need a word of explanation. Metabolic incompatibility occurs, for example, when a food is rich in phenylalanine (an essential amino acid, and therefore desirable for normal individuals) and is made available to children with phenylketonuria; gross imbalance would obtain in the situation wherein a food high in, say, saturated fat (and therefore replete with energy) was offered to subjects at risk for coronary artery disease (pretty well everybody, in fact). Taking the broadest view held by the opponents of GMFs, these could be considered obnoxious on the basis of all categories above except the first, and even then, if scientists ventured to engineer a novel mould to ripen cheese, say, it would be a candidate for inclusion.

Opponents of GMFs cannot yet point to a disaster, but the fact that hitherto there has been none does not mean that such will never happen; and every technological advance, ranging from steam engines and ocean liners to atomic power stations, has imported mishaps which could have been foreseen but in many cases were not sufficiently protected against. Some conceptual difficulties arise as a consequence of the science involved, for GMOs are extremely heterogeneous entities. They may be classified, for example, according to their possible pathogenicity - in other words the potential sale of an engineered tomato is one thing, of a yoghurt drink containing bacteria engineered to act as a vaccine in the gastrointestinal tract quite another matter. In respect of the latter, there are separate regulations for what is termed containment, classifying laboratories by the degree to which they can isolate microorganisms from the outside world, and these are germane at the stages prior to any engineered microorganism coming to the market.

Of course, one view is not take any risks whatsoever with the diet, again the precautionary principle, now well embedded in environmental law (as above). The other view is that some risk is inevitable, but can be minimised, and indeed quantitated by rigorous analysis. Thus there are a number of logical steps towards this end, namely:

(1) hazard identification,

(2) dose/response assessment,

(3) exposure assessment

(4) these latter two to be used to calculate risk of disease or defect, as incidence in a relevant population.

(Note that the items are quite different to assessment of risk to the environment as discussed above.) Such steps were designed for, *inter alia*, pesticides, but the case can be made that there are other, extra hazards specific to GM food technology, and that (1) – (4) above just do not apply, or at least are inadequate. For a start, in respect of item (4), no diseases or defects associated with GMFs are known, apart possibly from allergic reactions, a matter for ongoing controversy. The hazards unrepresented in conventional foods, then, are:

A Marker genes (discussed above) rather than the GMOs themselves getting out of control in the sense that they may.

B Genes which have been inserted into foodstuffs being taken up from the human gut and entering the human genome. This is possibly the easiest to counter - as pointed out previously we ingest millions of discrete genes from our food plants and animals (not to mention those from contaminating insects, and bacteria), the quantum reckoned to be about one gram per day from a normal diet, and none of the genes has ever been shown to enter the human genome. As usual there is a caveat: phage (i.e. virus) DNA has been shown to link covalently to mouse DNA despite the fact that on feeding, 95% of it was destroyed in the mouse gut.[33]

In any event food science has several concepts in response, most preceding the advent of the genetic revolution:

(1) A foodstuff may be 'generally regarded as safe' (GRAS). This applies to ingredients like sugar (sucrose) and salt (sodium chloride). They have been used for millennia and for that reason the same concept is unlikely to be ascribed to GMFs for some time, especially in Europe.

(2) The doctrine of 'substantial equivalence', to reiterate, is the assumption that a novel food is directly comparable to an existing food, which is known to be safe. The concept appears to have originated in the US National Academy of Science but was adopted readily by the OECD and WHO/FAO, not to mention the FDA, as useful tool, and has been applied to GMFs when thought appropriate. In Europe the concept was redefined in 1997 - only highly refined oils and carbohydrates are considered equivalent.

However as a concept substantial equivalence has not failed to generate considerable controversy and has been criticized as 'unscientific ', in that the degree of difference between a natural food and its candidate GM equivalent has not, it appears, been defined, and that it would be prudent, rather, since the interaction of GMFs with pesticides, predators and fertilizers is unknown, to subject them to the normal battery of genetic, biochemical, toxicological and immunological tests. Critics maintain that substantial equivalence just means 'familiarity'. On the other hand defenders of the concept point out that using if this line of reasoning (that conventional scientific tests of safety should

33   Schubert, R, Renz, D et al 'Foreign (M13) DNA ingested by mice reaches peripheral leukocytes and spleen' [1997] *Proceedings of the National Academy of Sciences of the USA* vol 94 at p 961.

be applied) were to be adopted, then every new conventional crop or seed variety would have to be separately tested for toxicity when it has been treated with every herbicide, pesticide, fertilizer, and attacked by every predator. As a compromise, substantial equivalence can sensibly be regarded, not as a safety assessment in itself, but as step preliminary thereto.

There is however a very cogent objection to substantial equivalence, especially when it is propounded by Big Agri. Companies developing GMOs/GMC/ GMFs try to patent them as inventions. This implies a claim that they are novel, that is, unknown previously to science, and that their development has involved one or more inventive steps. This being the case, how can they be substantially equivalent? There seems to be a tendency, by advocates of this mode of assessment, to have it both ways. Monsanto and other 'agritech' companies have identified genetically-superior strains of crops in the East and have made moves to patent their genes, with the view, presumably, of introducing these genes into other strains. This has raised hackles. The *South China Morning Post* described an application for a patent, by Monsanto, for a high yielding strain of soya, as ' nothing short of scandalous '. Yet Monsanto all the while tries to maintain an ethical stance. The yellow rice mentioned above [1] was developed by a Swiss institute partly by using technology licenced from the Monsanto. The company has offered these licences royalty free, particularly to the International Rice Research Institute in Manila, so that the technology can be applied to vitamin A deficiency alleviation at the earliest possible date. Even in that connection there is a snag. Monsanto, for its technology, had in its turn been forced to use the technology of other corporations, and indeed proprietary DNA from other sources, and it is the owners of these who might well hold up the technology transfer.

(3) The perceived ability of the transferred gene, in say fish or fruits, to enhance the survival abilities of the recipient organism. If the latter, though, it would raise concerns as to a possible weed-like habitus, as discussed in the environmental context. But a gene which makes an animal bigger and stronger it cannot at first site be likely to be harmful if taken up, in some way, by humans. If taken up by rats, that is quite another matter!

(4) Mammals as indicators of their own biosafety. That is, if a gene is inserted into a farm animal, and the animal appears healthy (as opposed to merely being more massive), how can the same gene harm

humans even if (as is highly unlikely) it could find its way into the human genome?

Numbers (3) and (4) are rather similar, and that the answer to all of them, in terms of the opponents of GMFs, is that by the time you would be in a position to assess their significance the damage might already have been done. (The precautionary principle rears its head again!)

Summary of 5.5

- Like other foods, GMFs may harbour hazards, probably the most prominent of which is the presence of novel allergenic proteins.

- Hazards can be identified and quantitated by a sequential process of analysis.

- GMFs may pose extra problems in that they may disperse marker genes in some way, and conceivably their genes may enter the human genome (both of these now largely discounted).

- The safety of GMFs can also be addressed in terms of:

  - GRAS

  - substantial equivalence

  - enhanced survival of the species providing the food.

5.6 Food Labelling and Genetics

Legislatures which have addressed the question of food labelling forbid manufacturers from claiming that a product can prevent or cure a specific disease (in UK the Food Labelling Regulations, 1984). There is ministerial or administrative discretion to reclassify a product as a pharmaceutical should such a claim be substantiated. Thus in the US Japanese rice was (naturally) classified as a food but when an 'anti-cedar', genetically modified variety, claimed to prevent hay fever without the need for vaccination, was proposed for the market, it was reclassified by the FDA as a pharmaceutical.

Labelling merges into advertising, but no food producer or retailer dares to flaunt GMFs on billboards or during television commercial breaks at this time. The public, unless they elect to sally forth and stamp on GMCs in the fields like Lord Melchett, have contact with GM technology only at the point where they go into the market to choose food. As has often been pointed out, they are then utterly dependent on the information printed on the items offered. The pressure for more information as such has come from the public and from consumer groups, initially in respect of the various additives (the so-called E-numbers), for by long tradition legislators have not been concerned to prevent people eating what they choose.[34] Regulations on labelling have come been late in the day. The persuasive authority on GMO labelling ought to be the Codex Alimentarius since this body is supported by internationally garnered funds, but at the time of writing it has not been able to produce recommendations, principally because of the US objections to any sort of stringency in the matter.

In the US it is the FDA which is responsible, under the FDCA, for the labelling regulations. Again, its approach has always been on the minimalist side, merely mandating that the label must be accurate and 'material'. There must be special labelling if the composition of the food differs significantly from its conventional counterpart (the 'substantial equivalence' rule again). If a GMF contains a protein that is potentially allergenic then information to this end must be put on the label. Hitherto the policy has been to regulate on a case-by-case basis. In 2004 there were signs of a shift in attitude. The FDA, the USDA, EPA, the Institute of Medicine, and the National Research Council formulated a report entitled *Safety of Genetically Modified Foods: Approaches to Assessing Unintended Health* Effects.[35] The title betrays the unease - the document advocated greater scrutiny of GMFs, particularly 'postmarket surveillance.' It did not specifically call for labelling, however.

In the EU, directives promulgated in the 1980s led member countries to revise their food safety legislation, and there was a general requirement that food must not be falsely or misleadingly described or presented either in statements about the product or in pictorial illustrations. It is a universal requirement that the manufacturer, and if appropriate the distributor, should be identified. In general, there are criminal sanctions against claims on labels which are false, misleading or deceptive.[36] Ingredients must be listed in order of weight; there must not be claims that the food will cure or alleviate any disease, and an expiration date must be provided (if only for various specific foods, like milk). There are no regulations in any of the member countries

---

34   It is generally true that governments do not try to control what people eat, safety and adulteration concerns aside, but this may not pertain forever. The epidemic of obesity is causing such strains on health services that there have been serious suggestions about banning fattening foods, or restrict their consumption by vulnerable groups.

35   <httpp://www.nowfoods.com/index.php/Home/cat/action/itemdetail/item_id/40871&TPL>.

36   Coghlan, A 'Named and Shamed' *New Scientist* 4th April, 1998. The regulations for UK are summarised on <http://binas.unido.org/binas/Regulations/summary/uk.html>; for other countries substitute the name for 'UK' in the site name.

to mandate a 'nutritional information panel', that is, a list of ingredients in relation to the recommended daily intakes, sometimes called daily values. However it is notable that most of the big international food producers provide these and local producers are encouraged to follow suit.

These provisions apply generally. On the advent of GMFs, there was debate in many countries as to whether they fell short of mandating as much information as might be thought desirable. The food industry in Europe was of the opinion, predictably, that labelling need only be minimal, but consumer and environmentalist groups wanted comprehensive labelling on any product which was even remotely contiguous with GMOs. Consumers in the EU appear to be among the most cautious in the world, disdaining at least two potentially beneficial results of widespread use of GMOs, namely the provision of extra (soya) high quality protein as an additive (infant foods, for example) and a reduction in the application of herbicides to plant foods when growing in the fields. In general there were no labelling regulations for GMOs in the EU before May 1997 but in that year Novel Foods Regulations 258/97 mandated that relevant information be given on the label if there was not substantial equivalence. This did not apply to non-packaged food such as tomatoes (which might or might not be transgenic) and the regulations did not go so far as to state that a label, should the food contain an ingredient such as soya bean meal, must state whether this was derived from a GMC or not. Now Directive 1830/2003 governs the issue. (It was followed by 65/2004.) The label must state if a GM component, authorised for marketing in the EU, constitutes more than 0.9% of the total product, in that it is recognised that there may well be technical reasons why an adventitious component up to this level may be unavoidable. There is however a transitional period exemption for products containing trace levels of GMOs which have not been authorised for marketing in EU - this predicates a lower threshold of 0.5%.

The regulations also apply to restaurants, which is a potential difficulty - a dash of soya sauce, for example, may have been derived from GM beans, so the chef has to carefully select ingredients which have no taint of GMOs, or if he prefers to use them, make special notes to that effect on the menu. One can imagine the great Escoffier, in the Ritz, holding up his hands in horror and exclaiming 'What next?'.[37] The regulators even took cognisance

---

37   Evaluations of the regulations can be found in: Sampson, note 22 above; also Burchett, P 'A castle in the sky: the illusory promise of labeling genetically modified food in Europe' [2004] *Pennsylvania State International Law Review* vol 23, at p 173.

of the modern tendency to order food by phone, when the onus is on the caller to enquire as to the GMO status of the dish ordered.

The labelling must entrain

- List of characteristics modified, together with the method of doing this if the new food lacks equivalence to existing products.

- List of characteristics which renders the novel food no longer equivalent to one pre-existing (here enters the substantial equivalence provision).

- Any entity (in a novel food) not present in the existing food which has implications for health (for example presence of a potential allergen).

- Any material (in a novel food) not in existing foodstuff giving rise to ethical concerns (For example, the transfer of swine genes to any foodstuff which might be sold to moslems).

- A list of any organisms genetically modified by techniques of genetic modification.

If it happens that there is no preexisting product then all that is stated is that there must be adequate information to make sure that consumers know the nature of the product. (It is however difficult to envisage such a situation. Can scientists produce a completely novel fruit?)

Australia and New Zealand introduced, in 2000, joint standards for the mandatory labelling of GMFs and in their economy and clarity these might well serve as a guide for others.[38] Products are assigned to either Division 1 or 2. Essentially, the former are allowed into the two countries with appropriate licencing, and would include, for example, animals (not in themselves GMOs) which have been fed GMCs like soya bean protein. Division 2 applies to labelling and a product must be identified, on sale, as a GMF if:

(1) It contains novel DNA or protein

(2) It has altered characteristics, namely if:

(a) genetic manipulation has produced significant modification

(b) there is a significantly raised level of a toxicant

(c) it contains new allergens

---

38   <www.anzfa.gov.au/foodstandardscode.> .

(d) the intended use of the food is distinct from its previous use.

(e) modification has raised ethical, cultural or religious concerns.

This seems clear enough, except that words 'significant', 'ethical' and 'cultural', among others, will have to be interpreted - ultimately, in the instance of a serious dispute, judicially.

Summary of 5.6

- The food industry awaits recommendations from the Codex Alimentarius on the labelling of GMFs.

- There is resistance to informative labelling in the US, but attitudes appear to be changing.

- The EU mandates strict standards for labeling foods containing GMFs, but recognises that adventitious GM ingredients need not be notified if below a threshold value.

Chapter 6

International Law

6.1 Background Matters

Inevitably this is the shortest chapter, for good reason - if domestic law must perforce catch up with technology, and if international law lags behind domestic law, as is habitually remarked,[1] there may not be much to write about. However it seems that there are some matters of importance to link genetics and DNA to the international scene. The nature and generation of a genetically modified organisms (GMO) or living modified organisms (LMO) was dealt with in Chapter 1 and its presentation or processing into a genetically modified food (GMF) in Chapter 5, there being international facets to these topics. The Convention on Biological Diversity (CBD) tends to use the term LMO which, in that it does not intrinsically imply genetic modification, is wider than the alternative, GMO, but it is also more restrictive in the sense that the entity under consideration must be viable. A special set of legal problems arise when there is transfer of any of these from one country to another in that governments (some of them) exist to protect their public, and MOs/LMOs/GMFs are regarded as potential mass toxins (at least by that public), the more so as they can exist in the form, not just of mammals or plants, but insects, bacteria and fungi. Modified viruses, which are not usually considered to be organisms as such, rather self-replicating entities, must also be taken into account. The ramifications arising are considered below, but in a preliminary way the relationships between the relevant gene technologies and international law can be listed as:

(1) The existence, or non-existence, of safeguards concerning the export, for commercial or other reasons, of a GMO/GMF. (An imported GMF might turn out to be allergenic; a modified virus vaccine might cause the disease it seeks to prevent; or a plant purported to be containable might escape into cultivated fields and

---

1 This is not the place for a general discussion on whether international law is 'law' and further, how much it is influenced by municipal law, and vice-versa. The standard textbooks seem to indicate that municipal, especially equitable (*ex aequo et bono* in international language) sources are important for the development of international law. Harris, DJ *Cases and Materials on International Law* (Sweet and Maxwell, 5th edn, 1998) p 48. Harris dismisses the Austinian view that international law cannot be 'law' because it does not recognise the commands of a sovereign, rather he maintains that it is observed just as readily and consistently as national law.

become a noxious weed.) This is the province of the CBD and its associated Cartagena Protocol.

(2) Accidental transboundary release of GMOs. The Cartagena Protocol is relevant to this aspect also.

(3) Deliberate transboundary release of GMOs. This elides into warfare or terrorism (para 6.5) and immediately suggests some analogy with international law in so far as it prohibits poison gas warfare.

(4) GMO modification of, or damage to, the *res communis,* the components of the planet owned by all, which inevitably is shrinking.[2]

(5) Damage by GMOs to a state's own territory or population in such a way as to cause international concern.[3]

If the items in the list are considered to be real hazards then the most direct corrective would be the international treaty, coming into force after a predetermined time and/or an agreed number of ratifications,[4] and

2 Fisher, DG *Environmental Law* (Law Book Co, 1993) p 194. International lawyers distinguish the res communis (that which is collectively owned) from the res nullius (that which nobody owns at present, but could be claimed.) In the case of the former, some components are expanding, namely water, as the glaciers melt, and another, air, is shrinking as we face exponential global pollution.

3 There have been no cases involving GMOs, but an instructive analogy might rest with the South East Asian hazes, the worst of which occurred in 1997 and 2006. The forest fires in Indonesia transmitted choking black smoke to Malaysia and Singapore, smoke that was fatal to a number of citizens with less than healthy respiratory tracts and which also disrupted the rice harvests. It is generally agreed that corruption and inefficiency precludes any remedial action by the Indonesian authorities. Beyond sending some of their own firemen and make severe representations, the two countries suffering the drift of smoke could do nothing about the situation. If the two countries gained advance notice of the fires starting, could they invade Indonesia and put them out, in a preemptive strike which is till controversial in international law. A start has been made on criminalising damage to the environment in Europe via the Council of Europe's 1998 *Convention on the Protection of the Environment through Criminal Law*; it is open to signature by non-member states of the Council, but it is difficult to envisage a country like Indonesia doing so.

4 As a reminder, when an international treaty is being negotiated or promulgated, those states which intend to adhere to it do so by 'signing' it. They become legally bound by it after 'ratification' domestically and it comes into force when a prescribed number of countries have ratified. In some countries, for example the USA, ratification is the responsibility of the legislature, which is why the president can habitually sign treaties which never become law there; in other countries, such as UK is the prerogative of the executive ('crown [or royal] prerogative') nominally the head of state, actually the government of the day. There is a good brief explanation in Robertson, G *Crimes Against Humanity; the Struggle for Global Justice* (Penguin Books, 2nd edn, 2002) p 87.

constituting 'hard' international law under which the *pacta sunt servanda* doctrine applies.[5] Subsidiary to this core are some interlocking concepts - *customary international law* (the accepted practice of a majority of states) *ius cogens* (rules, as against genocide, for example, which are too fundamental to be breached; the Vienna Convention on the Law of Treaties mandates that can be no derogation from humanitarian clauses in treaties) and *opinio juris* (rules which can be identified in writings). We need also to consider when the *erga omnes* doctrine might apply to the matters in hand - when a state perceives that it must take action against another state which has breached a fundamental rule of international law, but is not itself affected by the breach, its action is considered by some authorities to be legal under the *erga omnes* doctrine. (Not by the House of Lords, though, apparently; in *Jones v the Ministry of the Interior of the Kingdom of Saudi Arabia* (2006) it held that 'there is no evidence that states have recognised ... an obligation to exercise universal jurisdiction over claims arising from alleged breaches of *ius cogens*.'[6]) To these venerable tenets of international law, more modern concepts, which appear in the following pages, must be considered. Chief among these are prior informed consent, which seems to be the same as advance informed agreement (AIA) and the precautionary principle. This last was mentioned several times in Chapter 5, for of course the same topics/ ideas tend to crop up in various contexts.

In respect of DNA, some aspects of international law are in a nascent stage. For example, after the Indian Ocean tsunami in 2005 there was an immediate necessity to identify victims, many of whom had been holidaymakers far from their home countries. Interpol, one of the products of international administrative law, was called in to help, but remarkably, many samples were sent to a laboratory in Sarajevo. Of course, there is much experience of victim identification in that area following the mass executions in the recent Balkan wars. There is a question, not yet resolved, as to whether diplomatic representatives could demand access to specimens which may or may not be derived from their own citizens.

---

5 If international law seems overburdened with Latin the retort might be that even if 'dead', it remains an international language. Interestingly, the Finnish authorities during their recent presidency of the EU attempted – with a degree of seriousness difficult to ascertain - to reintroduce Latin as a means of intercommunication. For an international law Latin glossary see <http://www.law.uga.edu/~bodansky/courses.International_Law/ glossary.html>.
6 *Jones v The Minisiter of the Interior of the Kingdom of Saudi Arabia* [2006] UKHL 26.

6.2 The Convention for International Trade in Endangered Species (CITES)

CITES is the senior international instrument in the context of DNA technology in general.[7] It deals with undesirable international exploitation of natural resources, some of which can be listed (with brief examples) as:

Food - caviar scarcity due to sturgeon overfishing; excessive turtle exploitation.

Traditional medicine - rhinoceros horns, bear paws traded internationally

Pets - exotic reptiles and snakes smuggled and traded

Forests – unsustainable logging for ramin and teak.

Furs and skins - skins from wild reptiles made into handbags and shoes

Tourism - ivory and turtleshell carvings, coral jewellery as souvenirs.

CITES was put up for signature in Washington in 1972; unusually, only ten ratifications were predicated for coming into force - a measure, perhaps, of the urgency with which the delegates viewed the problem. It has almost universally been incorporated into domestic law, even in the US. Indeed this is predicated by Art 8, which states that 'The parties shall take appropriate measures to enforce the provisions..... [and to] .... penalise trade in, or possession of, such specimens ...' Presumably such wording as '...legislation will be introduced...' is avoided to enable compliance by those states which rule by decree. The word 'penalise' however is abundantly clear. The animals and plants with which trade is prohibited are gazetted into three Appendices, the first of which represents the most endangered species. The Conferences of Parties (COPs), held very two or three years, are devoted mainly to arguing about transfer from one list to another, alternatively entry or deletion. COPs 13 met in 2004 and in 2007 and by art 12(xii) simplified procedures for time-sensitive biological specimens, including DNA or other diagnostic samples. COP 14 met in The Hague in June 2007 and its recommendations are still embryonic. There is no enforcement or penalty system (the framing of such being an urgent ongoing task), however the mandatory domestic enactments of the parties to the convention harden it in that sense. This does not mean that the parties to the treaty totally ignore domestic violators. Some of the sanctions, or quasi-sanctions, include:

---

7   CITES's site is <www.cites.org>.

- the Secretariat informing all the other parties about a breach by one party.

- the Secretariat refusing to cooperate with the offending party.

- boycotting CITES related trade with the offending party.

- censorious visits by the Secretariat.

One imagines that compliance is patchy, but some states are quite zealous. In Singapore, to take an example, both export and import of a gazetted species, or their parts, can attract a fine of US $ 3250 plus a custodial sentence. To take the record of one year at random, in 1998 630 animals were seized by the relevant authority, most of them kept as pets. The *New Straits Times* (Malaysia) reported in 2005 that the police had arrested a man found in possession of python meat and crocodile tails worth US$ 2000. It is a matter of opinion as to whether such penalties are proportionate. One supposes it is easy enough to recognise a crocodile tail, although ascertaining the exact species might be difficult. The DNA technology enters when enforcement officials find pieces of tissue which are difficult to identify in themselves. They must ask themselves: is this the tail of a cat or a lemur? They send samples to veterinary laboratories which keep databases of animal DNA sequences similar to those constructed in other circumstances by the police. The analogies to human forensic databases are quite clear, except that in general the CITES enforcement officials will usually be concerned to identify species, not individuals. In a recent Italian case, as an example, poacher was convicted on the basis that blood on a knife seized from him matched that from the carcass of an animal he had killed.[8] This was a species identification, but the DNA technology has advanced to the point where individual animals can be tracked. From 1999 to 2003 South Korean fishermen reported 458 minke whales trapped in nets, ostensibly accidentally, which can be legally sold for their meat. Scientists, on the basis of DNA sampling, identified more than 800 individuals, so not all the deaths were accidental. There appears to be no record of any prosecution. A microsatellite-based technology, exactly parallel to that used to identify criminals (Chapter 2), was successfully applied in China to the identification of bones from individual tigers.[9] As in human forensics, the DNA technology will progressively enhance probative standards.

8   Lorenzini, R 'DNA forensics and the poaching of wildlife in Italy: a case study'. [2005] *Forensic Science International* vol 153, at p 218.
9   Yan, C, Bo, I et al 'Individualisation of tigers using microsatellites' [2005] *Forensic Science International* vol 151, at p 45.

Summary of 6.2.

• CITES is the international instrument for the protection of endangered species.

• CITES enforcement officials will progressively use DNA technology to identify species and even individual animals.

6.3 Transboundary Movement of Genetically Modified Organisms

There have been many both accidental and deliberate transfers of organisms to environments ill equipped to contain them. In the days when the world's communities were largely isolated from each other these were infrequent, but they could be disastrous. The transmission of the strain of plague bacillus endemic in China but new to Europe caused the deaths of one third of its population in the Black Death. The Indians in Hispaniola were wiped out by Spanish influenza and smallpox. Rabbits were introduced into Australia and have never been effectively controlled. The list today, indeed, is almost endless; botanically, rhododendrons from China took over large tracts of the Scottish Highlands, including almost the entire island of Mull. Kudzu, a creeping vine from Japan, infests large tracts of the southern states of the USA. No doubt there are reverse effects, West to East.

The role of the Convention on Biological Diversity (CBD)

A growing awareness of the danger to biodiversity highlighted by the International Union for the Conservation of Nature (IUCN) in the eighties led to an initiative by the United Nations Environmental Protection Agency (UNEP), which culminated in the formation of the Biological Diversity Group at the UN Conference on the Environment and Development (the 'Earth Summit') in Rio de Janeiro in 1992.[10] There grew, within the negotiations for the CBD, a group calling for an international binding treaty on the safety of LMOs. Progress overlaying the text of the convention itself was possible because the CBD like CITES is an example of a framework treaty, one which sets down principles but leaves the details to be worked out by conferences of working parties (COPs), which are usually heavily influenced by scientific progress. (The Framework Convention on Climate Change signed at the Erath Summit is even specifically labelled as such.) CBD came into force on 29th Dec 1993, when 30 nations had ratified it.

10 The CBD website is <http://www.biodiv.org>. For liability and redress specifically see <http://www.biodiv.org/programmes/socio-eco/liability/work.asp>.

Arts 8(g) and 19(3) are relevant to LMO safety. The former refers to the regulation of the multifarious risks associated with LMOs (which have been listed as 1-5 above) and the latter calls for a protocol setting up procedures for their safe handling and transfer, especially in respect of the conservation of biodiversity. Turning to 8(g):

> [Each contracting party shall...] establish or maintain means to regulate, manage or control the risks associated with the use and release of LMOs resulting from biotechnology which are likely to have adverse environmental impacts that could affect the conservation and sustainable use of biological diversity taking also into account the risks to human health.

Article 19 reads:

> The parties shall consider the need for ... a protocol setting out appropriate procedures... in the field of safe transfer, handling and use of any LMO resulting from biotechnology that may have adverse effects on the conservation and use of biological diversity.

Thus the triple heads of danger to humans, danger to the environment, and danger to genetic resources are covered. Also relevant is art 8 (j), which however does not mention LMOs as such but mandates equitable sharing of the benefits arising from traditional knowledge. This is also apposite to genetic material - if a company acquires a plant which expresses a valuable drug, and the company isolates the gene responsible for the synthesis of that compound, then according to 8(j) any commercial benefit arising from it must be shared with its originators. A 'sharing' provision is also incorporated into art 15 – it suggests sharing of genetic resources. The phrase used is 'units of heredity', in other words DNA.

Art 14 goes on to state that the COPs will address "the issue of liability and redress, including restoration and compensation, for damage to biological diversity, except where such liability is a purely internal matter." These phrases reconfirm that (a) this is a framework treaty (b), as usual there is respect for sovereignty, and (c) that that there is no enforcement mechanism in the text itself. The later articles suggest negotiation and arbitration, ultimately reference to the International Court of Justice, but since that body, in turn, has no punitive powers this hardly carries redress and enforcement any further. Some writers do refer to the CBD as 'hard' international law, but this only reinforces the uncertainty surrounding her concept.

The Cartagena Biosafety Protocol

The COPs in turn engendered the Open-ended Ad Hoc Working Group on Biosafety (OEAHWGB). This was originally expected to complete the main body of its work in 1998 and to lay recommendations for the Protocol on Biosafety at the meeting of the ministers (of the countries party to the convention) in Bratislava later that year. Unfortunately no agreement could be reached and a continuation meeting in Cartagena in February 1999 was also without conclusive result. The problem seemed to centre round the question of AIA, that is, agreement between importer and exporter of GMOs on possible hazards. One group of signatories, (the 'Miami Group') importantly including the US, wished this to be the responsibility of the importer. Their reasoning was that countries with a highly developed agricultural biodiversity need to ensure that any international regulations do not limit their flexibility to take domestic measures to manage LMOs appropriate to their national interests. Other, mostly developing countries, did not accept this. There was also no consensus on regulations for *commodities*, i.e. LMOs/GMOs for processing and consumption, not breeding. There was also argument that the eventual Protocol, being a list of mandatory procedures, should not override other international agreements such as those under the WTO.

Agreement was subsequently reached at Montreal in January 2000.[11] The Protocol is still eponymised as 'Cartagena', however, in honour of the efforts of the hosts in February 1999. Naturally, the Protocol makes turgid reading (like the present paragraphs, probably) and this may be due to what has been described as ' being laden with ambiguity'. If this is true it is not surprising, for the document is a compromise between the Miami group and the other hundred-odd countries. Its main features can be summarised under four heads:

(1) The precautionary principle (art 1) It allows countries to refuse GMO imports if they feel the need to apply the precautionary principle, that is if there is any uncertainty about safety, then the products should be kept out. However such refusals must be based upon 'credible' scientific evidence, which is a term almost impossible of interpretation.

---

11   The Cartegena website is <http://www.biodiv.org/biosafety/protocol.asp>. See also Duall, E A 'Liability and redress regime for genetically modified organisms under the Cartagena Protocol' [2004] *The George Washington University International Review* vol 36, at p 173; for the Montreal agreement see <www.biodiv.org/biosafety/iccp.asp> It appears that there were in fact five blocs fighting in the ring, (1) the Miami group, (2) the EU, (3) 'Like minded' (4) 'Compromise ' and (5) Central and East European.

(2) The necessity for a 'clearing house' for the exchange of information, for example about what types of GMOs specific countries are prepared to import (art 20).

(3) The strict application of AIA to GM fish, seeds and plants which are to be released into the environment (art 7). It was decided that the Protocol and the WTO regulations were to be mutually supportive, thus assuaging the concerns of the Miami group.

(4) AIA does not refer to LMOs intended for direct use as food or feed, or for processing (art 11). In other words, in such circumstances there is not likely to be any environmental hazard in the absence of any release. Whether the 'food' itself is acceptable, of course, will be depend on other factors domestically, dealt with in Chapter 5. The problems being faced by the Open Ended Technical Expert Group, in its turn a body appointed by the COP, pertain to the presumably tedious business of devising appropriate documentation and tracing to ensure that LMOs for food or feed can be identified as such.

Sooner or later a problem will arise in that if, after AIA is served and an import licence is granted, and the precautionary principle is observed, and then a GMO causes environmental damage, what is the redress under international law? At the moment, it seems little. However art 27 takes the process incrementally further in that it mandates the establishment of a process for "…international rules and procedures in the field of liability and redress for damage resulting from transboundary movements of LMOs", to be completed within four years. The subsequent OEAHWG on Liability and Redress is still in session at the time of writing. It met in 2005 in Montreal and reviewed, within its terms of reference, other international instruments which do incorporate enforcement and/or arbitration, including the Antarctic Treaty System, the International Atomic Energy Agency and the International Civil Aviation Authority. (At the Cartagena meeting itself an even more formidable list of international bodies was suggested as models for redress. These included *inter alia*: the European Convention on Civil Liability for Activities Dangerous to the Environment; the International Convention for Civil Liability for Oil Pollution Damage; the Convention on Civil Liability for Nuclear Damage. This is merely to point out that there is a vast array of international law with sanctions working away relatively harmoniously; international lawyers often cite them as examples of the quiet success of most multinational bodies, in distinction to such others as the UN General Assembly, notable for its discord.)

Other international organisations concerned with LMOs/GMOs and genetics

These international bodies deal variously with food, environmental safety, databases etc – what they have in common is interboundary pleadings. From the legal point of view it is again important to distinguish those which are merely declaratory and exhortative from those which have some binding force. The ones below come into the former category.

(1) The Codex Alimentarius. There is a joint WHO/FAO Consultation Committee on Biotechnology and Food Safety and their sub-agency, the Codex Alimentarius, sponsored a meeting in Japan in March 2001, attended by 165 nations, to try to draft safety standards for GMFs, but the meeting foundered on the issue of traceability. Some countries maintained that traceability is unnecessary and in any case too expensive. Agreement appeared to have been reached, however, on standards to be set for pre-market approval.[12] (This is a reiteration of a point in Chapter 5).

(2) WTO has decided to adopt the Codex in respect of its policy on food. Its own protocol, the Agreement on Sanitary and Phytosanitary (SPS) measures entered into force along with the WTO itself in 1995.[13] This deals mostly with pests, diseases, contaminants and toxins but it has the avowed aim of restricting the use of unjustified measures to protect human and plant health for the purpose of trade protection. It does not develop rules in itself but encourages governments to establish SPS consistent with international standards – the so called harmonisation effort. Any attempt by its member countries to restrict trade in GMOs, which in some eyes fall into the category of contaminants (and which seems to be the case generally in the EU and implicitly in the Cartagena Protocol) may well be held to be illegal by the WTO. Only a government can bring a issue to the WTO, but if it makes a ruling, then it is binding.[14] In summary SPS covers:

- scientific assessment of risks involved

---

12   The Codex site is <www.codexalimentarius.net>.

13   For a good explanation of SPS see <http://www.wto.org/English/tratop_e/sps_e/spsund_e.htm>. Also http://www.cid.harvard.edu/cidtrade/issues/spstbt.html>. There is a further, related, set of provisions known as *Agreement on Technical Barriers to Trade* (TBT).

14   The dispute of relevance here is the objection brought by Canada and the US in 2003 in respect of the refusal of the EU to allow imports of GMFs, alleging breaches of the SPS agreement, specifically arts 2,5,7 and 8.

- scientific evidence of reduced risk

- recognition of different ways of achieving the same risk level.

The experts involved emphasise that the free exchange of information is an important safety mechanism and this includes advance notification. That is, a potentially affected country should be informed immediately in the event of any adverse effect of the use of an organism with novel traits which could affect it. Paragraph 47 of the document goes on to catalogue the types of information to be provided. This includes, obviously, a description of the novel traits introduced into an organism – for example, antibiotic or pesticide resistance.[15]

(3) The FAO Code of Conduct on Biotechnology. FAO established a Commission on Genetic Resources for Food and Agriculture[16] which sourced information from no less than 400 experts worldwide. It forwarded its report to the CBD and is still working on its code of conduct.

(4) The UN Environmental Program (UNEP) statement entitled International Technical Guidelines for Safety in Biotechnology dates from 1995.[17] UNEP also took the initiative in forming the Information Resource for the Release of Organisms (into the environment) (IRRO). It established, by correspondence with the Microbial Strain Data Network (a scientific contact group) that no such database previously existed.[18] Obviously if the progress of regulation of release of GMOs into the environment is to be monitored there will have to be some central register of such events. The information resource was established on commonsense principles, but notably took the view that information on release of non-genetically modified organisms should be included and indeed should not be confined to microorganisms. The secretariat, based in Cambridge, UK is to concern itself substantially with the construction and maintenance of easily accessible electronic databases.

---

15   Antibiotic and pesticide resistance is dealt with in Chapter 5 generally.
16   The relevant FAO site is <www.fao.org/ag/cgrfa/Biocode.htm>.
17   UNEP/CBD/BSWG/2/3 (Background Documents on Existing International Agreements Related to Biosafety) Retrieved on < http://www.biodiv.org/biosafe/bswg2-3html> and <http://www.biosafetyprotocol.be /UNEPGuid/UNEP_I.html>.
18   An informative IRRO site is < www.nal.usda.gov/pgdic/Probe/v1n3_4/inter.html>. See also Kirsop, BH and Kritchevsky, M 'Development of the information resource for the release of organisms into the environment' [1993] *Annals of the New York Academy of Sciences* vol 173, at p 700.

(5) The Organisation for Economic Cooperation and Development (OECD). In 1984 the OECD commissioned a report later published in 1992 as Safety Considerations for Biotechnology.[19] This dealt mainly with risk - its nature, appreciation thererof, and the harmonisation of these concepts within member countries.

(6) UNESCO's Universal Declaration on the Human Genome and Human Rights (1997) in its art 12a states that benefits from advances in biology, genetics and medicine, concerning the human genome, shall be made available to all, with due regard for the dignity and human rights of each individual. It is notable how often the phrase 'human dignity' is mentioned and is assumed to be self-explanatory. This was followed by the International Declaration on Human Genetic Data (2001) This instrument in its preamble gives a particularly impressive list of antecedent conventions and agreements to the topics it addresses. The declaration in arts 8 and 9 deals with consent, which has previously been a primarily a matter of domestic medical law. It should be 'prior, free informed and express.' The jurisprudential interest here as ever centres on the degree of enforceability, which of course is nil. Embryonic sanctions are implicit in the obligation of parties to report on the implementation to the International Bioethics Committee As a pointer to the future, proteomic data (information concerning individual proteomics including their expression, modification and interaction) are included in the strictures (Preamble and arts 1, 2 and 8).[20]

The list above cannot be said to be exhaustive in terms of all of those organisations troubled by LMOs - the pervasive character of biotechnology has brought it on to the agenda of practically every agency of the UN and not a few regional groupings, like the North American Free Trade Association (NAFTA) and the Association of South East Asian nations (ASEAN). There is necessarily a large amount of overlap in the various reports and recommendations; the multitudinous documents produced, found easily on the Internet, constitute a turgid and repetitive read for the specialist only.

19 OECD: *Recombinant DNA Safety Considerations* (OECD, Paris: 1986). Also: <OECD.org/LongAbstract/02546,en-2649-34537-23754865-1-1-1-37407,html>.
20 The relevant UNESCO site is < http://portal.unesco.org/en/ev.php-URL_ID=17720&URL_DO=DO_TOPIC &URL_SECTION=201.html>.

Summary of 6.3

- The preservation of biodiversity in general became a pressing international issue in the early 90s, leading to the CBD.

- Its offshoot, the Cartagena Protocol on Biosafety, mandates the precautionary principle, a clearing house for information, and advance informed agreement for release of GMOs.

- Many other UN agencies and supranational bodies such as OECD have also issued guidelines in respect of the handling of GMOs internationally.

- In general these are advisory/declaratory documents.

- The Cartagena Protocol too still lacks an enforcement mechanism.

6.4 International Procurement of DNA

'Procurement' is used here rather than 'theft' to avoid any sort of prejudgement. Notably, the CBD in its art 15(1) recognises state sovereignty over biological resources. Thus one cannot just go into a foreign country and abstract plants, animals, or genetic material. Many states, such as Malaysia and India, have put in place very stringent criminal law as a sanction against this, the modern phenomenon of 'biopiracy'. This is another emotive term (like 'frankenfoods') which can be defined as the appropriation of the natural or genetic resources of rural and/or indigenous communities by individuals or institutions seeking exclusive monopoly control over these resources.[21] The terms 'biocolonialism' and the 'vampire project' have also been used, and these are equally unhelpful.[22] However, whatever their appellation, such

---

21   Stenton, G 'Biopiracy within the pharmaceutical industry' [2004] *European Intellectual Property Review* vol 26, at p 17; Editorial 'Gene prospecting in remote populations' [1997] *Nature* vol 278, at p 565. See also Blakeney, M 'Biodiversity rights and traditional resource rights of indigenous peoples' [1998] *Bioscience Law Review* vol 2, at p 82, in which are listed 19 conferences and/or organisations which have objected to 'bioprospecting' and/or 'biocolonialism' (however defined).

22   Whatever the precise language used, 'biopiracy' has made researchers more cautious. The potential of the 'gene police' was brought home to Dr Carol Jenkins when she was working in New Guinea and was arrested while boarding a plane to go to a conference, on suspicion of appropriating a human cell line potentially valuable for the therapy of leukaemia. She was later exonerated. Now researchers take precautions. The discoverer of leptin (a hormone potentially valuable in treating obesity) Dr Jeffrey Friedman of Rockefeller University, is looking for genes which predispose to the thrifty genotype (the type of individual who lays down fat to provide for future starvation) on Kosrae, an island in the Federated States of Micronesia. He is said to be operating entirely with the cooperation of the locals.

activities still offer considerable scope for the biological entrepreneur. There are two arms to such projects - first of all the collection of the genetic material from plants with a potential for health promotion or drug development (and there seems to be much scope for exploration here since according to some authorities only 1% of tropical plants have been tested for medicinal value).[23] Secondly, there is the search in tribes or otherwise isolated groups for genetic material which seems to have given some protection against disease or conferred some otherwise desirable characteristic. There is in this latter area a nexus to genetic triumphalism - the view that genetic research will provide all that is necessary for the cure of human ills. Researchers who incline to this view can be regarded as the latest wave of explorers, for their efforts take them to distant lands and exotic locations. Many others have reservations about the utility of such ventures. 'Genetic research will undoubtedly lead to important discoveries and new forms of treatment. However such benefits are a long way off and require large investments with potential benefits for a few high risk individual (and researchers). This leaves little to promote the health of the minority'[24] - and - 'It seems that the adaptive significance of most within human variation is obscure, except for example for skin pigmentation and sickle cell trait eye colouration, the epicanthic fold in Chinese, hair texture, and taste variation.'[25]

All this abuts the world of commerce. On the other hand, there is a notable project set up with purely research aims. One of the stars of twentieth century population genetics is Professor Luca Cavalli–Sforza, who with a few others conceived the idea of recording the genetic constitutions of endangered ethnic groups – "endangered" in this sense meaning not annihilation as such, but rather the likelihood of soon being assimilated into the modern world, with concomitant dispersion of culture and interbreeding with more dominant groups. As Cavalli-Sforza put it on behalf of the Human Genome Diversity Project (HGDP):

> Population growth, famine, war, and improvements in transportation and communication are encroaching on once stable populations. It would be tragically ironic if, during the same decade that biological tools for understanding our species were created, major opportunities for studying them were squandered.[26]

23 Fullick, A. 'Spice and Life' [2002] *New Scientist* Dec 7th, at p 34.
24 Pearce, N and Foliaki, S 'Genetics, race, ethnicity and health' [2004] *British Medical Journal* vol 328, at p 1070.
25 Marks, J *Human Biodiversity: Genes, Race and History*. (Aldine de Gruyter, 1995) p 23.
26 A good HGDP site is <www.stanford.edu/group/morrist/hgdp/faq.html>. (The project

The idea was taken up by Dr Walter Bodmer of the Human Genome Organisation (HUGO), which agreed to support it. HUGO does not concern itself with ethnic groups, but has been constructing a genome common to all humankind. Certainly the HGDP can be viewed as an offshoot of the HUGO which was completed (to the satisfaction of some) in 2001, but it turns out that the DNA sequenced in the official effort, came from a few American and European scientists. It has been pointed out that an 'indigene' might well wonder aloud why his DNA was disdained. The founders of HGDP argue that they are trying to rectify this anomaly.

Although the aims of the HGDP are stated to be the advance of anthropology and the understanding of patterns of disease, among others - such as bridging the gulf between the sciences and the humanities, the project has links to tradeable property, and it soon became apparent that the commercial potential of the DNA collected by the HGDP and the genetic information potentially disclosed by it might be considerable. Since the HGDP is committed to non-commercialisation, the results of its surveys initially were deemed unlikely to be patented, but if they were not, the information gathered would be made freely available to commercial companies, then these could independently obtain samples of DNA and cell lines which it could then patent quite legally, assuming some minimal input in the direction of inventive step. It seems then that the HGDP might be forced to undertake preemptive patenting. It is a hard fact that whatever ethical unease a person or organisation feels about patenting something, if this is not done there is nothing to stop somebody else from filing an application. (see the note on the Newman patent application (p 167). The fact that the information was available to the public (and therefore the novelty requirement destroyed) will not help, for the interloper might be able to maintain that, apart from an input of some bright idea, he is a bone fide inventor in showing that the utility claim has not been in the public domain hitherto.

The originators of the HGDP frequently made the analogy, when discussing the ethics of the project, with the loss of the world's indigenous languages. However when entering the sphere of patents and commercialisation, this analogy cannot be sustained. There is no hint, no possibility that endangered languages, if recorded or even rescued, could be put into the marketplace. In contrast to linguists, the HGDP scientists found themselves very much out on a limb, being accused of motives assumed to have disappeared in

---

was initiated in Stanford University.) Cavalli-Sforza is quoted by Posey, D and Durfield, G in *Beyond Intellectual Property* (International Development Research Center, Ottawa, 1996) p 163.

concordance with the various UN conventions on the abolition of slavery. This last word has been explicitly cited:

> ... today the architects of the programme – a group of geneticists and anthropologists with irreproachable academic and political credentials – stand accused of being pawns in a conspiracy to develop race-specific biological weapons. The atmosphere surrounding the work is thick with suspicion...a medical researcher whose ongoing study in the Caribbean was abruptly shut down by charges that he would use his subjects' blood samples to clone a race of *slaves* [my italics].[27]

If 'slavery' is taken literally, then recourse might be had to the 1956 UN Supplementary Convention on the Abolition of Slavery, the Slave Trade and Institutions and Practices Similar to Slavery, unlikely as this might seem. If the language above seems extravagant, it was in no way contradicted by the meeting which led to the Declaration of Indigenous Peoples of the Western Hemisphere regarding the HGDP, held in 1995: 'We demand an immediate moratorium on collections and/or patenting of genetic materials from indigenous persons and communities by any scientific project, health organization, governments, independent agencies, and individual researchers.'[28] The text goes on roundly to denounce the NAFTA, GATT and the WTO. Their stance finds sympathetic voices in that NGOs use language like 'colonial pillaging' of, for example, seeds from a Congo plant called *Aframomum stipulatum* by a Canadian Company, Option Biotech, to make an anti-impotence drug marketed as Bioviagra, and bacteria from Rift Valley in Kenya by the US Genecor International used to give jeans a faded look.[29]

Thus, it appears that indigenous peoples see the HGDP as a real threat. They are backed up by the UNESCO International Declaration on the Human Genome and Human Rights (see para 6.3). The indigenous groups who discount the value of information on their genomes are also aware that there still exist a large residue of 'native' specimens in the museums of the West, that is skeletons, skulls,shrunken heads, weapons, costume jewellery, carvings and votive objects, and they assume that DNA is only a modern extension of such appropriations. The physical DNA taken will be owned by the project organisers, presumably, as well as the information contained in it, prior to it being published in scientific journals, when it will in a sense be owned by the whole world, rather like the specimens in the museums.

---

27   Gutin, JC 'The end of the rainbow' *Discover*, Nov 1994, at p 71.

28   <www.anku.uaf.edu/IKS/declaration.html> .

29   Buncombe, A *The Independent*, 17th Feb, 2006.

One point, often overlooked, is that outwith the HGDP, 'mining' of DNA in indigenous populations has been going on for many years; this has been in the sense of collecting haplotypes, or groups of genes, mutations in which are characteristic of one population or another, and one disease or another. (Much effort has gone into detecting haplotypes typical of diabetes and heart disease, for example.) It is possible for anyone unfortunate enough to be accused of (human) biopiracy to argue that haplotypes have been collected from numerous indigenous populations over many years, and this activity has aroused little or no opposition. The vast amount of data on blood groups and human leucocytic antigen (HLA) types come into the same category. Nonetheless the results of haplotype mapping as published in the scientific journals are as susceptible to commercial uptake as is the more complete genetic information envisaged by the HDGP. The Hapmap Project, a multicentre cooperative study to record millions of haplotypes in various populations, based mainly on SNPs, states that its findings will be released free into the public domain.[30]

In reference to the CBD, it clear from arts 15 -17 that it aims to restrict free and easy access to genetic resources in the 'Third World' (although of course that term is not explicit in the text.) Art 15 recognises that access to genetic resources rests with national governments and is subject to national legislation; a party outside the boundaries of a country seeking its genetic resources must obtain prior informed consent. Thus there is looming conflict between the CBD and TRIPs, which seeks to be extremely enabling from the point of view of the biotechnology companies. As has been articulated by one authority:

> The agreement on TRIPs sets minimum standards for intellectual property. Membership of WTO carries with it the obligation to comply with TRIPs, which in its preamble recognises intellectual property rights as private property rights. The fact that GMOs can be privately owned under a set of property rights that have been globalised through inclusion in the trade regime raises a set of complex moral, economic and regulatory issues. For example, many patented GMOs are closely based on naturally occurring organisms that could be said to be in some sort of intellectual commons or under the stewardship of an *indigenous group* [italics added]. In either case, a public asset has fallen into private hands. ... Through the CBD the international community committed itself to assert open-ended principles that would pattern the development of national regulation aimed at the

---

30   The hapmap site is <www.hapmp.org>.

"fair and equitable sharing of benefits arising from the utilisation of genetic resources".[31]

Unhappiness in the US about the CBD is said to be most prominent in the pharmaceutical and biotechnology industries, which fear that they will be excluded from the genetic resources of countries with an ecology still to be exploited commercially. A possible solution, or partial solution to the impasse is to create a world patent system. This would provide an opportunity to incorporate requirements laid out in the BDC concerning access by the government of the country providing a genetic resource used in a foreign invention, as well as prior informed consent, benefit sharing, protection of traditional knowledge, and technology transfer. Such harmonisation awaits the ratification of the draft Substantive Patent Law Treaty promoted by WIPO. To put genetics in a wider context, one has to note that others interested in the commodification-cum-patenting of indigenous resources include not only the pharmaceutical industry in its entirety, but also zoo and aquarium keepers, herbal medicine advocates, slimming clinics, ethnobotanists, the seed industry, horticulturalists, and the manufacturers of cosmetics - quite a list!

Summary of 6.4

• State sovereignty over biological and genetic resources is recognised by the CBD.

• Indigenous natural and genetic resources are thought to be potentially vulnerable to BigPharma, seeking (a) medicinal plants per se and (b) genes in plants and animals which may aid drug design.

• The HGDP has fallen foul of indigenous groups in the face of these suspicions.

• Exporting indigenous plants and animals attracts severe penalties under domestic law in many countries.

31   Drahos, P 'Genetically Modified Organisms and Biosafety' [1999] *Bioscience Law Review* vol 2, at p 40. For similar comments see Blakeney, M 'Biotechnology, TRIPs and the Convention on Biological Diversity' [1999] *Bioscience Law Review* vol 4, at p 144 and Toumi, E 'Ego TRIPs'. [2002] *Patent World*, October p 22; Keating, D 'Access to genetic resources and equitable benefit sharing through a new disclosure requirement in the patent system: an issue in search of a forum' [2005] *Journal of the Patent and Trademark Office Society* vol 87, at p 521. See also discussion in Chap 4. 2 herein.

6.5 Molecular biology and warfare

Molecular biology of course is merely the latest input into warfare. Bacteriological warfare of a sort has been practiced from time immemorial by throwing rotting corpses and dead animals into wells and propelling them over the walls of besieged cities (Kaffa, Crimea in the 14th century). One of the nastiest allegations is that American Indians were given gifts of blankets impregnated with the smallpox virus in order to avoid the trouble of fighting them (the Indians). In modern times the public has been educated on the sinister roles of such entities as anthrax (a bacterium), ricin (a protein) and sarin (a relatively simple chemical).[32] Missiles loaded with DNA are difficult to envisage except in the case of the DNA viruses (smallpox, herpes and papilloma are DNA viruses) if a means can be found to keep them intact on impact. Scientific information on biological warfare is sparse since any achievements naturally become classified. However we know that the US Centers for Disease Control have identified several classes of biological warfare agents under their category A, including anthrax, smallpox, plague, tularaemia, botulism and viral haemorrhagic fevers. These would be dealt with, clinically, by the standard approaches to bacterial and viral diseases. The nexus with molecular biology is that apparently there are ongoing attempts to engineer these agents to make them more virulent, or more selective, or more easy to control. Regarding this last, obviously an infective agent if engineered to prostrate the enemy, must not be allowed to spread to your own soldiers. Thus during the trial of Wouter Basson in South Africa during 1999-2000 it was claimed that his organisation had been attempting to genetically modify organisms so that they would selectively infect non-whites.[33] Relatively mild genres of warfare can envisaged, for example increasing the virulence and penetrance of diarrhoea producing amoeba which would spread quickly among an enemy and incapacitate it to the extent that it could be overrun and captured. For an attempt at envisaging such a scenario, see Box 6.1.

---

32 Leaving aside the species names of the agents, an abbreviated list of diseases potentially resulting from terrorism or warfare using bacteria are: anthrax, plague, brucellosis, tularemia, Q-fever, cholera, glandular fever and melioidosis. Ricin has recently been thrust to the fore again after it was found in a South Carolina post office and in the White House mail room: Audi, J, Belson, M et al 'Ricin poisoning' [2005] *Journal of the American Medical Association* vol 294, at p 2342. Protein toxins would generally have to be injected, but if the molecule is small enough it can be administered by nasal inhalation. Notably, there is no known vaccine or antidote for ricin.

33 See <en.wikipedia.org/wiki/Wouter_Basson.> Basson was acquitted on all 46 counts, apparently by a judge sitting alone, to the disgust of those who considered themselves to have been his targets.

War and terrorism are not as distinct as they once were. So far, Al Qaida and other terrorist groups have spread their message with nothing more subtle than high explosives and hijacked aircraft. Commentators have expressed hope that tomorrow's terrorists do not include those with PhDs in molecular genetics. It is possible to buy DNA base sequences through the Internet. (It is not necessary to buy the physical DNA, if the base sequence for a specific application is known, the physical DNA can readily be synthesised.) It is suggested that any biotechnology company should check sequences it supplies against a list of those sequences known to be dangerous, otherwise it might be operating against the battery of antiterrorist legislation recently introduced in Europe and US.[34] Screening gene sequences for danger (viral virulence for example) can be done using software from the Craic Company in Seattle.[35] The US National Science Advisory Board for Biosecurity set up in 2004 advises the US government on which advances in technology can be useful to terrorists, presumably with a view to banning the exchange of information about them. There is more administrative law on the way.

International law and weaponry

The law regarding weaponry is said to be one of the longest established areas of military law and rests on two cardinal principals of customary law. There are two established prohibitive norms:

- Prohibition of the use of weapons which cause unnecessary suffering, suffering unnecessary for the pursuance of victory. This is another example of the use of a proportionality principle in law.

- Prohibition of weapons inherently indiscriminate – those which cannot distinguish between military objectives and the civilian population.

Crossbows were banned at the Second Lateran Council of 1139, but only in respect of Christians fighting among themselves. Arquebusiers were sometimes so anathaemised that they had their heads chopped off on capture.

---

34   Aldhous, P 'The bioweapon in the post' *New Scientist* 12th Nov, 2005 at p 8. This paper notes that a scientists working for the wildlife division of the Australian National Research Agency set out to make a contraceptive vaccine to control plagues of mice, and ended up with a deadly mousepox virus that resists vaccination, thereby creating a recipe for smallpox. Also, generally, Byrnes, ME, Klug, DA et al *Nuclear, Chemical and Biological Terrorism* (Lewis Publishers, 2003). For a measured assessment of the threats of bioterrorism see King, NB 'The ethics of biodefence' [2005] *Bioethics* vol 19, at p 433.
35   The Craic Corporation website is <www.craic.com>. It is reported to provide software which allows DNA suppliers to screen sequences which are potentially harmful.

Box 6-1 GMOs at War

Neighbouring countries 'A' and 'B' are traditionally on bad terms. Only 'A' has a highly developed biotechnology industry and is known by 'B' to be engineering an amoeba which causes a debilitating diarrhoea. It is suspected that this is to be released into 'B's water supply with the aim, inter alia, of neutralising its army. The defence authorities in 'B' therefore commission a laboratory in a rogue state to engineer one of the influenza virus strains to make it super-virulent. When the wind conditions are favourable, 'B' releases the virus, stabilised as an aerosol, over the border into 'A'. It then invades and occupies 'A' and brings in mercenary scientists to try to alter the germ line in 'B's ruling caste to make them produce more serotonin and therefore become lazy and placid. Fearful of further release of the virus, a great power 'C' attacks both 'B' and the rogue state in order to destroy all stocks of it. At an early stage 'A' sought condemnation of 'B' in the Security Council and it subsequently complained to the International Criminal Court about the genetic outrages perpetrated on the ruling families. 'B' in turn complained to the Security Council about the invasion by 'C'. 'A' also seeks monetary compensation from 'B' in the International Court of Justice.

Possibly the GMOs do not throw up new issues of international law, but they certainly illustrate its principles. Since the Kellog-Briand Pact of 1928 (to which 'A' and 'B' may not be parties, however) war as an instrument of policy has been illegal. However almost certainly both countries are members of the UN and should adhere to art 2(4) of the Charter which forbids the use of force in settling international disputes. (An interesting debate might arise as to whether release of viruses constitutes 'force.') Of course 'B' will point to numerous instances where 2(4) has been disregarded with impunity.

'B' will further argue that its actions constituted a preemptive strike, or alternatively self-defence. (The opposition, 'A' were probably guilty of the same intentions, leading also to the *tu quoque* defence unsuccessfully pleaded by the Nazis at Nuremberg.) It considers preemptive strikes legal under international law and may have a good case. But it would have to prove that an attack on it was imminent. (Then we have arguments on what is meant by 'imminent'.) It might also argue 'provocation', but it would have to be pointed out that this is a concept in domestic law, not international law. The question arises as whether 'B's actions were proportional to the perceived threat. Even if it can sustain this principle, its attempted manipulation of the genome of citizens in 'A' will have to be examined under the provisions of the Geneva Conventions especially the Protocols I and II of 1977. 'Crimes against humanity' emanating from Nuremberg might also be adduced. Now, under the provisions of the International criminal Court any war criminals in 'B' could be indicted if named by 'A' or by the prosecutor in the Hague *proprio motu*.

If 'B' and 'C' are parties to the CBW then both are clearly in breach of it . Art 13 does permit derogation in the face of 'extraordinary events..... jeopardising the interests of the country', if three months notice to all concerned parties and the

Security Council provided. 'B' might well argue 'extraordinary events' but is in breach of the notice requirement.

The action by 'C' might be legal under the *erga omnes* doctrine, or obligation. It benefited, or was intended to benefit, the international community as a whole. 'C' will cite the *Barcelona Traction* case should this become an issue.

The International Court of Justice can award monetary reparation under art 36 (d) of its charter but has no power to enforce compliance. In any case 'B' might just refuse to be a party to the action, as did the US in the *Guatemala* case. Alternatively however, 'A' might merely seek monetary or other compensation through a formal peace treaty. Traditionally this was the way wars ended, at the Congress of Vienna in 1816 for example, but since the debacle of the Treaty of Versailles in 1919 they have fallen into disfavour. Victorious states in modern times, as in Iraq in 2002, prefer the unconditional surrender.

Lastly, one has to assume that 'A' and 'B' are not members of the EU – such actions as described would then be completely unconscionable.

All these issues are dealt with in the standard texts on international law. See for example Harris, D *Cases and Materials on International Law* (Thomson – Sweet and Maxwell, 5ᵗʰ edn, 1997).

Killing at a distance was unconscionable to the prelates then, so what would they have made of ICBMs? The above two tenets may well be *opinio juris*, the received doctrine, but they are breached so often they can hardly be considered *jus cogens*. Despite attempt to produce smart bombs, the latter in particular has been consistently ignored to the point where area/mass bombing, for example, has progressed (if that is the right word) to customary international law. It is difficult to conceive of GM weaponry as being other than non-selective. A virus or a bacterium cannot distinguish a soldier from a civilian any more than can a bomb, with the caveat that it appears to be an aim to produce agents to target specific groups.[36] However art 51 (2) of the 1977 Protocol 1 to the Geneva Convention of 1949 states: ' The civilian population as such, as well as individual civilians, shall not be the objects of attack. Acts or threats of violence the primary purpose of which is to spread terror among the civilian population are prohibited.'

---

36   The first instrument to refer to biological warfare was the *Protocol for the Prohibition of the Use in War of Asphyxiating, Poisonous or other Gases, and of Bacteriological Methods of Warfare*, Geneva, 1925. The use of viruses, for example the smallpox virus, was not envisioned at that time. The reference guide to the Geneva conventions is <http:www.genvaconventions.org/>.

Para 4 of the same art 51 states that ' Indiscriminate attacks are pro-hibited …' which means striking at military objectives and civilians without distinction.

Turning to point A above, specific prohibited categories in the past were dumdum bullets and projectiles fired from balloons, these attracting the attention of international law at the 1907 Hague Conference on arms limitation. In modern times the appropriate language is that of art 35(2) of the 1977 Protocol 1: 'It is prohibited to employ weapons projectiles and material and methods of warfare of a nature to cause superfluous injury or unnecessary suffering. '

A potential problem is that DNA based weapons might not necessarily be covered by the language in the various protocols. A modified bacterium to cause chronic diarrhoea in an opposing army, for example, might not be considered to cause unnecessary suffering. If a modified bacterium infected only a certain racial or age group it might not be considered indiscriminate. For further guidance, we must look to two other instruments, the Convention on the Prohibition of Development, Production and Stockpiling of Bacteriological (Biological) and Toxin Weapons and on their Destruction (1972) ('the Biological Weapons Convention', BWC) and the Convention on the 1993 Prohibition of the Development, Production, Stockpiling and Use of Chemical Weapons and on their Destruction (the 'Chemical Weapons Convention', CWC).[37] Progress on negotiating these was hindered by disputes about the linking of chemical and biological weapons. The US and UK maintained that these two genres were distinct, the biological weapons presenting less intractable problems, and their point of view eventually prevailed. The CBW was roundly criticised for the use of 'indeterminate language in its provisions' which in effect reduce it to 'soft international law'.[38]

The BWC eventually came into force in 1975 and 169 states are now parties, the CWC in 1997 with 181 parties. (The Geneva Conventions are the champion, as it were, with 194 parties in 2006 - all the sovereign nations in the world). Art 1(1) of the BWC states that parties to the convention will not 'develop, produce, stockpile, or otherwise acquire or retain'….. 'microbial or other biological agents, whatever their origin or *mode of production.* The italicised words are obviously entered include bioengineered bacteria and viruses (and for that matter moulds, tapeworms, mosquitoes or anything

37   The text of the BWC can be found on http://www.state.gov/t/ac/trt/4718.htm.
38   Beard, J 'The shortcomings of indeterminacy in arms control regimes: the case of the BWC' [2007] *American Journal of International Law* vol 101 at p 271.

else which might be harmful). Unlike the CWC, which has an inspection mechanism, there is no procedure for checking or indeed punishing those parties who are in breach of the BWC. Indeed the US under the Bush administration withdrew from it in 2001 on the grounds that it was not serving the interests of national security - this is indeed allowed by art 13 in face of 'extraordinary events'. In any case it is suspected by almost all commentators that the CBW is widely ignored in many countries. (The US also passed a Bioterrorism Preparedness and Control Act in 2001, largely directed towards financial support for the stockpiling of vaccines and drugs - there the prospect of biological warfare is taken very seriously indeed.) As a tangential issue there appears also to be no international mechanism for investigating outbreaks of disease suspected to be a result of violations of the BWC, that is accidents affecting a local population rather than some hostile incident. An obvious investigatory agency would be WHO but it is generally accepted that it does not have the funds to undertake such a role. There is particular concern about the engineering of the smallpox virus as a biological weapon.[39] Although smallpox as a disease was eliminated in the human population in the 1980s, the virus can now be synthesised *de novo*, a fearful prospect when all young people lack immunity. It is questioned, even, as to whether modern day physicians can even recognise the disease. Further concerns are whether the virus can be engineered to cause the disease in those who have been vaccinated, that is to evade the antibodies generated by vaccination.

Further to the possibility of the military using GMOs, 1977 Protocol 1, art 55 forbids destruction of the environment in the course of warfare. The environment provides food, of course, and it has always been a military objective to sap an enemy's strength by cutting this off, hence the time honoured siege and blockade. Potato blight and cereal rust could be engineered to devastate an enemy's food supply and precipitate surrender. No doubt it is a good thing that this be banned, but it is difficult to understand how it is morally different from maritime blockade. Reprisals may not be taken on the environment, according to art 55 (2). This means that a GMO destructive to any aspect of the ecosystem may not be used to punish a population deemed to be in breach of some rule propounded by an occupying power, say. Implicitly, not all reprisals are illegal.

As a final note, the use of GMOs as weapons might be held by many international lawyers to fall foul of the 'de Martens clause', originally a product of the 1907 Hague Convention but now embodied in art 1, para 2 of

---

39   Breeze, RG Budowle, B, et al (eds) *Microbial Forensics* (Elsevier, 2007).

Protocol I: 'In cases not covered by this Protocol or by other international agreements, civilians and combatants remain under the protection and authority of the principles of international law derived from established custom, from the principles of humanity and from the dictates of public conscience.'

From the point of view of international humanitarian law specifically, biological warfare presents a nice moral dilemma. As a combatant, is it worse to be incapacitated by severe diarrhoea caused by a genetically modified coliform bacterium, and have to surrender due to dehydration and weakness, than to surrender after both your legs have been blown off by high explosive? Fritz Haber, who developed the poison gas programme for the Germans during 1914-18 and who received the Nobel Prize in 1918 maintained that gassing was a more humane mode of waging war than high explosive. Who in the twenty first century would be so dogmatic as to disagree?

Summary of 6.5

- Biological warfare has always existed, but the potential to modify organisms to make them more deadly poses a new threat.

- Acquiring potentially harmful DNA sequence information through the post is at present unregulated.

- In international law, GMOs which cause unnecessary suffering and/or are indiscriminate are prime facie illegal.

- The BWC however exists as an extensively ratified international instrument prohibiting the use and stockpiling of biological agents, presumably including GMOs.

- In any case the use of GMOs in warfare may fall foul of the de Martens clause, as enunciated in the Geneva Conventions.

Index

Please note that specific references to cases are under the heading 'Cases' and specific acts/statutory instruments under the heading 'legislation'

268

278

UNIVERSITIES AT MEDWAY LIBRARY